"In this first history about the underground abortion network in the west, Alicia Gutierrez-Romine explores abortion providers and those who sought them during the anti-abortion statute era in California. Well-researched and accessible, this volume illustrates how the past truly informs the future."

—KARLA STRAND, *Ms. Magazine*

"Gutierrez-Romine's important book on illegal abortion reminds us that those who have historically been labeled as 'criminals' cannot—and should not—be understood outside the context of the society and the circumstances in which they lived."

—ERIN N. BUSH, assistant professor of U.S. and digital history at the University of North Georgia

"Alicia Gutierrez-Romine skillfully walks the reader through the complicated world of criminal abortion and, in the process, reveals how racialized logics, changing family values, and evolving legal frameworks created the post–*Roe v. Wade* world we inherited. This transnational account offers rich historical context while insightfully illuminating dozens of fascinating individual stories of women's choice—and lack thereof. *From Back Alley to the Border* is an urgent and eloquently argued contribution to contemporary debates about the value of life, family, and reproductive freedom."

—SUZANNA KRIVULSKAYA, assistant professor of history at California State University, San Marcos

FROM BACK ALLEY TO THE BORDER

FROM BACK ALLEY TO THE BORDER

CRIMINAL ABORTION IN CALIFORNIA, 1920–1969

Alicia Gutierrez-Romine

With a new afterword by the author

University of Nebraska Press | Lincoln

© 2020 by the Board of Regents of the
University of Nebraska
Afterword © 2023 by the Board of Regents of the
University of Nebraska

Portions of the book have previously appeared in "Abortion and Intimate Borderlands," in *Beyond the Borders of the Law: Critical Legal Histories of the North American West*, ed. Katrina Jagodinsky and Pablo Mitchell (Lawrence: University of Kansas Press, 2018).

All rights reserved

The University of Nebraska Press is part of a land-grant institution with campuses and programs on the past, present, and future homelands of the Pawnee, Ponca, Otoe-Missouria, Omaha, Dakota, Lakota, Kaw, Cheyenne, and Arapaho Peoples, as well as those of the relocated Ho-Chunk, Sac and Fox, and Iowa Peoples. ∞

First Nebraska paperback printing: 2023
Library of Congress Control Number: 2023938703

Set in Arno Pro by Mikala R. Kolander.
Designed by L. Auten.

To the women whose stories inspired these pages

CONTENTS

List of Illustrations — ix
List of Tables — xi
Preface — xiii
Acknowledgments — xv

Introduction — 1
1. From Back Alley:
   Butchers and the Underworld — 15
2. Regular Physicians, Irregular Circumstances:
   Loopholes and Scandals — 45
3. Inconceivable Blackness:
   Race, Medicine, and Contraception — 75
4. "The Mid-Wife Type":
   Wicked Women Abortionists — 93
5. The Pacific Coast Abortion Ring:
   Organized Crime and Criminal Ambitions — 111
6. After PCAR:
   Surveillance, Repression, and Restriction — 139
7. To the Border:
   "Tijuana Abortions" and Legal Vagueness — 161
   Conclusion — 193
   Afterword — 203
   Notes — 209
   Bibliography — 239
   Index — 251

ILLUSTRATIONS

1. Abortion arrest, Gloria June Weisbrod, 1953 — 99
2. Abortion suspect, June Jackson, 1958 — 105
3. Signal Oil Building, 1920 — 120
4. Jewel Inez Joseph in court, 1935 — 127
5. Body of teenage bride found, 1959 — 167
6. Abortions as a percentage of Los Angeles County Coroner's Office caseload — 181
7. Patients prepped for abortion operations, Montclair Hospital, 1971 — 190

TABLES

1. Los Angeles County Coroner's Office abortion cases, 1927–38   69
2. Los Angeles County Coroner's Office abortion cases, 1938–54   153
3. Los Angeles County Coroner's Office abortion cases, 1954–70   177

PREFACE

I came across the topic of abortion while researching what I thought would be a very different dissertation. I never imagined I would spend the better part of five years researching and writing about it. While pursuing my doctoral degree in history at the University of Southern California, I expected to write a dissertation about physicians in Southern California after World War II. After my comprehensive exams I received funding from my department, and I was on my way to the California State Archives in Sacramento, where I planned to examine physician license revocation files. However, in what turned out to be a fortuitous rookie mistake, I forgot to request archivist permission to view documents that had not yet been released.

Frustrated but unwilling to wallow in self pity and waste a week in Sacramento, I requested physician license revocation files that had passed the seventy-five-year waiting period; those I could look at. In the midst of being upset with myself, I began to notice a pattern. Repeatedly I came across files with the phrases "criminal operation" or "illegal operation" listed as the reasons for license revocation. I was confused and intrigued. I did not quite understand at first. In my naïveté I wondered why people were performing operations illegally. I thought physicians decided when operations were necessary. What made an operation illegal? What kinds of operations were at issue here? Why were illegal operations so common? Why would a physician perform them if they were illegal? And why were so many physicians performing illegal operations when it seemed likely that their licenses would be revoked?

After diving into these files, I soon discovered that "illegal operation" and "criminal operation" were euphemisms for abortion. Immediately I was intrigued. Having come of age in the period after *Roe v. Wade* I never really considered what the social, historical, or even medical landscape had looked like when abortions were illegal. And now, suddenly, I had all these archival boxes that were trying to tell me.

I continued to follow the illegal abortion "thread" until I discovered documents about the Pacific Coast Abortion Ring (PCAR)—a 1930s abortion mill. At the end of my first day, I remember walking back to my hotel as I excitedly emailed William Deverell, one of my dissertation advisers, asking if he knew anything about PCAR. He responded right away. He said he was not familiar with it and encouraged me to find out everything I could.

It was after that email exchange that I knew I had found my dissertation. Somewhere—in those old folders that I was looking at because I had made a mistake—was my dissertation. I just needed to write it. The rest of my week at the state archives I gathered as much information as I could. After further trips to Sacramento, I was able to see the rest of the documents and the bigger picture. That dissertation has now turned into this book, and the timing has become more significant with the recent surge of conservative efforts to eliminate women's access to safe, legal abortion.

We are again at a critical moment in the history of women's reproductive rights, as were the scholars who wrote on the history of abortion in the 1970s and 1990s. Conservatives are continuing their efforts to control women's bodies; we are at a crossroads in the legal history of abortion and perhaps at the beginning of a new period in its history in the United States: recriminalization.

The next few months and years will no doubt demonstrate the extent to which women's reproductive choices have been constrained. I have always hated any phrase that suggests "history repeats itself." I thought we were too intelligent to allow women to return to the back alley. There are probably other people have who never had to wonder what abortion was like before *Roe*. Others perhaps might have forgotten. Perhaps if I tell this story, we can be motivated enough to prevent a reappearance of the pre-*Roe* days.

ACKNOWLEDGMENTS

Since this manuscript began as my doctoral dissertation, it seems only fitting that I first thank my dissertation committee members for their guidance and encouragement. Each member brought a specific quality to this project. I owe a debt of gratitude to Shana Redmond for her incisive comments and keen eye; to George J. Sanchez for his faith in me and his reminders to look at the big picture; and to William Deverell for his eternal patience and encouragement. I appreciate them more than I can fully articulate in words. I would like to thank the University of Southern California's History Department staff for all of their work and organization and the USC Dornsife College of Letters, Arts and Sciences for its generous funding.

I would like to thank my husband for his moral support, for making sure I had a comfortable environment in which to work, for sometimes being too eager to tell people about my research, and for the occasional reminder to be tough and suck it up. I would like to thank my family, friends, and colleagues for sitting through countless conversations over coffee or dinner where I rambled about this project to no end.

I would like to extend thanks to my colleagues at La Sierra University's College of Arts and Sciences and, more specifically, my colleagues in the Department of History, Politics, and Sociology. Thank you for providing me with a collegial environment and the resources to be successful during this publication process. I would like to thank the students in my Winter 2018 "Pressing Issues in Society" class. Though they didn't realize the topic was reproductive justice, they jumped in and made it one of the most fun and intellectually stimulating classes I've ever taught. Likewise, the students in my inaugural HIST 466 class (Reproductive Health, Justice, and Politics in American History) were very supportive and intellectually curious. I'm so happy I was teaching this class as I made these final revisions. I am also grateful that I had the opportunity to participate in two symposia that forced me to push the limits of this project and conceptualize it in new ways: "Laying Down the Law: Critical Legal Histories of the North American West," organized by the University of Nebraska–Lincoln's History Department and Center for Great Plains Studies and Southern Methodist University's William P. Clements Center, and the New Scholars Series at Bates College, "New Approaches to Gender and Migration in the United States since 1900." These two symposia introduced me to other scholars with similar thematic interests, and I appreciate their comments and collaboration. I would also like to extend thanks to Bridget Barry and the staff at the University of Nebraska Press for making my first manuscript experience a breeze, and I would like to extend my thanks to Bojana Ristich for patiently editing everything.

Many thanks to Thomas Long for being my eternal mentor, and to Annalisa Zox-Weaver for her editorial comments on my introduction. I am incredibly grateful for the help I received from Broderick Dunlap, who was my undergraduate research assistant at La Sierra University and is now doing amazing things at Johns Hopkins University. I would also like to thank Jerry Crow for helping clear up a few things about Dr. Galen Hickok once I realized that this story also included identity theft; Marques Vestal of the University of California, Los Angeles, for helping me gather information about Dr. Mathew Marmillion; and Fran Johns, Patricia Maginnis, Glynn Martin, and Joan Renner for taking the time to respond to my email inquiries. Dr. Christopher Rogers and the rest of the staff at the Los Angeles County Coroner's Office; the staff at the California State Archives; Dr. David Grimes of the University of North Carolina's School of Medicine; Julie Yamashita, the archivist at the Lanterman Historical Museum Foundation; and Patterson Smith were all instrumental in helping me access resources, data, and archival evidence. On a more personal note, I am extremely grateful to Dr. Robin Beers and Linda Heisig for trusting me with Laura Miner's personal effects.

Last, this project would not have been possible without generous support from USC's History Department, the Tomás Rivera Policy Institute, the Institute of Humane Studies, two Roberta Persinger Foulke Fellowships, a grant from the National Endowment for the Humanities–Institute for California and the West, several awards from the USC Graduate School Academic Professional Development and Enhancing Diversity in Graduate Education program, and a College of Arts and Sciences Research Grant at La Sierra University.

FROM BACK ALLEY TO THE BORDER

Introduction

> Every person who provides, supplies, or administers to any woman, or procures any woman to take any medicine, drug, or substance, or uses or employs any instrument or other means whatever, with intent thereby to procure the miscarriage of such woman, unless the same is necessary to preserve her life, is punishable by imprisonment in the State prison not less than two nor more than five years.
>
> —Laws of the State of California, 1935

It was late in 1961 when Mrs. Eleanor MacDonald discovered she was pregnant again.[1] MacDonald was a waitress and a mother of three when she made the decision to go to Tijuana, Mexico, for an illegal abortion. On that fateful day in October, MacDonald and a friend drove approximately 125 miles from her home in Long Beach, California, to Tijuana, where she had the procedure. They returned to Long Beach immediately, and along the way MacDonald fell ill. Her condition worsened, and she was taken to the hospital, where she eventually died.[2] When physicians performed an autopsy, they realized the abortionist had removed only the fetus's head. An investigator described the scene as "repugnant ... beyond the decency of description."[3]

When MacDonald had her abortion in 1961, the procedure was illegal in California. Nevertheless, some women were able to acquire the procedure legally when their physicians determined it was medically necessary. Abortion was illegal in Mexico, too, and had been since the Mexican government had criminalized the practice in 1931. Because MacDonald did not pursue her *legal* options in Long Beach, it is unlikely she had an existing condition or the financial resources to acquire or negotiate a legal abortion. If MacDonald had received a legal (that is, therapeutic) abortion in Southern California, she would have had a standard hygienic medical procedure under the care of licensed physicians and nurses. If her situation had been otherwise, her story would have likely remained a closeted secret—known only to herself, her physician, and her partner, and it would likely not be in the text of this book.

If abortions were illegal in California *and* in Mexico, why did MacDonald pursue an illegal abortion across a national border rather than closer to home? One of the purposes of this book is to explain how MacDonald, and other women like her, came to make such a choice. If the procedures were equally illegal, what made the prospect of a Tijuana abortion more appealing than an illegal abortion in the States? *From Back Alley to the Border* is a history of abortion in the American West with an emphasis on California and the borderlands. California sits at an interesting intersection in the history of abortion nationally. Before states like Alaska, Hawaii, New York, and Washington *legalized* abortion, California decriminalized it, recognizing its existing law as flawed and paving the way for *Roe v. Wade*. At the same time, California's location—particularly its geographic continuity with Mexico—has made it a unique site in the history of race, sex, and politics. If we trace the history of criminal—that is, illegal or unsanctioned—abortion from the notorious "back alley" to the U.S.-Mexico border, this continuity—from the back alley to the border and from California to Mexico—is unmistakable. After 1953 the number of American women who crossed into Mexico for abortions spiked. American women's demand for this procedure created a thriving black market in Mexican border cities, and American women in California readily crossed the border in search of what they could not easily obtain in the States.

This book builds upon the work of previous scholars who have studied the history of birth control and abortion in the United States. Many of the earliest works on this topic emerged in response to the women's liberation movement, including Linda Gordon's *Woman's*

Body, Woman's Right: A Social History of Birth Control in America, James Mohr's *Abortion in America: The Origins and Evolution of National Policy*, and Kristin Luker's *Abortion and the Politics of Motherhood*. These scholars lived and wrote in the era of the *Roe v. Wade* (1973) decision, and their firsthand experiences in this period likely informed their perspective. The most significant book on the history of abortion since 1985 has been Leslie Reagan's *When Abortion Was a Crime: Women, Medicine, and the Law in the United States, 1867–1973*. This was the first book to provide a systematic study of the entire period of abortion criminalization, not just a broad study on contraception, abortion law, or public discourse over abortion.

Kristin Luker had previously argued that women were surprisingly silent about abortion laws and failed to speak out against them: "Even the Depression, which gave rise to the most profound social and political change this country has seen, failed to create a movement to liberalize or repeal abortion laws."[4] However, Reagan found that women spoke in secret, quietly among their female networks, until the 1960s, when they finally started speaking openly about abortions in the context of the women's rights movement: "Metaphors of 'silence' and 'speaking' implicitly refer to women's ability to speak in specific forums from which women have been excluded.... Emphasizing the 'silence' surrounding abortion inaccurately represents the history of abortion and ignores what women did say in *other* arenas.... They did not proclaim their abortions in open political forums, but they did speak of their abortions among themselves and within smaller, more intimate spaces."[5]

Yet these "other arenas" do not tell the whole story either. While women did speak openly within their female networks, they were often forced or compelled to speak publicly too. In placing abortion recipients on the stands in the courts of the 1930s, the prosecution effectively disrupted the status quo that had limited public abortion discussions to fatality stories. After the 1930s, when abortion became a specialized procedure, mortality decreased. Consequently more women were likely to face public exposure after an illegal abortion. It was women's desire to remain silent that prompted them to find abortions where they could be anonymous and invisible. After the 1950s that place was the U.S.-Mexico borderlands.

This book attempts to focus on individuals. While medical organizations and law enforcement agencies leave behind a plethora of reports, documents, and sources, the stories and perspectives of the women who sought abortions and the providers who performed them are often lost or filtered through the lens of these other organizations and institutions. This is especially true of women who had illegal abortions since the combination of illicit activity and shame essentially erases them from the historical record. This book looks primarily at the experiences of white American women in California who acquired illegal abortions—whether locally or across the border in Mexico. Though this book may look at the border between the United States and Mexico, Mexican women do not figure in the story as presented here. This story is about a black market that emerged for the consumption of white American women and speaks little about Mexican women who may have been involved or who may have acquired abortions in these border spaces after this black market was created.

Many of the women whose stories are told in this book died in the process of getting an abortion—not because abortions were inherently unsafe but rather because the legal landscape forced these women to acquire medical procedures under conditions that provided them with few protections. Under the circumstances these women's voices are often silent in the courtroom, where they exist only as props in narratives that both center on them and render them invisible at the same time. However, this is true only to a certain point. The use of antibiotics and the rise of abortion specialists drastically reduced mortality, even for illegal abortions, thus allowing some women to have a voice in the courtroom—whether they wanted to or not.

From Back Alley to the Border places at its center the rise and fall of an infamous abortion ring that operated in the waning years of the Great Depression—the Pacific Coast Abortion Ring (PCAR)—and by looking at the case of the *People of the State of California v. Reginald L. Rankin, et al.*, it illuminates the role this organization played in the penalization of illegal abortion providers and recipients in the years before decriminalization and legalization.[6] This case is a turning point. Before it most of the women in this book died from their abortions. After this case most of the women lived. The case and the physicians involved weren't magical catalysts for medical care. Rather this case highlighted that illegal abortions could be safe when performed using hygienic procedures (and in conjunction with antibiotics when they became widely available) and that women who had illegal abortions could provide testimony in court. Furthermore, this case was resolved shortly before most legal abortions moved almost exclusively into the hospital. After the case everything changed for women seeking abortions, for providers of abortions, and for agents of law enforcement attempting to uphold the law. It was not causal, but it was a watershed to everything that happened with abortions after. It was the first significant change in the process by which suspected violators of the abortion statute were found, tried, and convicted in the history of abortion criminalization in California.

In 1937 Reginald Rankin and a collective of physicians and abortion specialists were charged with multiple violations of California's abortion statute. Before this case, safe, successful abortions were seemingly invisible to the public.[7] Because of their illegality and because of the public shame often associated with illicit sex, few women spoke openly about their abortions. Furthermore, the stories of abortion that did come to light were those that were fatal. Since abortions came to the public's consciousness only under those circumstances, it appeared that *all* abortions were dangerous. Before PCAR California physicians who performed abortions often relied on the law's ambiguity to justify performing the procedure and to avoid culpability for performing abortions that turned fatal. However, as medical technologies progressed, the procedure became less dangerous, and police had fewer opportunities to arrest providers of illegal abortions. Decreased mortality is the context that frames PCAR's significance. While PCAR was a large, coastwide criminal syndicate, it was also safe. The ring, which was in operation from 1935 to 1936, not only provided newspapers with titillating fodder, but it also contributed to local abortion restrictions in the form of increased surveillance, reduced standards of evidence, stricter enforcement of therapeutic abortion laws, and even federal investigation into abortion activities. PCAR showed that abortions could be safe. Rather than liberalize abortion laws to make way for the abortion specialist or abortions on demand, law enforcement chose to crack down on abortion providers and made abortion an easier crime to prosecute, changing the landscape for women seeking abortions and for providers of illegal abortions.

After the PCAR defendants were tried and convicted in the *Rankin* case, women who sought abortions essentially had two options: acquire a legal abortion by petitioning hospital therapeutic abortion committees and defer to their judgment or take a chance with an illegal provider. However, since the *Rankin* case had opened the door for stricter enforcement of the abortion statute, fewer physicians were willing to perform the procedure unless the patient had a clear, justifiable reason or condition. Ultimately strict interpretations of the abortion statute funneled women to potentially unsafe illegal abortions, and the men and women who continued to perform illegal abortions had to find new ways to work under the radar of law enforcement and professional medicine.

Providers of illegal abortions played a critical role in exposing and exploiting the faults in California's abortion statute. When possible, I will use the term "providers of illegal abortions." This term indicates that the procedure itself was illegal for a specific instance. It does not make a claim about the professional status of the person who performed the procedure. It thus encompasses everyone from physicians performing abortions for extra income or non-therapeutic reasons to abortion specialists who lacked medical credentials to untrained, unlicensed abortionists.

California's nineteenth-century abortion statute was stagnant and unrepresentative of women's needs in the twentieth century. Legislation on abortion was integral to controlling women's bodies and behaviors at a time when women were challenging their place in society by claiming the right to vote and moving into the workplace in greater numbers. In the absence of the social control of women, abortion legislation stood as a satisfactory alternative. State legislators, therefore, remained uninterested in decriminalizing the procedure or loosening the legal reins associated with it. As a result abortion providers continued to profit. When heat from law enforcement compromised abortionists' ability to do their jobs, they modified and transformed their methods of serving their patients in order to delay or avoid arrest.

Even if increased restrictions forced providers of illegal abortions to retreat into the shadows, women were still willing to pay for abortions whatever the ramifications might be. Therefore, abortionists simply developed new ways to serve their patrons and stay in business. It was the abortionists' creativity and deliberate exploitation of the law's loopholes that took them across the border into Mexico. Eleanor MacDonald, whose abortion story opened this introduction, had become an unfortunate statistic and another victim of California's abortion statute, whose strict enforcement would compel women to seek their abortions in Tijuana in order to exercise control over their lives and bodies.

Only when the medical black market in border cities became visible did other Americans see the risks that women were undertaking in order to terminate their unwanted pregnancies. Only when the number of American women seeking accessible—yet potentially dangerous—abortions across the border grew did Californians realize the need to liberalize their existing abortion laws. It should also be noted that public concerns emerged primarily when white women were pursuing abortions or when white women were at risk. The easing of abortion laws became possible when a danger to white women and white nuclear families was at the fore. When poor women and women of color were at risk (for example, after the Hyde Amendment passed in 1976), most public discourse was directed at policing morality or preventing taxpayer dollars from aiding women of color.

When risk to white women and their families combined with calls from physicians and women's rights advocates to liberalize existing abortion laws, providers of illegal abortions challenged California's abortion statute to such a degree that in *People of the State of Cali-*

fornia v. Belous (1969) the California Supreme Court ruled that its nineteenth-century statute could no longer stand. Though *Belous* resulted in a victory for women in California, its effects were felt beyond state borders when it resulted in an onslaught of legal actions elsewhere. Women, physicians, and lawyers saw the *Belous* case chip away at the foundation upon which most states' abortion statutes had been built.

In order to highlight the significance of the *Rankin* decision in 1937 and to show how it differed from earlier abortion cases, chapters 1–3 examine five abortion cases before 1936: the stories of abortionists Galen R. Hickok and Henry Lee Mottard and the abortion-related deaths of Delphine Walsh, Vera Nelson, and Margaret Scott. These sensational cases generated ample coverage in local and national presses. They were noteworthy incidents that incited hatred and disgust of the illegal abortionist, sympathy and pity for the girls involved, and sometimes empathy for the physicians caught in the middle. These episodes represented the dangers of the illegal procedure. These chapters also illustrate the pursuit and investigation by law enforcement of abortion deaths, social concerns about women, and a genuine interest on the part of the medical community to monitor and police its members. While the contemporary public may have been able to read into young women's concerns and motivations for pursuing an illegal abortion, these stories ultimately stood as cautionary tales to other women who would want to avoid a similar fate.

While chapter 3 discusses the abortion that resulted in Margaret Scott's death, it also offers a narrative of Dr. Mathew Marmillion, the Black physician convicted of performing the procedure. The chapter addresses the Black experience in the medical field, as well as community discussions centered on contraception and abortion. It exposes some of the difficulties that Black medical professionals faced when compared to their white peers, and at the same time it can offer some insight into their patients' experiences.

Chapter 4 discusses female providers of illegal abortions. At the most basic level this chapter is an attempt to remind the reader that women's participation in abortion was not limited to the role of either patient or victim. The chapter demonstrates that the medical profession and the public viewed female abortionists as particularly deviant. It shows that female abortionists had a precarious position in the industry—in many ways like their Black counterparts. Because some were midwives—and many more were assumed to be—the medical field was also interested in monitoring them. Female abortionists were explicitly targeted, and most had little social or political influence to challenge this targeting. This chapter also explores Laura Miner's experiences as a provider of illegal abortions to explain why some women went into this line of work. Furthermore, Laura Miner will reappear in two subsequent cases.

Chapter 5 focuses specifically on PCAR. This chapter traces the history of the ring, describes how it functioned, and walks the reader through its discovery and trial. It highlights the connection between illegal abortions and the criminal underworld, but it also shows PCAR's efficiency, high standards, and sense of consumer responsibility. This chapter may leave the reader conflicted—on one hand deeming the syndicate's leader, Reginald Rankin, a rogue for the way he conducted business and on the other hand appreciating that he provided many women with safe, sanitary procedures.

The years after the *Rankin* case saw a dramatic shift in how women acquired abortions. Chapter 6 revisits some of the *Rankin* defendants—namely, Rankin and Miner—and shows their failed attempts to continue providing abortions after PCAR. After the dissolution of the ring and after had Rankin served his sentence in San Quentin, both served time—Rankin in Reno, Nevada, and Miner in California's Tehachapi Women's Prison. Upon her release from Tehachapi Miner never returned to the abortion business, but Rankin did.

Chapter 7 takes us back to Reginald Rankin. With fresh vigor he found a new method of providing women with the procedure they desired. In Southern California mobility became an abortionist's greatest asset. Blessed with geographic proximity to the Mexican border, Rankin and his new accomplice, Dr. Roy L. Buffum, employed an unusual tactic to evade arrest: they decided it was in their best interest to conduct their business in nearby Mexico, outside the reaches of American law. They were initially convicted of violating California's abortion statute; however, they successfully reversed the decision in a 1953 appeal, *People of the State of California v. Buffum*, effectively undermining law enforcement and the medical community and opening the floodgates for women to acquire their abortions in nearby border cities.[8] While women had traveled outside of the country to obtain abortions before the 1950s, recent developments in transportation made the *Buffum* case especially significant to Southern California women at the time. Traveling outside the country to receive an abortion had become much easier than it had been decades before. Furthermore, the *Buffum* case shifted the epicenter of Mexican abortions. Before 1953 wealthier women who went to Mexico for illegal abortions would likely fly to Mexico City to get the services of licensed physicians. After *Buffum* the epicenter shifted toward the border between California and Mexico and became accessible to nearly any woman who could afford a bus ticket, a night at a motel, or even just the gas to get as far as the border.

"Tijuana abortions" became synonymous with illegal abortions in Mexico regardless of the city in which they actually took place. More significant, "Tijuana abortions" gained a reputation for illicitness, and their pervasiveness fueled a sense of paranoia. Chapter 7 discusses *People of the State of California v. Belous*, a 1969 case in which a reputable obstetrician referred a client to an abortionist because he feared she would turn to "butchery" in Tijuana. The *Belous* case forced the California Supreme Court to reevaluate its abortion statute and its supposedly liberal Therapeutic Abortion Act. By the middle of the 1960s Californians increasingly sided with efforts to relax existing abortion laws—particularly when these were combined with the concerns of heterosexual middle-class couples regarding genetic abnormalities and fetal deformities in the wake of the thalidomide and German measles scares. When the California Supreme Court ruled in *Belous*, the court's reasoning was grounded in these changes, and it ultimately found the nineteenth-century law "void for vagueness."

The cases mentioned here are significant because they illustrate another point: women spoke publicly about their abortions as early as the 1920s and 1930s.[9] Because of decreased mortality, increased use of antibiotics, medical specializations, and the ability to locate patients through medical paperwork, prosecutors who subpoenaed patients and put them on the stand disrupted the process of limiting public discussions of abortion to fatality stories.[10] When prosecutors placed women on the stand during and after the *Rankin* case, women had to speak publicly about their abortions. While their initial placement on the stand was not by choice, once they were up there, the women spoke for themselves. Despite prosecutors' efforts to circumscribe their narratives, women had an opportunity to speak out.

Placing abortion recipients on the stand created a problem: it ruptured several stereotypes about abortions. First, it challenged the notion that abortion recipients were naïve, seduced, unmarried young women. Second, the women were on the stand because they were alive. Abortion specialization had dramatically reduced the number of fatalities associated with the procedure. No longer disembodied, abstract victims, abortion recipients spoke for themselves—even if they did not want to. Decreased mortality and increased specialization meant more women were likely to experience public exposure after an illegal abortion and were more likely to stand trial and divulge the most personal details of their lives. They were no longer just volunteering information about their abortions with women in their networks; instead these women were being forced to speak out about their abortions before a judge, jury, and a room full of strangers, including the press. It was their desire to remain silent and anonymous that had driven abortion-seeking women across the border. It was only in the context of the civil rights movement in the 1960s and 1970s that women saw an opportunity to raise their voices for change. It was in this context that "Tijuana abortions" represented the extremes women had gone through because of their second-class status in society.

Though California women did not have abortion on demand before 1969, they claimed ownership of their bodies and exercised the conscious choice to have an illegal medical procedure. Nevertheless, the law seriously affected their access to safe procedures. But lack of political action or organization did not mean that women had resigned themselves to having limited control over reproduction.[11] Women recognized that citizenship, enfranchisement, and legal equality were hollow and meaningless if women could not control their bodies. However, because women who wanted abortions were pushed into the black market and outside the bounds of legal medicine, their choices were stigmatized and for some women proved dangerous or fatal.

It will become clear that this book relies heavily on court and law enforcement records to tell this story. Using documents from agents of the state can be cause for concern when looking at the experiences of women and people of color or simply because this book also explores illegal and illicit activity.[12] Historian Paul Gootenberg's assessment of drugs and their flow across borders and his analysis of the language that the state employs when alluding to them can be used similarly to address illicit transborder abortions. Gootenberg noted that the media and many agents of the state exaggerate the development of illicit organizations "on the Third World side of borders" while paying little attention to the white, American, or First World demands that have created them.[13] Such an assessment emphasizes both the racialization and spatialization of vice and perpetuates essentialist arguments about the people who live or operate in these spaces. In this case the existence of the abortion mills on the *Mexican* side of the U.S.-Mexico border effectively makes an Other of anyone who occupies that space or who uses that space to provide these services.

Furthermore, as the state is devoting its resources to policing such places and practices, it is also relying on tropes and myths to explain why people—women—would "transgress . . . behavioral or social boundaries" by eschewing motherhood and opting for an abortion in Mexico (I have again applied Gootenberg's ideas to these transborder abortions).[14] As a historian, I have attempted to read these court documents with an eye for empathy and humanity. I tend to concede on some data presented—dates, times, and persons or parties involved. However, when it comes to motive, I try to make clear when the state is making assumptions and when I am making assumptions. Ostensibly assumptions are often all we have when piecing together stories from women who died from their procedures. As much as I may try to avoid "talking like a state," when writing about these women, there is no way to fully escape statist language either.[15] In the end these sources and documents are invaluable, if flawed. This book is simply my interpretation.

From Back Alley 1

Butchers and the Underworld

> It is not my place as a health writer to go into the morals, ethics, or legality of abortion.... We all know that it is illegal, but let us not shut our eyes to the fact that it is done. We have a situation here somewhat analogous to bootlegging. We regret it—yet only fools say that the nation is not consuming colossal quantities of bootleg. The same is true of abortions.
>
> —Philip M. Lovell, 1931

In 1923 a twelve-year-old boy in Boston discovered a suitcase floating in the Merrimac River. Because this was in the midst of Prohibition, the boy believed the suitcase was an abandoned case of liquor—perhaps a shipment discarded by a rum runner. He fished it out of the river, but to his horror the suitcase did not hold a cache of liquor; rather, it held a young woman's mutilated corpse.

The coroner determined that the woman had died from an illegal abortion and that her body had been mutilated after the fact. The article painstakingly described the "cheap black imitation leather suitcase" in which her abdomen, legs, and hands were discarded.[1] Descriptions of her clear skin and missing head served to incite fear and warn the public of the dangers of illegal abortions and their providers. The woman, the article asserted, had been "cut up by [an] expert."[2] For the disturbingly curious readers whose whetted appetites demanded more detail, it continued:

> The torso and arms made a heavy bagful, but when the two clasps were fastened and the lock in the center snapped shut, the bag contained much air and as a result it floated, instead of sinking....

The person who threw it away overlooked the air chamber created, which offset the weight of human flesh.... There was little doubt ... that the cutting was done by a man who knew how to wield a knife or scalpel. While those in charge of the investigation would not declare that in their opinion it was the work of a registered practitioner, it is known that they have not eliminated professional men.... The severing of the arms at the shoulders and the neck and vertebrae was cleanly done. The cutting of the body and spinal column near the waist line was also a clean job, with the exception of two jabs in the abdomen. Considering the character of the knife work for the balance of the operation it is believed that the two rough spots were done on purpose to convey the impression that the cutting was done by an amateur.[3]

This story served as a warning. The assertion that a trained medical professional was responsible and had dismembered the body meant that even members of the medical community could not be trusted. If the woman had died at the hands of a medical professional, it suggested that the procedure itself was dangerous, for even a skilled practitioner could not save her. Stories like this highlighted abortion's inherent dangers, while descriptions of a dismembered body and references to the criminal underworld simultaneously connected abortion to other heinous crimes. The young boy who had retrieved the suitcase thought he had caught a cache of liquor. Instead he caught a glimpse of the black market and the criminal underworld.

There were other instances when abortion was linked to the criminal underworld. In this chapter we will discuss two shady figures: Dr. Galen R. Hickok and Henry Lee Mottard. Neither of these men was a legitimate medical professional, yet both made their livings providing illegal abortions. Both men were allegedly responsible for botched procedures that resulted in fatalities. What made these men stand out was the attention that law enforcement paid to their places of business. These men were among the first to adopt the clinic model, which centralized abortion procedures in one organized locale. Both of these men were villains from the perspective of the American

Medical Association (AMA), and they embodied the trope of the back alley butcher.

The newspaper article quoted previously and the cases of Hickok and Mottard demonstrate the slippery reasoning of most members of the media and the public when discussing illegal abortion. Rather than a perception of abortion as a medical procedure that was legally out of reach, abortion was regarded as a crime on a par with murder. The Progressive era's moralistic attitudes had permeated reporting and directly affected the way abortions were covered. Few reporters saw patients as willing participants in abortion, and most regarded the women as naïve and brainwashed, not fully recognizing what they were doing, or under the influence of some morally repugnant man. This outlook was in stark contrast to the way that alcohol consumption was reported during Prohibition, even though the two were occurring simultaneously.

Before we can begin our twentieth-century story, we must go back a few centuries to understand how public views of abortion changed over time. It is important to realize, first, that for most women long ago, abortion was simply another method of birth control. While abortion is the center of many moral debates today, it was rarely seen as a moral issue through much of the late nineteenth and early twentieth centuries. Outside of the medical field few Americans saw fetuses as persons, and most of the "pro-life" language so prevalent in the anti-abortion debate today was created by physicians and later coopted by political conservatives late into the twentieth century.

Abortions have existed since time immemorial, but the only things that have changed are how women procure them and how the law treats both the procedures and the women who seek them. Abortion was not always considered a deviant practice of fallen or seduced women. Instead it was a remedy. In the seventeenth and eighteenth centuries, for example, it was common for women to take herbal remedies such as savin, black root, or pennyroyal to induce miscarriage.[4] Such practices were common regardless of region, race, or ethnicity. In the Anglo-American colonies women and midwives believed that abortion restored balance and regularity to women's bodies. When a woman missed her period, she was "obstructed." Getting rid of the obstruction by means of abortion was an at-home procedure that returned balance by bringing about menses.[5]

Long before the organization of the professional medical field in the nineteenth century, Anglo-American society accepted abortion so long as it occurred before "quickening."[6] Quickening, or the sensation of fetal movement, occurred as early as twelve or thirteen weeks in some women or as late as twenty weeks in others. After quickening, society considered induced miscarriage "a crime, because the fetus itself had manifested some semblance of a separate existence: the ability to move."[7] Once quickening had occurred, there was a "moral obligation to carry the fetus to term."[8] Before quickening there was no way of knowing whether a woman's "obstruction" was a pregnancy or something more dangerous, so the woman was not faulted for attempting to remedy the obstruction. Once quickening occurred, though, the "obstruction" had announced itself for what it was: pregnancy.

As far as moral outrage is concerned, in Anglo-American colonies abortion was usually considered deviant only in that it was an attempt to cover up sex outside of marriage. While abortion occasionally provoked discussions about sexual purity and courtship, it rarely prompted discussions about fetal life.[9] As other scholars have noted, it was not always possible for colonial assemblies to "establish pregnancy, let alone determine whether gestation had been *intentionally* terminated."[10] Furthermore, only the woman could attest to whether she had experienced quickening; thus it would mean that she was the arbiter of determining whether her abortion was illicit. Her word—whether true or false—framed her actions. Regardless of whether an induced miscarriage was an attempt to restore regularity or to cover improper relations, early Americans were overwhelmingly uninterested in penalizing it.[11] Furthermore, that so much weight was placed on women's testimony would at least suggest that women were trusted and not regarded suspiciously.

As the eighteenth century gave way to the nineteenth, production moved from the home to the factory, and American society gradually shifted from family-centered and agrarian to modern and industrial.

This period was also an era of transition in the abortion business. While there had been some early discussions concerning the morality of abortion, the market revolution facilitated the dissemination of information through advertisements, print media, and other literature and created more opportunities for the public to speak out on this previously private procedure.[12] Early home catalogs and almanacs offered drugs for sale or recommended home remedies for women to deal with their unwanted pregnancies. They suggested means and remedies relevant for women in the primarily rural United States; for example, the women could use plants or herbs, lift heavy objects, or take violent falls.[13] The regular mention of such products and remedies suggests that abortion was commonplace. Nonetheless, by the 1820s and 1830s some territories and states began to introduce anti-abortion measures.[14]

Many legislators imagined laws against abortion as a form of consumer protection. Westward migration in the nineteenth century had created an opportunity for unlicensed medical practitioners to thrive beyond the major metropolitan areas associated with the professional class of physicians. With distance between themselves and major cities like Philadelphia and New York, many self-taught or part-time "physicians," or quacks, took up the practice of medicine and began prescribing various treatments and remedies.[15] Abortion legislation in the United States grew incrementally alongside the nation's steadily evolving technology, both medical and industrial. Some of this evolution resulted in new, untested methods of performing abortions that were crude, barbaric, or dangerous when performed by inexperienced hands. Nevertheless, high infant and maternal mortality made abortion in the hands of a skilled practitioner a safer procedure than childbirth, and some women may have seen it as a favorable alternative to potential injury or death from carrying a pregnancy to term.[16] But depending on geographic location, some women had no choice but to resort to untrained professionals.

The growth of this pseudo-professional class—of naturopaths, osteopaths, chiropractors, and other "irregulars"—resulted in efforts to organize and legitimate the medical profession. Indeed though the early nineteenth century produced some of the earliest anti-abortion laws in America, these laws overwhelmingly punished the person who had provided the abortion—and *only* if the abortion occurred after quickening.[17] For example, in 1859 Julia Moore came before a Nevada County, California, grand jury. She was accused of performing an illegal abortion on Ms. Lucy Nutall.[18] According to the indictment, Moore had fashioned a hook-like instrument out of a piece of metal and used it on Lucy Nutall. Ms. Nutall died on September 2, 1859, probably from a septic infection, a common cause of death stemming from illegal abortions before the 1930s. The abortion was a violation of California's Crimes and Punishment Act.[19] The Crimes and Punishment Act—California's first legislative code—criminalized abortions *only* when performed by nonmembers of the medical community. It read in part as follows:

> Every person who shall administer or cause to be administered or taken, any medicinal substance, or shall use or cause to be used any instruments whatever, with the intention to procure the miscarriage of any woman then being with child, and shall be thereof duly convicted, shall be punishable by imprisonment in the State Prison for a term not less than two years, nor more than five years: *Provided*, that no physician shall be affected by the last clause of this section, who, in the discharge of his professional duties, deems it necessary to produce the miscarriage of any woman in order to save her life.[20]

Following efforts to organize and legitimate the medical field, the Crimes and Punishment Act and other early abortion laws represented a conservative effort to protect women from unlicensed quacks and even suggested that physicians could do no wrong. According to the act, a physician was not culpable for a fatal abortion if he or she believed it was medically necessary.[21] It therefore recognized licensed physicians' professional independence while demonstrating a relative lack of concern about the practice of abortion writ large. This statute's primary purpose was not to eliminate access to abortion; it was to punish unlicensed practitioners and prevent them from performing abortions.

Until the nineteenth century most existing methods of birth control remained unchanged: withdrawal, extended periods of nursing, abstinence, the ingestion of herbs and plants thought to have contraceptive or abortifacient properties, barrier methods such as condoms, the introduction of foreign objects into the cervix to induce abortion, and (in the most extreme cases) infanticide. Though withdrawal, extended nursing, barrier methods, and abstinence were common preventative methods with varying levels of effectiveness, abortion was different since it occurred after conception. While violent falls, lifting heavy objects, or the ingestion of plants or herbs to induce miscarriage may have been easier to hide from prying eyes—after all a miscarriage could have been hidden, considered accidental, or blamed on natural causes—an instrumental abortion typically required the assistance of another person and represented a conscious act. These were not accidental or attributable to everyday life. The complications that could result from instrumental abortions were not easily dismissed as the results of an accident or natural issue. They were evidence of deliberation and intent.

By the end of the nineteenth century, the days of women ingesting herbs and plants were past as more people moved away from rural areas and into cities. At the same time, abortion became medicalized in the sense that it shifted away from home remedies to drugs, medical instruments, and the assistance of presumed specialists. This became particularly true after the invention of the curette in the late nineteenth century.[22] Industrialization in the nineteenth century resulted in a vast array of devices, tonics, and medicines for women's health. Instead of plants, women ingested mail-order drugs they hoped would help, or they submitted themselves to invasive medical procedures performed by physicians or unlicensed laypersons. Prior to the Pure Food and Drug Act in 1906 there were no regulations for labeling or advertising patent medicines. The people who bottled and sold patent medicines could claim that the products would alleviate female maladies while including a disclaimer for pregnant women. By default these products became mail-order abortifacients. In addition, some abortionists would run ads claiming they specialized in women's health. Women seeking abortions frequently understood these ads by reading into what they implied rather than what they explicitly stated.

Such claims and ads appeared within a broader transformation that was occurring with reproductive technologies. Charles Goodyear's rubber vulcanization process—which Goodyear accidentally discovered in 1839 and later patented in 1844—was pivotal in this transformation. The once haphazard prophylactics constructed from various linens, intestines, or other raw materials now became part of their own systematized industry. The vulcanization process opened the door for a variety of other rubber contraceptive devices such as intrauterine devices (IUDs), diaphragms, and douching syringes.[23] Like the patent medicines to induce abortions, these early mass-produced contraceptives were available through mail order. Increases in printing technology and penny literature allowed for information about birth control and abortion to be widely disseminated. Advertisements for contraceptives, doctors who treated women's conditions, and patent medicines to induce miscarriage all made sex more visible in society.

Few opposed this visibility more than Anthony Comstock. Comstock, a member of the Young Men's Christian Association (YMCA), found birth control and abortion obscene, and he embarked upon a crusade against what he considered the causes of moral decline.[24] Comstock may have also had personal reasons for despising women who "casually terminated pregnancies" since he and his wife had suffered the tragedy of losing their only daughter when she was an infant.[25] Believing that commercialized sex degraded society, Comstock helped form the New York Society for the Suppression of Vice and later lobbied Congress for federal anti-obscenity laws. Comstock used his power in a war against the transmission of obscene material in 1873, when he helped pass the Act of the Suppression of Trade in, and Circulation of, Obscene Literature and Articles of Immoral Use—more commonly referred to as the Comstock Act—and he became a special agent for the U.S. Post Office. In this position he was able not only to target individuals for misuse of the mail, but also to engage in moral censorship, targeting buyers and sellers of contraceptives, medical quacks, and purveyors of immoral books and pamphlets.[26]

As early pharmaceutical firms and advertising companies profited from the unregulated market in the days before the Food and Drug Administration (FDA), physicians and non-physicians alike began to specialize in abortion. With specialization, abortion continued to remain a safer alternative to childbirth until the maternal mortality rate began to go down in the early twentieth century—coincidentally at a time when most deliveries moved into the hospital.[27] Abortion deaths were not always a direct result of the inherent dangers of the procedure itself; instead they frequently reflected the skill of the provider or the hygienic standards where it took place because most deaths were infection-related. Most women who obtained abortions in the late nineteenth and early twentieth centuries did so quietly, trusting the referrals of friends, sisters, coworkers, or trusted physicians; they moved on with their lives, never uttering another word about their procedure until one of their friends or family members found themselves in a similar situation. Many of these women survived. However, these were not the women who became topics of conversation in the popular press.[28] Sensational and highly publicized abortion-related deaths provided fodder for reformers, moralists, and physicians who believed that legalized abortion would gradually erode America's moral fabric.

Newspaper ads for abortionists and abortifacients often ran alongside sensational stories about young girls who had died in the aftermath of an illegal operation. For example, between December 1888 and January 1889 undercover reporters for the *Chicago Times* released a twenty-five-part exposé on criminal abortion that revealed the sordid details of villainous abortion providers and the dangers of the procedure. Two undercover journalists, posing as a couple, followed the reform movement sweeping across big American cities and transported their readers into the abortion underworld by exposing the compromised physicians, midwives, and law enforcement officers allied with the trade. Such abortion stories profited the newspapers since the stories "could dominate local newspapers for days."[29] Stories of criminal abortions, illicit relationships, jilted lovers, trunk murders, and cover-ups created a form of didactic pornography in which young, lovely white girls seemed to perish by the dozens. The sexual histories of women who had died from illegal abortions could no longer be concealed when their stories hit the papers. After all, their illicit sex was what had gotten them in the predicament in the first place. While these stories sold papers, they also functioned within a larger effort to regulate sexuality so that it conformed with marital, heterosexual, and reproductive ideals—presumably "good girls" who conformed to ideals about virginity until marriage and who engaged in procreative sex within marriage didn't end up in such a situation. These efforts to regulate sexuality in the late nineteenth century not only involved the criminalization of abortion, but also coincided with attempts to police prostitution, banish homosexuality, prevent the dissemination of "obscene" materials, and wrangle women's health away from female and "irregular" practitioners and toward the professional medical community.[30]

Dr. Horatio Storer was a religious New Englander and Harvard Medical School graduate. He held all the criteria to be considered a proper physician and stood as a quintessential example of an AMA member. Storer was also one of the first generation of American physicians to specialize in the burgeoning field of gynecology. He devoted his life to that specialty and wrote volumes on the diseases of women. Despite his many accomplishments and successes in the medical field, he is perhaps best known as the preeminent face of the anti-abortion movement in the nineteenth century.

Storer's anti-abortion campaign presented abortion as a moral issue in a way that it had not been before. As stated previously, abortion had been a nonissue in the eighteenth century and first half of the nineteenth century if it occurred before quickening. The campaign against abortion began around 1847, when the AMA was officially organized. Physicians and members of the public began to refer to abortion more frequently as "antenatal infanticide" or murder. In 1860, for example, Storer wrote, "By the Common Law and by many of our State Codes, foetal life, per se, is almost wholly ignored and its destruction unpunished.... By the Moral Law, the willful killing of a human being at any stage of its existence is murder."[31] Storer called abortion a moral wrong and challenged longstanding beliefs about abortion—specifically quickening. Storer argued that there was no difference between abortions that occurred before quickening and those that occurred after. In a rhetorical sleight of hand Storer asserted his own expertise—and that of other physicians—by suggesting that previous beliefs about quickening and abortion were backward and based on ignorance or superstition. Common sense dictated that "the foetus is from the very outset a living and distinct being."[32] Common sense, of course, belonged to the erudite physician. While simultaneously flashing their own credentials and denigrating those who performed abortions, Storer and other members of the AMA successfully pushed an anti-abortion agenda, and by 1880 all states had an abortion statute on their books.

While Storer and others in the medical field used the campaign against abortion to legitimate themselves and push irregulars out of practice, others pushed for abortion laws by claiming they wanted to protect women from back-alley butchers.[33] To an extent, the "focus on fatalities" did protect women by ensuring the investigations and arrests of the worst abortionists, yet criminalization and the AMA's moral campaign also made abortions more dangerous by making them harder to find.[34]

As stated previously, in the late nineteenth century there were marked efforts to regulate sexuality. Physicians' and politicians' efforts to criminalize abortion—while publishing negative effects of contraception and encouraging native-born white women's reproduction—coincided with a surge of Nativism that was in response to a growing immigrant and non-white population.[35] Native-born white women's use of contraceptives was an affront to American society in the face of a sharp increase in immigration from Southern and Eastern Europe. The declining birth rates of white women, compared with the purportedly high fertility rates of immigrant women, led to a political panic that linked white women's bodies to the success or failure of the nation. If white women continued to abort or use contraceptives, immigrants would take over.

In the face of several overlapping conflicts, physicians walked a tightrope. On one hand, they needed to legitimate themselves and eliminate their competition. On the other hand, they needed to do so in a way that would not alienate or offend their middle-class female patients. By focusing on their supreme expertise, physicians were able to shield their middle-class patients from complete ostracization. The women themselves were not evil or immoral. They simply lacked the understanding and education that physicians had. Instead in the war where "medical men [were] the physical guardians of women and their offspring," the real villains were those who continued to provide illegal abortions.[36] The AMA's anti-abortion campaign helped set the stage for the vilification of abortion providers through the first half of the twentieth century and lay the foundation for the stereotype of the back-alley abortionist.

Vilifying abortionists was an important part of the anti-abortion campaign; from the late 1800s through the early 1900s organized medicine tenaciously pursued this goal. Abortion providers had a reputation for being greedy, disreputable, and nefarious. They could afford luxury items and made tawdry displays of their wealth. While humble physicians healed the public, abortionists made their living providing black market services to fallen women. Since much of the AMA's denigration of abortionists hinged on publicizing the relationship between the procedure and the provider of an illicit procedure that could lead to crime (specifically murder), it made sense to link stories about fatal abortions to other segments of the criminal underworld.

Even though most women who received abortions were married, the most popular and sympathetic personification of an abortion seeker was a young, unwed woman.[37] This chapter arguably has a subtext on stereotypes. The foil of the conniving back-alley butcher, after all, had to be someone innocent and naïve. Progressive reformers had long claimed that cities were evil places for young women, so a description of abortion seekers as young, naïve, and unwed served the reformers' aims. Reformers claimed that unsupervised, immoral city life ultimately led to moral decline.[38] Away from families' immediate oversight, young women's moves to urban areas in the late nineteenth and early twentieth centuries disrupted patriarchal control over the family unit. For example, when Josie Leeman's story became public knowledge after her fatal abortion in 1881, the newspaper article traced her life from a comfortable Southern upbringing to the city, to a pauper's lot by way of a number of shameful relationships, and to an unfortunate encounter with an illegal abortionist.[39]

A similar narrative emerged when Guadalupe Garcia died from an illegal abortion at the age of twenty-three. A *Los Angeles Herald* article detailed Garcia's last days from information collected during a coroner's inquest. Garcia was described as "a young native California girl," and her story was "the old story of man's inhumanity—brutality rather—to woman."[40] Garcia grew up in Los Angeles and lived with her aunt downtown. When she got older, she left home to find work. When she was away from her family, "she encountered a betrayer, with the usual incidents, in her case a dual visitation."[41] In other words, the young woman had become pregnant with twins. The article continued:

> Appalled at the shame which awaited her, she sought out dark and devious methods to rid herself of this evidence of her fall, in this case, as in so many others, finding that the ways of iniquity and crooked medicine lead down to hell, which, in the language of the old testament, even in the case of so pious a man as David, meant death. . . . It is with keen regret that we note that the testimony seems to point to a physician who has hitherto stood high in this community—who has enjoyed our respect in common with that of most of our people—as the immediate agent in this poor girl's death. It is needless to barb an arrow to reach the heart of the betrayer of Guadalupe. If he possesses such an organ, it must have been wrung poignantly long before these lines will reach his eye.[42]

Unable to abide by the rigid social mores of her time, (which required virginity until marriage) and perhaps already shut out from respectability on account of her race, Guadalupe Garcia risked death to destroy the evidence of her deviance, and she lost this gamble.

To most reformers death by illegal abortion was a logical end to an immoral life that began when fathers lost control of their families' livelihoods and young daughters went off to work. As young women sought independence and moved to the city away from their families, they also found their ways into dance halls and vice districts. The rapid urbanization of society, and changes in American culture, would have catastrophic effects on unsupervised young women.[43]

Nevertheless, the early twentieth century looked promising. After the Great War the economy boomed, and consumers took advantage by buying cars, luxury goods, household goods, and appliances using lines of credit. Women in particular became the targets of advertising campaigns for household goods and clothes, and postwar factories began to mass-produce ready-made clothing because of the newly mobilized garment industry. Recently enfranchised, the "new women" of the 1920s cared more about independence and their economic prospects in this burgeoning economy.[44] Young white women—particularly those who had recently moved away from their nuclear families to pursue employment in the city—found more employment opportunities and a greater degree of independence than they had ever experienced before. The lack of surveillance helped move "courtship into the public world" and away "from the implied supervision of the private spheres—from the watchful eyes of family and local community—to the anonymity of the public sphere."[45] Even though women were typically paid less than their male counterparts, they felt independent as working women in the city, and part of this independence relied on their ability to control their own reproduction.

When Margaret Sanger opened the first birth-control clinic in the United States in 1916, she devoted herself to bringing the previously taboo subject of sexuality to the fore. Sanger, as well as the other editors of *Birth Control Review*, was a proponent of contraception, and she believed that men and women alike should fight for voluntary parenthood.[46] She repeatedly defied the Comstock Act in order to spread word about contraception. Sanger was aware of the dangers when poor women were forced to pay for cheap, back-alley abortions. Moreover, she had witnessed her own mother's misfortune. Sanger's mother, Anne, had conceived eighteen times, delivering eleven children and suffering seven miscarriages, before dying at the age of fifty.[47] Sanger believed it was better for women to have access to contraceptives so that they would not have to resort to the unregulated abortion underworld. Despite her endless legal battles, she championed her cause because she believed that if women were able to control their own bodies, they could engage in other cultural and intellectual pursuits. Because her desire was to liberate women from the shackles of eternal pregnancy and child rearing, Sanger's beliefs dovetailed with those of the newly independent, employed, and enfranchised woman of the 1920s.

Sanger was an advocate of birth control, but she drew the line at abortion. While many today would likely place abortion somewhere on a spectrum of contraceptive options, Sanger made an effort to distance herself from appearing to have a pro-abortion stance. Rather than advocate for abortion, Sanger and her peers stated that birth control was their primary objective; if women had access to contraceptives, then abortion rates would likely decrease over time.[48] Since Sanger and her allies approved of abortions only in instances of therapeutic necessity, their stance was moderate and technically fell in line with the professional medical community as well as most state laws—like California's.

Though professional medical organizations in California were fervently against criminal abortions, it was still difficult to bring an illegal abortionist to justice. Per the guidelines of the California Board of Medical Examiners (BME), every abortion complaint required two pieces of evidence in order to bring about punitive action. In order for a complaint to turn into an investigation against the abortionist, it was necessary to establish both proof of pregnancy and proof that something had been done to terminate the pregnancy in the absence of medical justification.[49] As practical as these categories were, they were incredibly difficult to ascertain if a woman had no complications from her abortion. Women were sometimes able to disguise the early stages of a pregnancy so that their friends, family, or even their partners may not have been aware of it, thus making proof of pregnancy difficult and effectively making the pregnancy disappear as if it never had been. Depending on what method a woman used to terminate her pregnancy, intent could be difficult to prove as well. For example, was a fall down the stairs accidental or intentional? If a woman had miscarried, was it because she had done something or because she had sought someone's assistance? Or was it *really* just a miscarriage? In addition, if the abortion was discovered, there was always the possibility that a trusted family physician could claim the woman had a condition that required an abortion. As a result, in the early twentieth century, it was very difficult to punish individuals for performing illegal abortions. However, prosecutors and professional medical societies had been able, with varying degrees of success, to prosecute abortionists in instances when a woman became critically ill or died from the procedure. When a woman died from an abortion, the coroner could establish pregnancy, proof that something had been done to terminate the pregnancy, or a preexisting condition if there was one. But the woman had to die to make the discovery possible.

Since abortion was a difficult crime to prosecute when it was safe and invisible and abortions usually became visible only when they were fatal, police relied heavily on dying declarations to gather evidence to help prosecute suspected abortionists. The organized medical community was aware that there were few alternatives when pursuing providers of illegal abortions. The *California State Journal of Medicine* even provided guidelines so that physicians could help obtain evidence to assist law enforcement. While a dying declaration had its own requirements—namely, the declarant had to state he or she was dying or knew he or she was dying—a solid abortion case had certain other requirements. First, the woman needed to testify that an abortion had been attempted or committed. Second, proof of pregnancy at the time of the alleged operation had to be established. Finally, a third party needed to corroborate that an abortion had occurred or had been attempted. According to the California Penal Code, "Upon a trial for procuring or attempting to procure an abortion, or aiding or assisting therein, or for inveigling, enticing, or taking away an unmarried female of previous chaste character, under the age of eighteen years, for the purpose of prostitution, or aiding or assisting therein, the defendant cannot be convicted upon the testimony of the woman upon or with whom the offense was committed, *unless she is corroborated by other evidence.*"[50]

Moreover, the California Penal Code essentially stated that a woman who attempted to procure an abortion was not *technically* an accomplice in the operation. On one hand, the code stripped women of legal responsibility and agency—perhaps to mitigate the fears that women were actively, deliberately seeking abortions. It also made it possible for the police to compel these women to testify against their abortionists because under existing laws co-conspirators could not testify against each other. On the other hand, the code reflected a sense of distrust between the law and the women who were caught seeking abortions. Together these seemingly contradictory sections of the law contributed to a sense of vagueness about abortion law and reflected the difficulty in prosecuting a known abortionist—especially if there was no one else to witness or testify to the operation.[51]

However, if a woman was slowly dying from her abortion, a significant portion of the investigation's success hinged upon a dying declaration. Dying declarations are a unique exception to the hearsay rule in America jurisprudence. According to the Federal Rules of Evidence, hearsay is a statement made outside of court, or while one is not under oath, and is offered as evidence or proof.[52] Rule 802 of the Federal Rules of Evidence states that hearsay is not admissible in court. Dying declarations are defined as statements made "under a belief of certain or impending death," and the statements themselves must relay information surrounding the "causes or circumstances of impending death."[53] Dying declarations are allowed as exceptions to the hearsay rule "so long as those making the statements know that they are dying and have no hope of recovery" and are dead at the time of the trial.[54]

The argument for the validity of dying declarations was initially religious, as individuals were unlikely to lie before death since it would inevitably invoke God's wrath. A dying person's statements were admissible, therefore, because it would be in their best interest to be honest.[55] Many considered dying declarations artifacts of the eighteenth and nineteenth centuries, though law enforcement continued to use them well into the twentieth century. They were relics of an era when physicians could do little for their patients as they watched them die slow, painful deaths. Unfortunately fatal abortion cases frequently fit that bill. For example, Natalie Romero died from general peritonitis nearly three weeks after a self-induced abortion; Hazel Scott died from septicemia two weeks after her abortion; and perhaps Allie Mae Sullivan was lucky that it only took her two days to die from the septicemia-induced endometritis following her abortion.[56] If the body could not be treated, last words and testimony might provide closure and justice. Sometimes abortion deaths were immediate. There were cases when inexperienced or unskilled practitioners ruptured the uterus and punctured other vital organs, resulting in hemorrhaging and death. However, most abortion deaths were the result of infections or incomplete abortions—when fetal tissue remained in the uterus—or resulted from the introduction of bacteria to the uterus through unsterilized medical instruments or an unsanitary environment. In most cases it was the infections that resulted from unsanitary or self-induced abortions that were fatal, and they did not result in immediate death. Death from infection was slow since most women avoided going to a hospital or physician until it was already too late. As a result, dying declarations played an important role in the ability to prosecute criminal abortions in the early twentieth century.

In theory dying declarations worked only when the declarant believed his or her death was imminent. The fear or "impression of almost immediate [death]" and not the actual "rapid succession of death" renders testimony admissible.[57] If the person making the declaration "had any expectation or hope of recovery"—even if he or she died soon after—the declaration was inadmissible.[58] Dying declarations relied heavily on religious assumptions, but even in their most secular defense, the threat of impending death was supposed to be enough to compel truth from the declarant. Critics of dying declarations claimed that the practice was dangerous since the declarant would not have to face a perjury charge and could use the declaration as a final opportunity to exact revenge upon someone; in addition, the family of the declarant could use the declaration to attempt to gain financial compensation.[59] Though dying declarations had their faults, investigators believed they were useful in abortion cases because these were often their only chance to gather information about providers of illegal abortion.[60]

If a woman who had had an abortion was dying, a fourth step was required: a representative from the district attorney's office needed to take the dying declaration. The declaration had to begin with a statement by the woman that expressed she was dying or knew she was about to die.[61] This step was crucial, and failure to begin a dying declaration with this statement could result in its dismissal. For example, when Dr. Emilienne Sattier Simon was charged with murder for the abortion-related death of Mrs. Annie Mott in San Francisco in 1910, the primary piece of evidence was Mrs. Mott's dying declaration, which had been taken "by an attaché" of the district attorney's office.[62] Despite the statement, the case was dismissed for lack of evidence. When the attaché from the district attorney's office began to take the dying declaration, "the San Francisco deputy failed to ask Mrs. Mott if she believed or had been apprised that she was near to death. This omission proved to be an irreparable defect in the evidence against Doctor Simon."[63]

Law enforcement's efforts to secure dying declarations often put physicians in limbo. If a woman sought help from a physician after a botched procedure, it would be that physician's legal responsibility to contact the authorities once he or she realized the woman had been operated upon illegally. Once the physician contacted the authorities, he or she would have to wait until the police arrived *before* he or she could begin to treat the patient. It's easy to imagine how difficult it would be for physicians to do their job while law enforcement agents were attempting to collect evidence, both parties negotiating space and time in order to fulfill their separate responsibilities. Sometimes delays turned what could have been an investigation into a matter of collecting a dying declaration—that is, sometimes a delay was the difference between the patient's life and death. Some physicians knew time was of the essence and attempted to treat the patient before the authorities arrived. While the physician might have claimed that he or she was doing the duty of a physician, law enforcement sometimes became suspicious, suggesting the physician had fabricated a story to cover up involvement in an illegal abortion. Fearing suspicion, some physicians refused to treat women who came to them after a botched procedure.

When the police conducted their investigations into illegal abortions, they demanded to know the name of the man responsible for the pregnancy, the name of the person who had performed the illegal operation, when and where the abortion had taken place, and how much the woman had paid for it, as well as other questions about her sex life.[64] This line of questioning may have felt punitive not only to the victim, but also to her female friends and family members, whom police also interrogated. Police often believed that these women could establish proof of pregnancy or at least provide the name of the man responsible for it. While the women were not subjected to a criminal trial or legal punishment for their involvement in procuring illegal abortions, they were required to undergo such invasive interrogations at their most vulnerable moments.[65]

The image of a young woman on her deathbed was particularly powerful. Deluded by a former love who had perhaps promised her marriage, a vulnerable, naïve, young single woman was an innocent victim. Young unmarried girls were too ill-prepared for all the evil that a city had in store. But what about married women, who represented the majority of abortion recipients? Perhaps the image of a married woman procuring an abortion was too damning. Married women who sought abortions were described as opportunistic or self-absorbed. But these women were too complicated to generalize about in newspapers, while young, unmarried women served as convenient tropes for reformers, newspapers, and law enforcement agencies.

In her analysis of abortion depictions in film, Heather MacGibbon describes two stereotyped representations of women seeking abortions in the 1920s: "prima donnas" and "martyrs" or victims.[66] Wealthy and heartless, prima donnas shirked responsibility for freedom. For example, in the 1916 film *Where Are My Children?* the prima donna has an abortion because she doesn't want a pregnancy to interfere with a party she plans to attend the following month. Prima donnas' desires to remain childless stemmed from selfish self-interest. They were negative representations of the "new woman." On the other hand, martyrs and victims were "youthful maidens" who had fallen "prey to the charms" of immoral men.[67] Martyrs and victims were the opposite of "new women." They were old-fashioned, innocent, and still believed in Victorian ideologies of virtue. They were naïve and gullible. The martyr in *Where Are My Children?* gives in to the sexual advances of the wrong man. When she becomes pregnant, her seducer escorts her to a doctor for an abortion, and she later dies at home alone.[68] Her innocence has betrayed her, and she dies a lonely death.

This trope still exists. *El Crimen del Padre Amaro* (The Crime of Father Amaro), a 2002 Spanish-language film with commercial success in the American market, conveys this same idea. The film, which is loosely based on a nineteenth-century Portuguese novel, stars Gael García Bernal as Padre Amaro, the newly ordained priest of a small Mexican town, and Ana Claudia Talancón as Amelia, the pious young woman with whom he breaks his vow of chastity. Amelia becomes infatuated with the priest, leaves her long-term boyfriend, and becomes pregnant with the priest's child. In an attempt to preserve the priest's reputation Ana begs her ex-boyfriend to take her back and marry her. When he says he is no longer interested, the priest arranges a back-alley abortion with the assistance of an eccentric female parishioner whose behavior errs on the side of *brujería* (witchcraft). Something goes terribly awry, and Amelia begins to bleed profusely. She dies en route to the hospital. The true story is concealed, and a false story is spread: Amelia's ex-boyfriend had gotten her pregnant and abandoned her, Amelia arranged a back-alley abortion, and Padre Amaro tried to save Amelia and her innocent, unborn child—but it was too late.

The martyr/victim trope relied heavily on a villain counterpart, whether that villain was the prima donna or the abortionist. Though the prima donna and martyr/victim tropes had emerged in the late nineteenth century with yellow journalism exposés, they gained new credence with the rise of the entertainment industry and organized crime. In the early twentieth century "the underworld" became "a staple of popular news reporting."[69] This is the context from which Dr. Galen R. Hickok's case emerged. Hickok was an interesting figure for two reasons: he was neither a doctor nor the real Galen R. Hickok. Hickok—and other abortionists like him—were telltale examples of how nefarious the abortion business was. The man who performed abortions under the name of Dr. Galen R. Hickok cared little about the women who sought his services or about the morality of abortion. His lack of formal medical training and his ability to fraudulently usurp another's identity further bolstered the idea that he was not a true physician or a practitioner of the healing arts; he was a liar, a murderer, and a ruiner of women. If Progressive era reformers needed to juxtapose an innocent victim against a diabolical antagonist in order to justify continued paternalistic interventions, Hickok was that antagonist.

The real Galen Hickok was born in Missouri in 1873. He went to Ottawa University in Kansas, where he earned his degree in 1895.[70] Soon thereafter he received his medical degree from the St. Louis College of Physicians and Surgeons. He began practicing medicine in 1900 and moved to the prairie town of New Ulysses, Kansas, where he was the only practicing physician for several years. Though he never lived west of Kansas, he was also registered to practice medicine and surgery in Arkansas, Colorado, Illinois, Iowa, Kentucky, Missouri, Nebraska, New Mexico, Oklahoma, and Tennessee; he occasionally visited patients in these states by special request.[71]

After practicing medicine for some time, Dr. Galen Hickok got involved in real estate. He opened a real estate office and eventually became president of the Southern Mortgage Company and a prominent figure in local government.[72] When he discovered that someone was fraudulently using his name and credentials in California for illegal activity, he did his best to clear his name. Despite his best efforts, newspapers and even the California BME continued to use *his* name when referring to the usurper abortionist. According to the real Dr.

Hickok, in 1902 his former assistant—a man with no recorded first name who went by the name of "Thompson," though his actual name was "Zangwell"—stole Dr. Hickok's legitimately earned diploma and resurfaced in 1904, when he used the stolen credentials to apply for a license to practice medicine in Nevada.[73] For the real Dr. Hickok's sake I will use "Zangwell" to refer to the illegitimate Dr. Hickok. It should be noted, however, that the documents use the name "Dr. Galen R. Hickok" for both the real physician and his usurper.

After fraudulently obtaining his Nevada license, Zangwell practiced medicine in the Nevada towns of Deeth, Ely, Gardnerville, and Midas. Around 1909 Zangwell and his family moved to Los Angeles, where his mother-in-law lived.[74] While in Southern California, Zangwell acquired a license to practice naturopathy. When called before the Naturopathic Association of California, Zangwell presented Dr. Galen R. Hickok's credentials and was able to masquerade as the Kansas physician yet again.[75] In Los Angeles Zangwell established connections with local abortion providers. Since he was already operating on the wrong side of the law—as an identity thief—it made sense for him to fall into the abortion industry. Abortions were illegal, but they were lucrative and relatively simple procedures considering that Zangwell had previously worked as an assistant to Dr. Hickok and likely had prior medical training.

Despite having some experience under his belt, once he was in California, Zangwell was frequently under BME investigation. Starting in 1911 Dr. Hickok's name began to appear regularly in newspapers and internal BME correspondence in connection with illegal abortions. That same year an attorney for the BME described Dr. Hickok as one of the worst abortionists in Los Angeles.[76] Zangwell repeatedly changed his address and business associates in order to thwart BME investigations. Since BME investigations at the time required current addresses, Zangwell's frequent relocations allowed him to stay ahead of the board. When an abortion went poorly or when he had been at one location for too long, Zangwell moved his business to a new location and effectively off the BME's map.

In 1911 Zangwell purchased land in Northern California, though it is unclear when he and his family moved there.⁷⁷ From 1912 through 1920 Zangwell maneuvered his way through periodic investigations and evaded incarceration. In 1912, for example, a nineteen-year-old woman in San Francisco named Dr. Hickok in her dying declaration.⁷⁸ Zangwell was arrested, booked, and charged with performing a criminal operation. He was later released on bail and did not serve any time. In 1913 he was arrested and charged with performing an illegal operation on Elsie Pickrell. Even though the judge increased bail from $1,000 to $10,000 because of supposedly incriminating testimony, Zangwell did not serve any time for performing this abortion either. Despite such legal troubles, Zangwell's illegal abortion business prospered. By 1916 he had a professional office in San Francisco and a partnership with a surgeon, Dr. Martha Allen Reinhart.⁷⁹ Zangwell even had enough money to purchase the McCloskey Castle in Salada Beach, California (now Pacifica, California). In 1916 Zangwell was arrested two more times. In her dying declaration Mrs. Alva McKean, a twenty-six-year-old bookkeeper at First National Bank, said she had paid "Dr. Hickok" $150 for an abortion on August 2. She became critically ill and died on August 30. Despite further arrests and investigations in 1917 and 1918, Zangwell managed to avoid jail time until 1920, when his "castle" became the center of new allegations.

Zangwell's decision to run a multi-bed clinic from the relative obscurity of his castle was a departure from the usual methods of running an abortion business from a doctor's office or residence. Since the castle was away from the city center, Zangwell remained mostly undisturbed. Women came and left his castle at night under the cover of darkness, and the castle was large enough for him to accommodate half a dozen patients at a time. It centralized his work in an early example of an abortion clinic and allowed him to maximize efficiency.

Upon hearing allegations that Dr. Hickok had contributed to the delinquency of a fourteen-year-old girl, police obtained search warrants and made their way to the castle, where they found three women recovering from operations. When police searched the premises, they found discarded, visibly charred human remains wrapped in newspaper.⁸⁰ The remains—determined to be those of a newborn child and possibly a woman—coupled with the presence of the three recovering women led to Zangwell's subsequent arrest for performing illegal abortions. As police continued to search the castle grounds, they found other articles of women's clothing scattered around the property, leading them to believe there were more bodies, though no additional remains were ever found.

Zangwell was charged with performing an illegal operation on Mrs. Bertha Casteel, one of the women recovering in the castle. Though Zangwell was charged only with the abortion on Mrs. Casteel, the other two women who had been recovering—Mary Cozzo and Irene Carpenter—also testified. Zangwell's attorney attempted to block their testimony on the grounds that it was immaterial, but the judge allowed it. Zangwell also interrupted the testimony several times before his counsel managed to silence him. The jury took just seven minutes to find Zangwell guilty, and he was sentenced to an indeterminate term of two to five years in San Quentin. Zangwell lost his appeal and was denied a retrial.⁸¹

Shortly after the initial trial the BME subpoenaed Zangwell to appear before the board and show cause why his license should not be revoked—even though the BME was now aware of the fraud and identity theft that had resulted in his possession of a medical license in the first place!⁸² The meeting between Zangwell and the BME was rescheduled at least once because Dr. Pinkham, the secretary-treasurer of the BME, hoped to have the real Dr. Hickok present. Zangwell did not attend the hearing, and after hearing testimony from patients that Zangwell had treated as early as 1909, the BME revoked Zangwell's license (obtained fraudulently) to practice naturopathy in California.

Word of discarded remains on the mystery castle's grounds made the Hickok case a national story, but it also served to reignite fears about illegal abortionists. The story of Zangwell/Hickok suggested that providers of illegal abortions were crude and barbaric or that a visit to an abortionist could result in death. Journalists' language even added to these fears. In the *Oakland Tribune* the "girls" were "rescued" in a raid of the "castle-like structure" that was "guarded day and night."[83] With this text it would seem as though the abortionist was holding unwilling girls hostage—not adult women—so that he could force abortions upon them. Instead it was most likely that these women were willing participants in this whole debacle—regardless of how unskilled Zangwell was. And it should be noted that even if Zangwell was a presumed butcher, after years of evading arrest and unflattering media coverage, his business was booming.

Shortly after San Francisco police had conducted their search at Zangwell's castle, a similar case appeared in New York, and Suffolk County Sheriff's officers began to search Henry Lee Mottard's farm in Long Island. Henry Lee Mottard performed abortions in a Manhattan office under the name of "Dr. Henry L. Green."[84]

In 1923 a forty-four-year-old Brooklyn woman named Annie Allison was found dead in the elevator shaft of Mottard's office building. Mottard claimed that Allison must have fallen down the elevator shaft to her death. As a physician, he signed the death certificate with the cause of death as "chronic cardiac nephritis."[85] However, another suspicious death in Mottard's office prompted law enforcement to exhume Allison's body and reopen the case. Upon further review it was revealed that Allison's body lacked the telltale signs of a tragic fall. She had no broken bones, bruises, or cuts that would be expected from such a tragedy. Upon her exhumation Dr. Charles Norris, the chief medical examiner, stated that in his opinion "a criminal operation had been performed. The cause of death [was] a hemorrhage."[86] If the two suspicious deaths (and potential cover-ups) were not enough, Mottard's former nurse implicated him in the disappearance of a missing infant, Lillian McKenzie.[87]

On August 18, 1923, Mrs. Ella McKenzie was window-shopping on Sixth Avenue in New York City with her three-month-old daughter Lillian. She decided to leave baby Lillian in her carriage on the sidewalk while she went inside a store to browse some more. While we might cringe at the idea today, it was apparently quite common and not frowned upon in 1923. After looking in the store for about ten minutes, Mrs. McKenzie went back outside, only to discover that her child was missing. Her screams alerted police, and a frantic search for the child ensued. Potential leads came and went, and eventually those dried up. The case slowly went cold. According to the nurse, Mottard claimed that the baby she thought to be Lillian was the adopted child of a Dr. and Mrs. Grofe.[88] The child was ill because the Grofes had been on vacation, and their babysitter was inexperienced. The Grofes were disturbed to find the child sickly when they returned. Lillian McKenzie was also a sickly child. In fact her sickliness fueled a sense of urgency because her parents claimed she required a special kind of formula. Police even published the formula she needed in hopes that the kidnapper could at least keep her nourished. It isn't clear why the nurse suddenly brought up Mottard's name since the investigation into Lillian's kidnapping had been ongoing, but it seemed like a strong lead, and police suspected that Mottard was somehow involved in Lillian's disappearance.[89]

Upon interrogation Mottard denied knowing anything about the McKenzie child, but he admitted to performing abortions at his farm.[90] After discovering this piece of information, Suffolk County Sheriff's officers acquired a search warrant based on the theory that they would find bodies buried on the property.[91] As the investigation escalated, police uncovered more details surrounding the Grofe child. As it turns out, the Grofes' adopted child had been born in Mottard's office. The mother was a young girl who did not want to keep the child.[92] Therefore the child could not have been Lillian McKenzie. Nevertheless, investigators continued to search the property.[93] In the search they found that Mottard had spent $12,000 on renovations for a private operating room, but there was no graveyard. Mottard was unable to come up with the $25,000 bail and remained in custody until early May 1925, when the court accepted $15,000 for his release.[94]

It is unclear what happened to Zangwell after he served his time in San Quentin or to Mottard after he got out on bail. "Dr. Galen Hickok" was paroled on October 4, 1924. In the 1926 San Francisco city directory his occupation was listed as tailor. In 1928 he was arrested for practicing medicine without a license, and he served time again. The Hickok family is listed in the 1930 San Francisco census but disappears from record thereafter (though members of the family maintained ownership of the castle for some time). In 1938 Max Hickok, Zangwell's son, appears to have followed in his father's footsteps. He was charged with the murder of forty-two-year-old Elizabeth Sowers when she accused him of performing a criminal operation in her dying declaration. He was convicted of second-degree murder, and in the 1940 census he was an inmate at San Quentin prison.

The cases of Zangwell and Mottard illustrate that law enforcement was better equipped to try abortionists when death or allegations of death were involved. Since abortion was a relatively invisible crime when performed safely, illegal abortions became visible only under such instances. Hence many of the discussions about abortion in the legal realm revolved around fatal cases. These cases also show that a bad reputation did not put an abortion provider out of business. In the black market women got the abortionist they could find or afford. Women who wanted illegal abortions did not have legal protection or access to sanitary treatment; their options were usually "take it or leave it." Black markets tend to be "wealth-sensitive," meaning that "poor people face the risks more often."[95] As a result deaths from illegal abortions were distributed unevenly and found mostly among poor women who had gone to cheaper providers who lacked proper credentials or skill. Women's desperation and a lack of alternatives kept even these practitioners in business, not their skill or reputation.

These cases also suggest that illegal abortion was not a huge leap away from other criminal behavior—at least in the minds of law enforcement or the public. In the sensational cases discussed here the abortionists assumed false identities and lied about causes of death. These men weren't just providers of illegal abortions; they were common criminals, not unlike bootleggers, mobsters, or murderers. Allegations of buried bodies, kidnapping, fraud, and identity theft made abortion just a stepping stone to other segments of the criminal underworld. In this line of thinking abortion was not a medical procedure; it was an illicit service and commodity. For example, in the film *Confessions of a Vice Baron* (1943), Willy Castello plays James "Lucky" Lombardi. Lombardi reflects on his life of crime the night before his scheduled execution. He recalls using aliases when pretending to be an aristocrat, running an abortion racket, pimping prostitutes, selling girls in the white slave trade, and eventually committing murder. To those watching the film abortion was inseparable from the rest of the criminal underworld in which he took part.

In practice the criminalization of abortion and loopholes thereto paralleled the enforcement of the Volstead Act, which initiated Prohibition. Those who wanted to exploit Prohibition's loopholes simply acquired their booze legally with medical prescriptions or became members of Catholic churches or synagogues, institutions that legally used wine in their services. American farmers put labels on their at-home juice making kits with warnings against leaving the juice out too long (in order to avoid fermentation), much like druggists in the Comstock era put labels on their drugs to "warn" pregnant women from taking abortifacients, lest they miscarry. Unregulated, illegal alcohol could be deadly for those producing or ingesting it. Thousands of Americans died from ingesting tainted alcohol, while others were injured or killed by distillery fires or noxious fumes. Deregulation in alcohol and abortion meant there were no consumer protections. Because of the disconnect between the law and the public's wishes, countless otherwise law-abiding citizens became criminals.

This chapter has linked the underworld and the abortionist. As most physicians drew a hard line at what was considered a legal abortion, others came in to fill the void. As a result abortion providers were sometimes unlicensed or unskilled. The chapter has also illustrated how the press maligned abortion providers by focusing on the criminal element, linking abortion to other crimes and using sensational reporting to sell newspapers. In these cases the villainous abortionists were at the center of the story. In the next chapters we will move from the villainous, unlicensed abortionist to regular physicians who performed illegal abortions. As the characters in our narrative change, the legal options change as well. No longer unlicensed back-alley butchers, these physicians used their status as medical professionals to escape harsh sentences. Their status also tended to shield them from the smearing that unlicensed providers faced. In addition, the chapters, shifting our focus to Southern California, will stress the vagueness of California's abortion law. Rather than standing as an insurmountable legal blockade, for regular physicians the law was often a minor hurdle that could be sidestepped.

Regular Physicians, Irregular Circumstances

Loopholes and Scandals

> The doctor's position in these [criminal abortion] cases is an unpleasant one, but a medical man as such is concerned solely with the proper treatment of the patient and the fact that she has been a party to a criminal transaction can have no place in regulating his conduct. His duty is to endeavor to save life regardless of the moral character of the patient.
>
> —Dr. John Campbell, 1921

After spending some time in Southern California, Dr. William A. Edwards concluded that its climate had the ability to cure a variety of ailments—from chronic pneumonia, tuberculosis, malaria, and jaundice to female disturbances and constipation.[1] When Dr. Edwards wrote this conclusion in the nineteenth century, he was not the only one to view California's environment so favorably. He followed on the heels of miners, travelers, and medical experts who had fed into the myth of California's healing climate. Boosters inflated these curative myths and spread them to wealthy invalids and consumptives. At the same time quacks, pharmacists, and "healers" sold various tonics, cures, and treatments, making California a place where people were constantly preoccupied with health and matters of the body. Physicians were instrumental in the founding of Los Angeles. Because of California's reputation as a place of healing, medicine was important to the state from the start, and medical associations in the state were constantly on the cutting edge of professional debates.

In the late nineteenth and early twentieth centuries sick individuals made up a significant portion of the newcomers to California and helped to spark the dynamic growth of not only a system of sanitariums but also a coterie of medical quacks and eccentrics who sought to capitalize on the growing population. For example, representatives from the Battle Creek Sanitarium in Michigan began negotiations for the creation of a sanitarium in Glendale in 1904, and the *Los Angeles Times* considered this a wonderful possibility for the city and region.[2] The descriptions of California as a health destination worked hand in hand with boosters' efforts. For example, in 1904 the Southern Pacific Company published its own tract to bolster the use of its rail lines. Aside from the sensational promotion of the climate, the tract explained that California's fruit had actually achieved perfection because the abundant sunshine resulted in sweeter, more delicious, and exceptionally nutritive fruit.[3] California fruit and vegetables were manifestations of the state's sunshine, wellness, and healthfulness.[4] California's burgeoning agricultural industry was also crucial to the image of California as a health destination.

This early focus on health in California contributed to the creation of some of the oldest medical societies in the United States west of the Mississippi River. Like the AMA, the medical societies in California—specifically in San Francisco and Los Angeles—emerged to dispel quackery and establish uniformity in a climate where charlatans preyed on the sick and naïve who had financial means. One of the earliest concerns of the Los Angeles County Medical Association (LACMA), for example, was the regulation and punishment of those who practiced irregular medicine or called themselves physicians when they lacked the proper credentials.[5] LACMA believed that advancements in the medical field, as well as additional medical contributions to society, were possible only through the separation of regular and irregular medicine. LACMA denied membership to any person who practiced irregular medicine, and any member who was found to have consulted with an irregular practitioner had his or her membership revoked.[6] In 1876 California passed the Act to Regulate the Practice of Medicine. This act required all persons to present themselves before their local board of examiners if they intended to practice medicine in the state. If an individual was unable to furnish a diploma from a recognized medical school, he or she was subject to an examination. Only after this process would the board determine if an individual was competent in the healing arts.[7]

Membership in professional societies had grown increasingly important in the American West for physicians, who used such memberships as "vital links" to physicians in the rest of the country.[8] This imagined community of physicians facilitated the creation of a standardized field with oversight. These professional associations, and the networks they forged, denied nonmembers access to the modernity and legitimacy that membership created.[9] Medical society members positioned themselves as protectors of the profession and used membership to legitimate themselves in a way that secured their collective statuses as regular physicians against a backdrop of irregular practitioners, such as Chinese medicine men, Black graduates of unrecognized medical colleges, and midwives.[10]

When California legislators drafted the state's original abortion statute, they did so before the growth of the state's fringe medical community and the rise of the AMA. The statute, quoted in part in chapter 1, was intended to protect women from unlicensed quacks, and it indicated that the state's legislators were on the cutting edge. The original specified the following: "*Provided*, that no physician shall be affected by the last clause of this section, who, in the discharge of his professional duties, deems it necessary to produce the miscarriage of any woman to save her life."[11]

An interpretation of this statute suggests that physicians could do no wrong. There was no penalty for physicians who performed abortions when they determined the procedure was medically necessary to preserve the life of a mother. If, for example, a woman had attempted her own abortion and had failed or experienced complications, a doctor might determine it necessary to complete the induced abortion for the woman's health and safety. An unintended consequence of this line of legal thought was that physicians had little to lose in the event that they came before a judge or the medical board. Financial or human-interest motivations, then, could spur otherwise mainline physicians to provide abortions; they simply had to say they believed the procedure was necessary. Minor legal obstacles, coupled with a potential for high profits, led to the rise of the physician-abortionist in California.

California was in the midst of rapid transformations during the first half of the twentieth century. Carey McWilliams has described the rapid population growth in Los Angeles as a boom "punctuated [by] major explosions."[12] Ambitious boosters sold California as a place of eternal sunshine where the future happened first. And they were successful in attracting newcomers. They profited by selling "deluded dreamers . . . a paradise that didn't exist."[13] Los Angeles became a tourist destination where the world came to winter or heal. While California's climate was enough to entice sojourners, tourism gradually gave way to planned subdivisions, housing, and suburbanization when the newcomers decided to stay. Increased industrialization in the 1920s facilitated the population boom as individuals came in search of jobs.

Three factors increased the migration to Los Angeles in the 1920s and 1930s: oil, movies, and the Great Depression. A surge in oil production during World War I had transformed Southern California's landscape and economy as fabricators struggled to construct pipelines fast enough to transport this liquid gold. The discovery of oil also echoed the tenuous relationship of the Los Angeles boosters with nature in the region. The constant battle to "civilize," control, or exploit the landscape was most visible in efforts to irrigate the desert and pave the Los Angeles River. All the efforts reflected a similar narrative. Los Angeles was founded on white modernity: the ability to control and organize nature. William Mulholland's ventures into the Owens River Valley, for example, contributed to the growth of the city. His plan to divert a body of water and manipulate nature in a time when most cities lacked running water reflected the boosters' truth that Los Angeles was a city of innovation, where the future happened first.[14] Efforts to make Los Angeles modern coincided with the making and remaking of its ethnic past. While whites in Los Angeles worked to pave the landscape and civilize nature (in order to make it suitable for whites), they also created a mythological past that effectively retold the city's racial history—the Spanish Fantasy Past. Much as the paving of the Los Angeles River had tamed the landscape and prepared it for incorporation into the American nation, the creation of a historical myth smoothed over a history of violence, conquest, and racism that had been integral to U.S. imperial ventures.[15]

Southern California's geography also played a role in the film industry. Though the history of film extends into the nineteenth century, it did not become a popular form of mass entertainment until the twentieth century. While film's early history begins on the east coast, by the 1910s a number of filmmakers had begun to make the journey west—among them D. W. Griffith, who is most famous for his film *Birth of a Nation*. Some of Griffith's earliest films, like *Old California* and *Ramona*, were among the first motion pictures filmed in California, and they also relied heavily on tropes of the Spanish Fantasy Past.

To early filmmakers Los Angeles was a safe haven. Some of the earliest producers who came to California did so to escape legal actions for violating patents. California was distant enough from Thomas Edison and the Motion Picture Patent Company that filmmakers and producers could practice in relative peace. In the rare event of legal action filmmakers had escape to Mexico as an option or last resort. In addition to the safety the state's distance provided, California's weather and landscape made it a prime filming location with year-round sunshine and the availability of nearly every type of nature scenery within a short drive. The proximity to the border and an almost endless supply of cheap labor didn't hurt, either. The introduction of sound to motion pictures helped transform the previously small colony of actors and producers into professionals and celebrities. Writers and artists also saw in Hollywood a place to make their mark and earn a living. Soon "Hollywood" became the motion picture capital, and motion pictures became the leading industry in Los Angeles from the 1920s through the 1940s.[16]

While some came to Los Angeles to create films, others came to star in them. As Hollywood spread its reach across the country, young women left their homes and day jobs to wait in lines at studios and get discovered. After seeing the "kaleidoscope of pretty clothes, automobiles, gay suppers, beach-bathing, and a million other things" in a picture show, their lives were never the same.[17] While the film industry attracted throngs of young women, newspapers lamented the pressures these women felt to look a certain way. In 1917 Dr. Lulu Hunt Peters's *Diet and Health with Key to the Calories* had already debuted and become a sensation, while her *Los Angeles Times* column, "Diet and Health," made her one of America's first diet and weight-loss gurus after she had lost seventy pounds by following her own protocols.[18] While other doctors and quacks usually referenced weight loss in conjunction with health concerns, Dr. Peters's dieting advice accompanied beauty tips, suggesting, if perhaps subliminally, that attractiveness and thinness were one and the same. Dr. Peters dispelled earlier conceptions that individuals were destined to be a certain size and instead argued that dieting, or "reducing," required perseverance and discipline. It was not for naught, though. Dr. Peters suggested that those who were intent on losing weight should smile and find comfort in the fact that achieving a goal weight would make them more attractive and help them "look fully ten years younger."[19]

Dr. Peters's daily column, "Diet and Health," continued where her book left off, providing her readers with daily advice and affirmation. Headlines like "It Won't be Any Easier Tomorrow" reminded her readers of the long road ahead. Readers wrote in and described their own weight-loss journeys. A certain Mrs. C. wrote that she decided to start reducing when, at the age of twenty-seven and at 163 pounds, she realized she looked more like "a nice, fat middle-aged hausfrau" than an attractive young wife.[20] Though Peters's daily column focused on health since she was using her medical credentials, her headlines gradually shifted from the likes of "What Shall We Eat to Keep Healthy and Strong?" to "Will Be Disgrace to Be Overweight: Dr. Lulu Hunt Peters' View of the Near Future" to "How Film Stars Keep Slim," and young women craving a job in Hollywood ate the columns up (if nothing else).

According to one Chicago journalist, Hollywood tourists could easily witness "the daily parade of the thousands of beautiful but starving girls who have come out to be stars in movies."[21] Rob Wagner's 1918

Film Folks described the conventional roles, plots, and components of "the movies." His lengthiest chapter, "The Movie Queen," followed the journeys of different young ladies in the quest for Hollywood stardom in an industry where looks predominated. Studios and employment bureaus would gather information from "potential Juliets": their age, height, weight, hair color, chest size, eye color, waist size, nationality, and previous experience. They would then categorize and file the girls according to "various heads, such as matrons, young girls, children, chorus types, fat, [and] thin" so that they could quickly find someone if a spot opened up.[22] Those who did get jobs often found themselves with "weight clauses" that could potentially nullify their contracts.[23] These weight clauses could vary from a temporary suspension until the actress "regain[ed] her earlier silhouette" to a "legal phrasing" stipulating that weighing over a specified amount would automatically release the actress from the contract.[24]

As the film industry grew, so did salaries, celebrity status, and requirements for actors and actresses. A supplemental textbook for the New York Institute of Photography included a chapter titled "Would You Screen Well?" which addressed the physical characteristics that would or would not work well under the camera's gaze. According to the chapter, long necks looked better on screen than short necks; "clear, white skin" looked better than all the alternatives; and women were best if they were under a height of five feet two inches. The chapter also stated that "a good figure counts for much on the screen. You must make allowances, in judging your screen value, for the fact that the camera exaggerates; that you will appear larger on the screen than you really are. Many an actress who looks beautifully slender off the screen does not dare eat what or when she wants; she must diet to keep thin enough for the camera."[25] If an actress gained weight and especially if she got pregnant, she risked losing relevance in a competitive industry where flocks of girls sought to replace her daily.

When, or if, these working girls got pregnant, they became prime consumers for the illegal abortion industry. Abortions in the early film industry continue to be a fascinating topic for those interested in Hollywood's early history. A recent article in *Vanity Fair* suggested that abortions were run-of-the-mill procedures for Hollywood starlets and that they were frequently arranged by the heads of motion picture studios to avoid scandal and to protect their investments in the actresses. Actresses such as Jean Harlow, Tallulah Bankhead, Jeanette McDonald, Judy Garland, and Joan Crawford had these procedures, though typically under the auspices of some other condition. For example, Harlow checked into a hospital "to get some rest," while McDonald had an "ear infection."[26] However, it wasn't just the actresses in real life who had abortions. They were also topics for the big screen. Films like *The Road to Ruin* (1928), *The Seventh Commandment* (1932), *Men in White* (1934), *Gambling with Souls* (1936), *Dead End* (1937), and *Race Suicide* (1937) highlighted the connection among abortion, illegality, vice, corruption, and death—much like newspapers had done in the nineteenth century.

In *The Road to Ruin*, the character Ann Dixon is a sweet, innocent girl with two loving parents. At school she befriends Eve Monroe, a wild classmate with a wealthy divorcée (and conspicuously absent) mother. Shortly after befriending Eve, Ann loses her virginity to Tommy, a classmate and friend of Eve's boyfriend. Ann is transformed from a sweet, innocent girl into a drinker and party goer. Ann eventually leaves Tommy for Ralph, a slightly older man. One night Ralph, Eve, Ann, and some of their friends are at a party that results in drinking, strip poker, and romping in the pool. Police break it up and take Ann and Eve to the station, where they are forced to undergo medical examinations. Ann is released as a "sex-delinquent," and Eve, also a "sex-delinquent," must stay for treatment since her Wasserman test is positive for syphilis. After seeing the error of her ways, Eve gains a new perspective on life. Ann, however, wishes she were dead since her medical examination reveals she is pregnant.

Ralph tells Ann he will not marry her and convinces her to have an abortion. He takes her to an abortionist, and she returns home after the procedure. Ann is feverish, and her mother grows concerned, but Ann claims it's just a headache. Tommy, Ann's ex-boyfriend, arrives at the Dixon home. He has heard of Ann's grave condition and wishes to extend his sympathies to her family. Ann's father explains that Ann is very sick and that there is no hope. She had "a clumsy, unsanitary operation... aggravated by some terrific shock." On Ann's deathbed her mother sobs and apologizes for having failed her. Ann grabs both of her parents' hands as she says, "It seemed like such a beautiful road, but it was only..." She dies before finishing her sentence, and the viewer realizes it was only a "road to ruin."[27] As abortion stories had been a way to sell newspapers, films became the new medium through which to tell those same stories. However, movies didn't just feature abortions; they also created an opportunity for the abortion industry to thrive.

As noted, the Great Depression was another factor that motivated migration to Los Angeles. Booster images of California survived long after the booster period. Perhaps as a testament to their efficacy, "Okies" and "Arkies" traveled west, believing they would at least fare better in the Golden State.[28] Though New Deal projects and legislation attempted to combat the economic downturn, unemployment remained a staggering problem. With few opportunities for subsistence remaining in the Midwest, some four hundred thousand Americans abandoned their homes and old lives and headed to California in search of prosperity. However, the Depression had affected Californians as well, and most Californians cared little for these migrants. Despite the best efforts of many locals to keep the newcomers out of the state, migrants continued to pour in.

Unable to stop the deluge, Californians looked for other ways to save state money during this period of economic uncertainty. Two of the cost-cutting endeavors were the repatriation of Mexicans and the eugenics movement. State officials used economic justifications to boost support for these projects.[29] Many American migrants—like Okies and Arkies—found their way into agricultural positions with other immigrants—Mexican, Japanese, Filipino, and Chinese. Unemployed whites put pressure on local government to hire "citizens" only, conflating whiteness with American citizenship. Some places enacted laws that made it illegal to hire aliens; others prioritized welfare and charity to native-born heads of households.

The presence of a sizable Mexican population disrupted the earlier agribusiness arguments that Mexicans were "homing pigeons" who would return to Mexico when the agricultural season was over; thus, they argued, Mexicans should be exempt from the quotas in the Immigration Act of 1924. But Mexicans were not returning to Mexico. Homing pigeons no more, Mexicans were staying, settling, and forming families in the United States. "Repatriation" became a campaign that reconciled racial scapegoating and racism with the purported fiscal demands of the Depression. In "repatriating" ethnic Mexicans—many of whom were in fact U.S. citizens—the government helped secure some of the limited resources for whites by eliminating non-white competition. Some Mexicans chose to return to Mexico on their own because they feared an increasingly hostile environment in the United States.[30]

Similarly the eugenics movement and initiatives for compulsory sterilization relied upon financial justifications. While Margaret Sanger's efforts to bring birth control to the fore may have unnerved some when her target audience was white, middle-class women, in other instances reproductive control did not generate the same vocal condemnation. In fact, at the same time that Margaret Sanger campaigned for increased access to birth control, there was an upsurge in the number of irreversible surgical eugenic procedures throughout the country.

According to California's eugenic sterilization law, which was enacted in 1909, physicians and superintendents in state institutions were able to authorize the sterilization of a patient if the patient had certain conditions or if it was thought that sterilization would improve the patient's condition. The law was expanded in 1917 to allow for the sterilization of those with "any 'mental disease which may have been *inherited* and is likely to be transmitted to descendants,' thereby allowing a more expansive and eugenics-based rationale for sterilization."[31] National institutions such as the Eugenics Records Office (ERO) studied family pedigrees, crime, alcoholism, and poverty and drafted model eugenic legislation in the 1920s to direct and control human reproduction. Using Mendelian theories of genetics and biology, early eugenicists believed that it was possible to curb social decline by manipulating reproduction—that is, by preventing the reproduction of "socially inadequate people," most of whom were poor, immigrants, or non-white.[32] By 1935 most American states had adopted some form of eugenic legislation, and many were animated to aggressively sterilize their unfit populations after the U.S. Supreme Court Decision in *Buck v. Bell* (1927).[33]

Social scientists and eugenicists believed that compulsory sterilizations were fiscally conservative and ethically and morally neutral (or even positive). In ordering the compulsory sterilization of the eugenically unfit or those who were likely to become (or produce) public charges, eugenicists argued they could save states thousands of dollars in institutionalization costs alone. Dr. Leo Stanley, the medical superintendent of San Quentin Prison, sterilized inmates in the 1930s, while others like Paul Popenoe—a sterilization-advocate-turned-marriage counselor—believed that families on welfare should receive contraceptive information and devices since they were unlikely to produce good quality citizens.[34] Poverty, of course, was the telltale sign of flawed character. The same factors that compelled the deportation of Mexicans facilitated the unprecedented way that "eugenicists linked biological inferiority to the abuse of state resources, a connection reinforced by the Deportation Agent and during the exclusionary purge of the Great Depression."[35] Most states used the Great Depression to justify and mobilize public opinion behind compulsory sterilization. Given the prospect of saving money on institutional costs, sterilization was a fiscally conservative choice.

Eugenic sterilization targeted individuals who exhibited mental or psychopathic disorders, yet an increasingly gendered approach emerged that targeted women who were considered loose, immoral, or unfit. While the criteria were broad, it is important to also consider the proliferation of essentialist and racist thinking in California eugenics. Racial ideas about biological difference, criminality, poverty, morality, and mental capacity often overlapped with who was considered a good candidate for sterilization. Previous scholars have established that California's eugenic programs disproportionately targeted the foreign born and that "Blacks and Mexicans were operated on at rates that exceeded their proportion of the population."[36] As a result, California created "the most activist eugenics movement in the country and even the world."[37]

So while eugenic sterilization had existed in California since 1909, the economic depression and the *Buck v. Bell* decision fortified physicians' convictions to interfere with women's reproduction, performing therapeutic abortions and sterilizations for eugenic, social, or even economic reasons. However, because of the eugenics movement, some women's reproduction was considered more valuable than that of others. White women of a certain economic or social status may have found it difficult to acquire legal abortions for reasons short of life-threatening illness. For non-white women in California who wanted an abortion, though, the eugenics movement posed an additional risk. The stressful financial conditions put physicians in a position where they believed they could reduce the state's social and financial burdens through abortion and sterilization. Women's bodies therefore possessed different meanings, and how physicians interpreted those bodies was often based on other factors.[38] In the eyes of the state Mexicans, the poor, the disabled, or those who were otherwise eugenically "unfit" were burdens to stressed public health and charity institutions.[39] As such, it would appear that contraception—writ large—was not the problem. Instead it was only a social issue when the women who wanted to avoid motherhood were young, native-born, white, and without disease or defect.

A cursory understanding of the dramatic changes outlined previously is necessary to bring us to our next cases. Our young victims in this chapter are Delphine Walsh—an up-and-coming Hollywood starlet—and Vera Nelson—who perhaps had aspirations to be one. Building on the previous chapter's discussion of abortion coverage in the media, we note that Delphine Walsh and Vera Nelson's fatal abortions were covered widely in newspapers at the time. However, unlike the women who sought the services of Zangwell and Mottard, these two women sought their illegal abortions from licensed physicians. Newspapers were unable to rely upon the same tropes and adjectives used to describe unlicensed quacks and liars, so the licensed physicians were described with more sympathy—particularly since these physicians usually argued that the young women had self-induced their own abortions before seeking medical care. Walsh and Nelson were not young girls who had to be "rescued" from the castle of a depraved abortionist; they were young women who—supposedly—had taken matters into their own hands and forced reputable physicians into a moral, ethical, and professional gray area.

In addition to discussing these two cases, this chapter also uses Los Angeles County Coroner's Office records to delve into the reality of self-induced abortions and abortion mortality in general. Ultimately the prevalence of self-induced abortions served as an effective cover or loophole for licensed physicians involved in illegal abortions. If a case came to trial, it was likely because the woman had died, and as a result it would be only the physician's word as to the cause of death. If the physician was prominent or sympathetic enough, any repercussions from an illicit abortion would likely amount to just a slap on the wrist.

Delphine Walsh was born to Mr. and Mrs. Thomas Dougherty in the copper mining town of Bisbee, Arizona, a town approximately ninety miles southeast of Tucson and near the U.S.-Mexico border. The town was one of the most profitable mining sites in the West and one of the largest cities between St. Louis and San Francisco. Delphine's father was a copper miner in an industry that thrived in the late nineteenth and early twentieth centuries. She was born shortly before a 1908 fire devastated the community. The town survived the fire and rebuilt, but even as the copper industry remained strong in the area, Delphine's parents soon found themselves unable to care for their young daughter. It is possible that her father was injured in the mines and was unable to keep up with the demands of a rigorous physical job.[40] Alternatively, it is possible that the Mexican Revolution, which lasted from about 1910 to 1920, had brought an influx of capable male workers to the border town, thus increasing job competition and driving down wages. Writing about the copper mines in Morenci and Clifton, Arizona (about one hundred miles north of Bisbee), Linda Gordon describes Mexicans as "ideal workers" in the mining industry because "their labor power fell on a different economy and society, Mexico.... The migrant laborer, straddling two nations and two economics, could view the dollars in his weekly pay envelope in terms of what they could buy in Mexico ... [accepting] wages half to two-thirds those of 'American' workers."[41] We may never know why Delphine's previously capable parents suddenly found themselves unable to care for their young daughter, but soon enough, Mrs. Mae Walsh adopted her.

Mrs. Walsh put Delphine in dance classes, and the young girl thrived. They eventually moved to Los Angeles. Delphine had hopes of fame and became popular rather quickly. She became a rising star in theater, working with Franchon and Marco, renowned Los Angeles producers, and touring with "Hollywood Scandals," a burlesque that did tours on the East Coast.[42] She became a Hollywood socialite, befriending actresses and other movie personalities. Just days before she died of complications from an abortion, Walsh was flown from Hollywood to San Francisco for a party. Clearly she was on the cusp of stardom.

Delphine Walsh died in 1929 in Glendale, California, following an illegal abortion.[43] To find the man responsible for her "condition" police and the BME searched Hollywood's motion picture and theatrical circles. They held interviews and interrogations with (among others) Mildred Harris, ex-wife of celebrity Charles Chaplin—perhaps much to the delight of newspaper readers everywhere. This was not the first time that the film community had come under scrutiny. The private lives of the members of the Hollywood circle again became public—and publicized as "free and easy," their exploits having already been explored and critiqued just a few years prior in the trials of "Fatty" Arbuckle.[44]

In 1921 Roscoe "Fatty" Arbuckle hosted a party at the St. Francis Hotel in San Francisco. Arbuckle was one of the most popular comedians of the silent film era and a top star at Paramount Studios. Word of the party spread through the motion picture industry. Two of the women in attendance that night were Virginia Rappe, an actress, and her friend Maude Delmont. Two versions of events describe what happened that evening. Delmont's version alleged that Arbuckle had sexually assaulted Rappe, inadvertently causing her death. Arbuckle (whose nickname "Fatty" did not stem from his svelte figure or penchant for portion control) weighed approximately 260 pounds. The prosecution argued that Arbuckle's heft atop petite Rappe caused her bladder to rupture.[45] Arbuckle, however, denied the allegations and claimed that Rappe had drunk too much and had fallen ill, her ruptured bladder stemming from preexisting conditions.

The incident and resulting trials split the motion picture industry, with "one group convinced of the big comedian's blamelessness and determined to aid him to clear his name, and the other equally determined to 'see justice done.'"[46] Lambasting Arbuckle, Henry Lehrman, a film director and Rappe's fiancé, exclaimed, "[This] is what results from making idols and millionaires out of people that you take from the gutter."[47] The trials brought intense scrutiny to Hollywood and the motion picture industry. One authority in the theatrical world remarked, "The Motion picture stars have been riding to a fall for a long time. The recent blackmail case . . . the suppressed story of a prominent magnate's affair with a local stenographer, and the Arbuckle arrest are only the beginning. The whole picture industry is aware of what goes on . . . [in] Hollywood. . . . Stories of drug parties, liquor parties, and other forms of debauchery by certain individuals at various parties throughout the country are no longer new."[48]

In the aftermath of Rappe's death—for which Arbuckle was eventually acquitted—the film industry went on the attack against allegations that it was a source of immorality. The *Billboard* newsletter urged that Hollywood "purge" itself of "those intruders whose actions have brought only discredit upon the film industry."[49] It continued: "REAL ACTORS and REAL ACTRESSES should pit their power against the invading army of infected worms, stamp them out and prove to the world that the motion picture colony . . . is not a retreat for the immoral and depraved."[50]

Critics and reformers believed that a thorough federal investigation of the film industry would reveal "debauchery behind the screen worse than that shown in the most extreme sex plays."[51] These reformers claimed that a small circle of men held the entire industry in their hands. As a result they were able to get away with arousing the public with immoral motion pictures, and they preyed on young women, whom they coerced to perform "immoral acts in order to retain their business positions."[52] This small oligarchy threatened to undermine the entire American system with immoral lifestyles, business practices, and films.

Scandals like those of Fatty Arbuckle—particularly when tied to an institution like the film industry—demand a certain "moral opprobrium" that often results in a "breach [of] institutional trust."[53] "Moral decay" and "a breakdown of moral consensus" characterized the early twentieth century.[54] This was most visible in motion pictures, which often represented changes in American sexual practices. Hollywood represented the antithesis of moral small-town life. It represented pleasure, consumption, and fantasy on the surface, but just below the surface cases like those of Fatty Arbuckle and Delphine Walsh demonstrated how false that façade really was. The American public was fascinated with the entertainment subculture. Its members "kept to themselves" as they formed a community where "the regular social classes were all confused, with crude stagehands and set builders assuming fraternity . . . with dramatic actresses."[55] This unique community of entertainers and celebrities titilated the interests of the reading public. Journalists clamored to find sensational stories about Hollywood.

Police secured a dying declaration from Delphine in which she named Doctors Paul Traxler and Roy S. Lanterman as the physicians responsible for her illegal operation.[56] Lanterman was no stranger to law enforcement in Los Angeles. He was a man of privilege. His family had founded the city of La Cañada, and his parents were able to provide him with an affluent upbringing. In 1906 Lanterman was sworn in as the Los Angeles County coroner, but he left the position disgraced after an incident with his mistress, a Mills Seminary graduate student with the moniker "Suicide Ida," a nickname that she earned after threatening to kill herself every time one of her boyfriends ended their torrid love affairs. Lanterman's lover, whose real name was Ida Hastings, called the police after she alleged that he had attacked her. When police arrived at the scene, Lanterman had already sequestered himself in the bathroom. When he finally emerged, police found him under the influence and in possession of two revolvers.[57] Though there were no charges for the alleged assault against Hastings, a local prosecutor demanded Lanterman's dismissal on the basis of an obscure 1880 law that called for the dismissal of public officials caught intoxicated while on duty. Lanterman resigned and was soon indicted on other charges—including the falsification of miscellaneous expense reports to the board of supervisors. Lanterman was initially sentenced to one year in prison, but the conviction was overturned upon appeal.

In 1916 Lanterman's name came up during the investigation into seventeen-year-old Elizabeth Johnson's illegal operation.[58] He claimed the allegations were part of a larger conspiracy to put him out of business.[59] He was indicted and found not guilty, but the BME revoked his license. Later, when Mrs. Regina Greenburg of San Francisco provided a dying declaration, she named Lanterman as the physician who had performed her illegal abortion. Due to a conflicting report she gave wherein she initially claimed to have performed the procedure on herself, Lanterman was found not guilty. In 1918 Lanterman was also accused of contributing to the delinquency of a minor when he took Marjorie Woodbury to Malibu for the weekend. Nevertheless, by 1921—after a successful petition drive—Lanterman was able to regain his medical license.[60]

While Lanterman had a number of run-ins with the law and medical boards, Paul Traxler did not. He was a relatively obscure figure until Delphine Walsh's death. Traxler was born in 1893 and was a veteran of World War I. Little else is known about the physician. In early May 1929 Traxler and Lanterman were accused of performing the abortion that resulted in the death of Delphine Walsh.[61] As noted previously, Delphine implicated the two doctors in her dying declaration, claiming that Lanterman had administered the anesthetic before Traxler performed the operation.

Once law enforcement officers had the names of the two physicians, they focused on identifying the man responsible for Miss Walsh's pregnancy. Police often interrogated women to find out the names of their lovers because of law enforcement's "implicit assumption" that women who had abortions did so "because their 'sweethearts' had refused to marry [them]."[62] Through arrests, investigations, interrogations, and prosecutions, the state "reinforced the norms requiring men to marry the women whom they impregnated."[63] This practice of penalizing men continued through the 1930s. Some former lovers were even sent to prison for their part—whether it was because of their refusal to marry the young woman or because they had provided money for an abortion. In Delphine Walsh's case newspaper subheads (such as "Identity of Dead Girl's Male Associate Baffles") and statements (such as "All clews [sic] to the man responsible for the condition of Delphine Walsh . . . have failed to identify him") support the notion that identifying Walsh's former lover was integral to the case and possibly misguided, given that it was a murder investigation.[64] Despite the police inquiry on her deathbed, Delphine refused to name the man responsible for her pregnancy.

By May 8, 1929, Southern California BME special agent William Byrne maintained that investigators had the name of a suspect, but they were keeping his name secret until they were able to locate and interrogate him.[65] The main clue, Byrne asserted, was a letter Delphine had supposedly received with a large sum of money.[66] Investigators believed the money was used to pay for the procedure and that the man who had sent it—a supposed millionaire in Vancouver, British Columbia—was responsible for her pregnancy. Dorothy Neff, one of Delphine's coworkers, said that she and Delphine had befriended a wealthy theater owner while they were working in Vancouver. Neff said that the man took a liking to Delphine and even promised to take the two girls on a trip with him to Hawaii. Investigators continued to search for the man and to question Delphine's friends. Nevertheless, the search remained fruitless, with investigators unable to find the actual letter or the mysterious Vancouver millionaire who had purportedly sent it.[67]

Traxler and Lanterman were charged with Delphine Walsh's murder, and local prosecutors prepared for trial. During the trial the defense argued that Delphine's dying declaration was inadmissible because she didn't really believe she was dying when she provided it. Furthermore, the doctors' counsel argued the defense had its own document, signed by Delphine, that indicated she had attempted her own abortion.[68] With the help of a surprise witness, Mrs. Arline Morgan, the office assistant, the defense had testimony that backed up its claim. Morgan testified that Delphine had attempted to perform her own abortion and had come to Traxler and Lanterman only when her condition worsened. She said that Delphine had admitted to self-inducing her abortion before the doctors administered the anesthetic and began treatment for the infection that developed from the partial, self-induced abortion.

The jury deliberated, and both of the doctors were found not guilty in the criminal court. However, their troubles were far from over. Within weeks of the jury's verdict the California BME called Traxler and Lanterman to a meeting on October 23 to present an argument for why the board should not revoke their licenses.[69] The Board dismissed the case against Lanterman because it did not believe it had enough evidence to charge him with "performing or aiding an illegal operation."[70] However, it voted to revoke Traxler's license. Traxler argued that he was not responsible for Delphine Walsh's death since he had taken the case after she had self-induced. Nevertheless, the BME believed sufficient evidence existed to assert that he *had* performed the procedure. Traxler appealed the decision and appeared before the Los Angeles Superior Court with a writ demanding that the BME void the revocation. At the same time the board decided to charge Lanterman with "unprofessional conduct" related to the Walsh case. Lanterman's license was revoked for these charges on February 6, 1930. Lanterman appealed, and by 1945 his name was back in the BME's directory of active physicians. Traxler also continued to appeal, arguing that his license revocation was a form of double jeopardy since the criminal court had found him not guilty.[71] The judge ruled that it was not double jeopardy; rather it was about protecting the medical profession and society. However, by 1945 Traxler's name was also back in the BME directory of active physicians in the state.[72]

Traxler and Lanterman were punished for their involvement in this case, and it is likely they experienced this punishment as a source of frustration and inconvenience. Nevertheless, within a matter of time both physicians were again considered respectable and reputable and had served out their sentences. When Lanterman died in 1947, there was no mention of any of his many legal troubles in his obituary. In fact he is still remembered as part of the founding family of La Cañada and is lauded for providing quality medical treatment to poor individuals for free during the Depression.[73] While there were in fact legal troubles for the physicians who performed illegal or fatal abortions, the appeals process was generous and gave the physicians the benefit of the doubt. If the physicians were punished, they did not stay out of business for long. Shortly after the Walsh case settled, another highly publicized abortion case stunned Los Angeles County. Eighteen-year-old Vera Nelson, a Los Angeles High School student, became the talk of the town when she died in Hermosa Beach, California, following an illegal abortion. The petite blonde, who the coroner believed was about six months pregnant, met her death at the hands of the reclusive Dr. William C. Fiske, a seventy-year-old physician in ailing health.

The Fiske family was having a normal day until Dr. Fiske didn't come home for dinner. With the whole family waiting to eat, Mrs. Fiske sent her son-in-law, Barney Briggs, to retrieve her husband from the office. When Briggs arrived at his father-in-law's office, he found the door locked and returned to the family home, believing that he must have missed the doctor en route. Fiske, however, had not arrived home by the time Briggs returned. The family ate dinner in his absence. Concerned, Mrs. Fiske and her son-in-law returned to the office. When Mrs. Fiske unlocked the door, they found the doctor lying on the ground, holding a gas tube, and attempting to asphyxiate himself. Briggs grabbed the tube from the doctor's grasp, but the doctor begged them to let him die. Briggs ran to the police station, and by the time he returned with the police, Fiske had turned the gas back on and had resumed his suicide attempt. Police turned off the gas and removed the tube from the doctor's mouth. Police found a note on the door that read, "Mr. Nelson—you will find me in the front room. It is gas-filled. Care! Operation failed. Too far advanced."[74] Vera Nelson's body was in the back.

As had been the case with Delphine Walsh, police immediately began a search for the young man responsible for Vera Nelson's pregnancy. Sifting through her diary, investigators wove together the story of a young, troubled girl who was popular with the boys at school but was unhappy at home and frequently mused about getting a job and leaving home for good. The newspapers depicted Vera as a spoiled, promiscuous girl who found solace in the company of the dozens of boys whose names appeared in her diary as objects of her amusement or affection.[75] Based on her diary entries, the police learned about a relationship with a young man referred to only as "Mac." The relationship had ended just days before she first visited Fiske on September 16, 1930.

Once Fiske recovered, he told investigators that Vera had come to him distraught. He said that she looked run down, worried, and stressed, and she pleaded with him that she could not be a mother. She visited Fiske two or three more times, begging for an abortion, before he finally relented. It was his pity for the girl, Fiske argued, that compelled him to help her.[76] Fiske refused to make any more statements, and he was not present at the coroner's inquest. The coroner found that Vera had died from an illegal operation. During the inquest Vera's mother testified that she thought her daughter was seeing Fiske for the treatment of a tumor, but when her daughter did not return the next day, she suspected something was wrong.[77]

Fiske was released from the hospital straight to the county jail. He was later freed on bond. His health continued to deteriorate over the course of the trial, resulting in multiple delays. When he took the stand during the trial, he testified that Vera had died because of an accident on his operating table while he was performing his "legitimate duties of a physician."[78] Fiske claimed that Vera had induced her own abortion and that he was simply helping her after complications had arisen. The defense also had evidence to support this claim. It presented a letter from one of Vera's friends, "Birdie." In the letter Birdie stated she had witnessed Vera's attempt to self-abort before her final visit with Fiske. The defense also hired a physician who testified that it was likely that Vera's death resulted from complications that had developed before Fiske began his operation.[79] The jury was deadlocked, with eight in favor of a guilty verdict. The judge immediately moved for a retrial the following February. However, rather than go through a new trial, Fiske pled guilty to manslaughter. Perhaps because of his age or condition, the judge accepted the plea and allowed Fiske to simply apply for probation, which was granted.

During the frenzy of Delphine Walsh's case, Harry Carr wrote about it in his popular column, "The Lancer":

> I don't know what the moral of the sad story is. Miss Delphine Walsh moved out of Brewery Gulch in Bisbee, Ariz., to Hollywood. Instead of fame she found a disgraceful death. The inference is that, had she remained in Bisbee, she would by now have been the proud and happy wife of a time-keeper in the copper mines and perhaps been the chairman of the sub committee on arrangements where the Rotarians next performed. Alas, I fear when their heels get high and they carry the same lip stick that Clara Bow uses and take the movie magazines home to bed with them, then Brewery Gulch and even the blissful domestic life in the cottage on the side of an Arizona mountain no longer has a seductive echo. I don't know anything that can be done with them except lock them up or let them come to Hollywood.[80]

To men like Carr the tragedies that befell Delphine Walsh and Vera Nelson were not their deaths. The real tragedy was the loss of patriarchal control due to the changing status of women. Feminist scholars have addressed how sexuality is central to discussions of inequality. Others have said that birth control liberates women.[81] A woman's decision to have an abortion, especially on her own terms, undercut male control over women's reproduction and sexuality. Abortion rejected what many men assumed to be women's primary social duty: reproduction. In a society where women's value rested in antiquated ideas about chastity, reproductive control made it more difficult to devalue or discredit women based on their virginity. Fear of pregnancy often functioned as a means to control women's behavior, yet birth control provided women with the opportunity to enjoy the same freedom in sexual relations as men—a fact that might have been troubling. If women abandoned their primary social duty as mothers in favor of sexual freedom, it could destroy society. According to Carr, increasing female autonomy and the glorification of Hollywood led to the demise of domesticity. Women no longer found happiness in the things that had previously fulfilled them—like living a life of "domestic bliss." For the "new woman" living a life of domesticity was no longer blissful.

The idea of prosecuting the men responsible for pregnancies was another attempt to grapple with some of the social changes of the era. The narrative that women sought abortions only if their lovers left them failed to give proper credence to women's own concerns or desires. Arguably this narrative suggested women had no genuine concerns or desires that conflicted with motherhood; their desire to abort was simply an emotional response to rejection. By searching for the men responsible for a pregnancy, law enforcement officials were emphasizing the importance of sex for procreation, but they were also urging men to step up and take their place as heads of families. Suggesting that women had abortions only because their lovers had left them was not only manifestly *false*, but it was also an effort to insert men into the abortion debate where they did not necessarily belong. It marginalized the legitimate concerns women had about their livelihoods and families. While some women may have chosen to have an abortion because their lovers had refused to share in the responsibilities of a child, more frequently it was a direct result of women's desires to exercise reproductive control over their own bodies.

Despite the fact that abortions were technically illegal, women continued to procure them—either at the hands of others or by their own means. A shared feature among the cases discussed in this chapter is that all the doctors claimed their patients had self-induced their abortions. Whether or not this was true for these individual cases, self-induced abortions were a reality that doctors witnessed, exploited, and had to grapple with. While the law could have prohibited a woman from getting a trained medical professional to perform an abortion, a committed, determined woman could perform her own abortion without having to ask for permission. Even when surgical abortion was at its peak in the 1930s, self-induced abortion remained a common practice, and in reality it was the most dangerous method of inducing a miscarriage, particularly when it involved self-injury or introducing instruments into a woman's body.

Annual reports from the Los Angeles County Coroner's Office allow us to piece together an image of the women who died from abortions from 1927 to 1938 (see table 1). In those years abortion was listed as the cause of death for 278 women in the county.[82] This number represented .514 percent of the 54,078 total investigations that the coroner's office conducted during that period. In comparison, alcoholism was the cause of death in 698 investigations (about 1.29 percent of the cases), and "motor vehicles" were responsible for 9,388 deaths (about 17.36 percent). In any single year from 1927 to 1938 abortions never accounted for more than .729 percent of coroner cases or less than .247 percent. The 1929–30 fiscal year recorded the highest number of cases, and the 1936–37 fiscal year, the lowest. Of the 278 abortion deaths during this period, 146 (52.52 percent) were classified as self-induced abortions, 30 (10.79 percent) as criminal abortions performed by medical professionals, and 102 (36.69 percent) as "other."[83] "Other" causes of abortion deaths included "undetermined," "spontaneous" (miscarriage), "caused by fall to floor," "criminal by known person," "criminal by unknown person," and "septic." Some were also categorized as "self-induced or criminal undetermined." It is possible that some of these "other" classifications could have involved medical professionals as well, but even if they did, they still represented less than half of all abortion-related deaths. Most of the women who died from abortions (245 or 88.13 percent) were between the ages of twenty and forty-five, and the remaining 33 women (11.87 percent) were under the age of twenty. In 1931 the coroner began to track marital status. From 1931 to 1938, 132 of the 166 abortion deaths in this period involved married women. Of the

Table 1. Los Angeles County Coroner's Office abortion cases, 1927–38

Fiscal year	Total number of coroner cases	Total number of abortion cases	Self-induced abortions	Abortions by physician or medical professional	Other	Age of recipient: 10-20 / 20-45	Marital status of recipient
1927–28	3,756	20 (.532%)	5	3	2 undetermined; 4 spontaneous; 1 by fall to floor; 5 by instruments induced by unknown person	7 / 13	N/A
1928–29	4,174	28 (.671%)	19 (2 partial)	2	2 criminal by known person; 1 criminal by unknown person; 1 by fall to floor; 1 spontaneous; 2 undetermined	0 / 28	N/A
1929–30	4,254	31 (.729%)	13	5	4 criminal by unknown person; 2 spontaneous; 1 by fall to floor; 6 undetermined	1 / 30	N/A
1930–31	4,603	33 (.717%)	17	4	1 by fall; 3 criminal by unknown person; 4 undetermined; 4 spontaneous	6 / 27	N/A

1931-32	4,604	28 (.608%)	16	4	1 criminal by known person; 3 criminal by unknown person; 2 spontaneous; 2 undetermined	4 / 24	23 married; 4 single; 1 divorced
1932-33	5,059	28 (.553%)	13	4	1 criminal by known person; 2 by fall; 1 criminal by unknown person; 3 spontaneous; 4 undetermined (2 criminal or self-induced; 2 self-induced or spontaneous)	3 / 25	24 married; 4 single
1933-34	5,083	21 (.413%)	15	1	3 criminal by unknown person; 2 spontaneous	0 / 21	18 married; 3 single
1934-35	5,315	25 (.470%)	15	2	2 spontaneous; 3 criminal by known person; 3 undetermined (self-induced or criminal)	3 / 22	18 married; 2 single; 4 widowed; 1 divorced
1935-36	5,377	29 (.539%)	13	4	2 criminal by known person; 1 criminal by unknown person; 5 self-induced or criminal undetermined; 4 spontaneous	6 / 23	23 married; 5 single; 1 divorced

1936–37	6,070	15 (.247%)	11	1 self-induced or criminal undetermined; 2 criminal by unknown person	3 / 12	9 married; 4 single; 1 widowed; 1 divorced
1937–38	5,783	20 (.346%)	9	4 spontaneous; 2 septic; 5 self-induced or criminal undetermined	0 / 20	17 married; 1 widowed; 1 divorced; 1 single
TOTALS	54,078	278 (.514%)	146 (52.52%)	30 (10.79%)	102 (36.69%)	33 (11.87%) / 245 (88.13%)	132 married; 23 single; 5 divorced; 6 widowed (of 166 abortions for which this datum is available)

Source: Los Angeles County Coroner's Office, annual reports.

remaining, 20 were single, 5 were divorced, and 6 were widowed. In sum, most women who died from abortion in Los Angeles County from 1927 to 1938 were married and between the ages of twenty and forty-five, and the abortions were self-induced.

These statistics further prove the falsity of the narrative that women had abortions only because their lovers left them. While the figures do not tell us about the quality of a marriage, threats of divorce, fears of intimate-partner violence, or estrangement, nearly 80 percent of the women who died from abortions were married. When Allie Mae Sullivan wound up on the autopsy table in 1936, it was not because her lover had left her after promises of marriage. The thirty-six-year-old mother of four was in poor health and on county relief, a situation the coroner couldn't help but note in his report as a contributing factor that may have compelled her to induce her own abortion.[84] Mrs. Sullivan was probably a very concerned wife and mother. She could not afford to support her existing children and probably did not want to worsen their lot by adding another mouth to feed. Suggesting that women aborted only because they had been abandoned marginalizes their legitimate concerns about their livelihoods and their families and trivializes women's actions and decisions.

Self-induced abortions, then, were a fallback for women and a safety net for doctors. For women such abortions could potentially solve their problems or get them just sick enough to have a doctor complete an induced abortion. In other cases, however, they killed women slowly. For licensed physicians who wanted to perform illegal abortions, self-induced abortions were a convenient scapegoat in the event they botched the procedures. They could claim that the women had attempted the procedure first, then came to the physicians ill, miscarrying, but unfortunately too late. With a woman dead, there was no one to speak for her or against the physician.

This chapter has provided statistics that begin to describe the types of women who died from abortions. We know that women of all races, ethnicities, and classes have obtained abortions throughout American history. Before the organization of the medical field most women went to midwives or self-induced. After the professionalization of the medical field most native-born white women who wanted abortions went to a physician first, while most poor and non-white women sought help from midwives or practiced self-induced abortions if they could not afford the fees of providers. As noted previously, successful self-induced abortions are among the most invisible abortions in society, and they continue to elude historians. However, we can infer that the number of self-induced abortions declined with the increase of medical professionalism but that this practice continued to remain "concentrated in the groups with the least resources: the poor, Blacks, rural, and unmarried."[85] Even as legal abortions became safer, advancements in medical technology did not necessarily extend to women of color.

The next chapter examines the case of Margaret Scott, a young Black woman, and Dr. Mathew Marmillion, the Black physician believed to have performed an abortion procedure on Margaret. It will illustrate the unique obstacles that Blacks faced in the medical field generally and in acquiring or providing abortions. It will show that while white and Black women had similar responses to unwanted pregnancies, the coverage of their stories was different. The Black press wrote about Scott's death as the community shifted its focus to preserving and protecting the integrity of Dr. Marmillion, a prominent community member and race man who was committed to Black uplift. While Traxler, Lanterman, and Fiske were all able to evade serious punishment, Marmillion was sentenced to a lengthy term and served most of it, suggesting that he did not possess the same leverage in the wider—or whiter—community.

Inconceivable Blackness   3

Race, Medicine, and Contraception

[We found in our] investigation that year that a large number of colored washerwomen, finding it hard to get the husks to feed and the rags to clothe their already large family of little ones, living in one room like stock rather than add to their burdens, resort to crime. This is also a fruitful reason of the slow rate of increase in the colored population. This state of affairs is not confined to Nashville. It is true of nearly all our large Southern cities; and whether we like it or not, the hard fact remains that the enormous death rate among us, together with our small birth rate, is one of the signs of the times that, unless our home life be radically changed, the Negro problem in America may be ultimately solved by the extinction of the Negro.

—H. F. Kletzing and W. H. Crogman, 1898

While abortions were legally out of reach for all women in California during the period under discussion, it is important to note that race created additional challenges for Black women who wanted abortions. This chapter situates abortion within a wider discussion of the Black Los Angeles community and the Black professional medical community. Previous chapters have detailed how the AMA spearheaded the campaign against practitioners of irregular medicine, how abortionists were considered nefarious, and how licensed white physicians charged with abortions were able to either negotiate more lenient sentences or rejoin the professional medical community by claiming that the abortions had been justified. However, Black physicians struggled to claim legitimacy and were often unable to access resources and influence outside of their own community. With that in mind, it makes sense to assert that Black women seeking abortions and Black abortion providers underwent far more hardships when it came to abortion. Historically race has informed how women perceive their own sex and reproduction and how society views those things as well. Often discourses about women's bodies and sexuality are racialized. Women's abilities to be chaste, pure, virtuous, immoral, or promiscuous depended on their race.

Before Emancipation enslaved women were unable to exercise control over their bodies. Their bodies belonged to their masters as either workers, sexual objects and concubines, or wet nurses forced to sacrifice their own milk to feed the children of their white enslavers. Nevertheless, reproduction—at times—was one small arena where they could exercise agency by using contraceptives, inducing abortions, or committing infanticide as a means of defiance, a form of economic sabotage, or simply a response to the sorrowful and complicated realities of slavery.[1] The ability to control their own fertility was a source of power for enslaved women and showed where slaveholders' power stopped.[2] However, this should not be misunderstood as a desire to stop conception altogether. While slaveholders wanted enslaved women to reproduce in order to line their own pockets and enrich themselves, enslaved people also wanted children in order to advance their own goals: to love them and to strengthen family bonds.[3] However, for Black women sexual violence was not just a relic of the times of slavery. After the Civil War and Reconstruction and through the civil rights era, the unpunished and uninvestigated rapes and sexual assaults of Black women remained a tool of racial violence and an inescapable reality that defined their gendered and racialized existence.[4]

In the aftermath of Emancipation Black women's reproduction remained at the heart of concerns about social mobility and economic progress. However, birth control was a Janus-faced issue in the Black community. While Black women were still more likely to have a higher birthrate than their white counterparts, an especially drastic decline in Black women's fecundity began at the end of Reconstruction and continued through the 1930s.[5] Some whites believed that Blacks were ill-suited for freedom and would become extinct outside of the institution of slavery. An editor in the *Nation* wrote the following:

> There has been considerable speculation as to the effect of freedom upon the physical condition of the former slave. By many it is thought that his ultimate fate will be that of the Indian, and for this opinion there seems to be some ground. That immorality and disease are *largely* on the increase cannot be doubted.... I will merely add one or two facts falling under my own observations. Of all the great contrasts between the past and the present in the South, I can truly say that *not one* has struck me more forcibly than the seeming *dearth* of negro children.... It might be supposed that some new Herod had inaugurated a slaughter of the innocents.[6]

The author added that while slave owners cared for slave children out of economic self-interest, the existing state of African American infant mortality was due in large part "to the persistent neglect of [the children's] mothers ... [and their] absolute indifference—a want of maternal instinct."[7]

Frederick L. Hoffman, a noted Prudential Insurance Company statistician, argued that if unremedied, the "excessive mortality of the colored race" would inevitably result in its extermination.[8] According to Hoffman, the data he gathered irrefutably proved that the slave generation was physically and morally superior to the post-Emancipation subjects he studied.[9] Identifiable factors contributed to the lower birth rate: migration, urbanization, poverty, and a public health crisis following Emancipation. Some of the most educated circles of Black elites were also preoccupied with these concerns.[10] Hoffman's own introduction, however, demonstrated his proclivity toward social Darwinist theories; while he hoped his work would draw attention to and enlighten "the relations between the superior and inferior races," the fact was that once "race deterioration" began, it was difficult to stop. Races in a downward trend "invariably [become] useless if not dangerous factors in the social as well as political economy of nations."[11]

In order to combat what Hoffman described as excessive crime, pauperism, and sexual immorality among "the colored race," at the turn of the century many Black reformers turned their attention to racial vitality and uplift—specifically in light of the popularity of the eugenics movement.[12] When goals for racial uplift intersected with Black women's sexuality, prominent race men and women—members of the Black elite dedicated to racial uplift—believed that birth control would equate to Black race suicide, while others argued that it would "help improve the economic and health conditions of blacks."[13] The *Journal of the National Medical Association* (*JNMA*), for example, argued that proper sex education should be tied to marriage licensing. By giving an engaged couple a marriage guide along with their license, "the limitations of parenthood to those desiring that holy estate would undoubtedly improve the breed."[14] Not only did the *JNMA* suggest limiting access to sexual education to married couples, but family planning (with an eye toward eugenics, as evidenced in the phrase "improve the breed") was also recognized as a key aspect of the proposed marriage guide. Critics of birth control among the Black community argued that the practice was "dysgenic" since it was a practice that was concentrated in the educated and upper and middle classes "that were better prepared for parenthood."[15]

In her study of abortion in the Chicago metropolitan area, Leslie Reagan found class differences among Black women's abortion practices. While more Black women than white women were willing to bear children out of wedlock, this tolerance for illegitimacy was "tempered by class."[16] Higher socioeconomic status in Black families and communities meant more unyielding standards of chastity. Class was an important distinction among African Americans in the period after Reconstruction. While united on the basis of race and perhaps in "common goals and outlooks," those who saw themselves as gatekeepers of African American racial progress were often at odds with their poorer counterparts, a difference that sometimes manifested itself in perspectives on sexual behavior.[17] Because of these patterns, it can be inferred that as education and class standing increased, so too did rates of abortion among Black women. Given the lack of consensus, Black physicians, reformers, club women, and ministers alike devoted considerable discussion to the issue of birth control. Margaret Sanger's Harlem clinic, for example, had a majority-Black advisory council made up of local Black professionals and community leaders who soon found that Black women wanted the ability to exercise reproductive control as much as white women.[18]

Like their white counterparts, many Black physicians held similarly conservative beliefs about abortion and women's reproduction. It is unclear whether the physicians in the National Medical Association (NMA) supported mainline medicine's rhetoric as a tool for legitimization, whether they genuinely agreed with mainline medicine, or whether they chose to accept or reject the rhetoric when it was convenient. The answer be complex and nuanced, but it is likely some combination of all three. For example, in an address before the Maryland Medical, Dental, and Pharmaceutical Association, Dr. Barnett M. Rhetta made a plea for the lives of the unborn. He argued that "the greatest enemy to society, the greatest criminal on earth ... [was] the paid executioner of the helpless child."[19]

Other Black physicians advanced arguments against birth control or race suicide by focusing on changes to women's status in society. Speaking before the annual session of the NMA, Dr. L. L. Burwell, a Black physician from Selma, Alabama, felt compelled to discuss women's fertility and its physical and moral effects upon the nation. He explained that women's sexuality and fertility were of "little interest" to society when in the "primeval condition." However, when society developed, the "highest valuation" was placed upon women's virginity. While women were no longer "chattel" and were now considered the "equal of man," changes in society had "allowed certain fashions to come in, which, if not checked, will bring her back to that primeval period when no shame was felt and no restraint was placed upon her wicked acts."[20] While Burwell discussed changing fashions in the literal sense of dress, he also discussed "the prevention of child-bearing" as problematic—particularly when performed by members of the upper classes. Like white counterparts who emphasized their knowledge and credentials while discouraging their clients from procuring abortions, Burwell employed a similar tone:

> There is no doubt that the frequent resorting to preventive means will destroy the health of woman. There is so much danger of septic poisoning which is so prevalent in these cases, with all of its attendant evil effects. If the races are to be strong healthy races, we must have strong and healthy parentage. . . . Woman has little knowledge of the effects on her physical being when she resorts to means of prevention. . . . If we are to preserve the health of our women and check the immoral influences which arise from this practice, we must agitate against the practice. . . . It is a fact that we want to maintain a hard, healthy race, and by the law of inheritance, a weak race physically and mentally cannot reproduce a strong, healthy race. To preserve our strength and health, it is very necessary to desist from everything which tends to lower and weaken our vitality.[21]

Burwell's own position as a Black male physician with an eye toward racial uplift allowed him to echo the sentiments of mainline AMA physicians unironically. His belief that contraceptives were dysgenic since their use among Black elites contributed to the group's decline also meshed perfectly well with the paternalistic view of AMA physicians as guardians of women and the views of educated professionals. However, we may suspect that Burwell's championing of AMA rhetoric may have been a way to prove himself as a legitimate physician.

While there were definite arguments on both sides about birth control in the Black community, there were legitimate concerns when it came to the application of birth control principles. In the wrong hands efforts to provide contraceptive services to Blacks often resulted in outsider efforts to control the Black population rather than allow Blacks to direct their own projects and education. For example, beginning in the 1930s some Southern states created publicly funded birth control clinics that were intended to lower the Black birthrate.[22] While these clinics may have helped some women exercise reproductive choice, the explicit goal of lowering the Black birthrate was developed by outsiders. Similarly Sanger's Birth Control Federation helped develop the Negro Project in 1939, which became subject to criticism for becoming "indifferent to the needs of the Black community."[23] Nevertheless, in the absence of other suitable projects or organizations, some prominent leaders saw such developments as at least a progressive effort, and some women took advantage of these options regardless of what the programs' intentions were.

Writing for the *Birth Control Review*, Dr. Charles H. Garvin, a Black physician and graduate of Howard University Medical School, argued that birth control would not decimate the Black population. Instead he argued that it could be a tool to elevate the standard of living for the Black community.[24] W. E. B. Du Bois held a similar view. Reformers who adhered to this school of thought argued that adequate access to contraceptives would not only raise the standard of living by spacing out pregnancies, but would reduce also the spread of venereal disease. Garvin suggested it would be better if Black families were encouraged to have only two or three children—spaced out at desired intervals—than to have a high birthrate plagued with high infant mortality and tired, constantly pregnant mothers who lacked the stamina to care for their families. Garvin believed that when used properly, birth control would allow Blacks to improve their condition and enter the prosperous middle and upper classes. He also argued that it was the role of the Black physician to enlighten the community on the benefits of birth control in order to secure "the wealth and the social felicity of the Negro group."[25]

Dr. Edgar Bass Keemer Jr. seemed to take the task of spreading information about birth control to heart. The physician moved to Detroit, where he became a well-connected abortion specialist— *the* specialist to whom many other Black physicians referred their patients. At the beginning, however, it was not obvious that this man would have a nearly forty-year career as an abortion specialist. In fact he refused the first woman who approached him for one. His wife, who was also a physician, urged him to perform the procedure for the young, unmarried woman. She empathized with her since Mrs. Keemer too had had an abortion while in medical school. Despite his wife's urgings, Keemer did not perform the procedure, and he later discovered that the young woman had committed suicide. The tragedy following his initial refusal propelled him toward his career. Keemer was unique in his sense of personal responsibility to his patients. His fees were minimal, ensuring that even poor women were able to afford the procedure, and if the procedure failed, he refunded the fees to his patient. If a patient grew ill or needed further care that he could not provide, he paid the fees to have her cared for at a hospital, and if she had to miss work, he even covered her missed wages. This genuine sense of responsibility likely spared Keemer from complaints or legal interference, neither of which he, as a Black physician, would have wanted.[26] Keemer went above and beyond the traditional bounds of professional medicine in order to stay in business, so he was able to have a long, successful career. Others, however, were not so lucky.

Dr. Oscar Wilson DeVaughn was born on November 14, 1883, in Douglasville, Georgia. He attended Morris Brown College in Atlanta before moving on to Meharry Medical School, where he earned his degree in 1915. He married a young woman named Eugenia, and the couple moved to Oakland, California, before he volunteered for the U.S. Army Medical Reserve Corps. DeVaughn reported for basic training and provided care to various Black troops and regiments. He was honorably discharged in 1918 and returned to Northern California to practice medicine.[27] His first brush with the law came in 1929, when he was charged with conspiracy to commit abortion.[28]

A young woman, a minor, went to work for a Mr. and Mrs. McCoy at their home. One day Mrs. McCoy was out of town, and it would appear that Mr. McCoy took advantage of that the situation. Whether the young woman willingly engaged in sexual intercourse with Mr. McCoy is unclear in the court opinion. Furthermore, our modern conceptions about date rape and consent do not translate well into the early twentieth century. What is clear is that McCoy served the young woman a glass of port wine, and she had no recollection of anything until 2 a.m., when Mrs. McCoy returned.[29] In a weird string of events it was Mrs. McCoy who actually took the young woman to DeVaughn just a few hours later. The prosecution argued that she did so for an abortion for the young woman, while DeVaughn's defense argued that this was just for the treatment of gonorrhea. The defense argued that the young woman could not have been pregnant from the encounter that had only taken place just hours before. Hence there was no abortion, and DeVaughn was eventually acquitted of all charges.[30]

Though he was acquitted of the charges in the McCoy case, DeVaughn would become entangled in another criminal trial shortly thereafter in 1934, when he was charged and convicted of second-degree murder after performing a fatal abortion on Louise Swartz.[31] According to court records, Mrs. Swartz, a married mother of two, discovered that she was pregnant in January 1933 and told her husband that she wanted an abortion because she didn't want any more children. Though her husband believed it to be too dangerous, he ultimately told her to do as she wished. On or around February 1, Mrs. Swartz and a friend entered DeVaughn's office while Mr. Swartz and their two children waited outside in the car. The prosecutors argued that it was at this point that DeVaughn took Mrs. Swartz into his office and performed a procedure. Mrs. Swartz returned every day for the next three days. Though her appearance was described as "pale and very sick" after each visit, her condition after the third day was alarming, and she was rushed to the hospital. At the hospital it was discovered that she had undergone an illegal abortion. Mrs. Swartz died on February 10, and the autopsy showed a blood clot and an infection in the uterus.[32] DeVaughn was arrested, put on trial, and found guilty. His medical license was revoked, and he served seven years at San Quentin before going on parole in 1941. He died the following year.[33]

In comparison to the punishments meted out to Traxler, Lanterman, and Fiske, DeVaughn's punishment was harsher. The court documents themselves list several instances where evidence was conflicting or nonexistent. For example: "There is no direct evidence as to what took place at this time"; and, "There is a conflict in the evidence"; and, "While the evidence is conflicting in some minor details..."[34] While the most logical conclusion is that DeVaughn performed the abortion, the evidence does not appear to have been held to the same standard as that for Traxler, Lanterman, and Fiske. Furthermore, in his appeal DeVaughn complained of "prejudicial misconduct" on the part of the district attorney, who in his final arguments used "certain language which it is claimed indicated that [the] defendant was a member of the negro race."[35] While the court was unable to locate the specific language, it argued that the language was not grounds for appeal since the "defendant was present at the trial and *could be seen by the jurors*."[36] In other words, it didn't matter if the language hinted that DeVaughn was Black since the jury could see him anyway. Likewise, the announcements in the *California and Western Medicine* journal regarding his imprisonment and license revocation make it clear his race was not invisible: "Oscar W. DeVaughn, colored, No. 56283—Murder, second degree (illegal operation) and subornation [*sic*] of perjury."[37]

At the same time that DeVaughn faced his legal troubles in Northern California, Dr. Mathew J. Marmillion faced similar problems in Southern California. In fact in the *California and Western Medicine* article quoted previously, Marmillion's name is listed right above DeVaughn's: "Mathew J. Marmillion, colored, No. 55160—Murder, second degree (illegal operation)."[38] Of the six medical professionals listed as newly incarcerated inmates of San Quentin prison, Marmillion and DeVaughn were the only two with the "colored" designation, and all six individuals listed were incarcerated for abortion or murders tied to abortions.

Mathew Marmillion was born in 1871 in New Orleans, Louisiana, and he grew up in a well-to-do family. His father was literate and was employed in a professional trade in the South during Reconstruction. Marmillion graduated from New Orleans University and went on to study medicine at Flint-Goodridge Medical College. The college, which began as a small institution and training school for Black nurses, had its share of financial struggles in its short history before finally closing its doors in 1911. The college was closely linked to a local Methodist Episcopal Church and received most of its initial funds from there. However, after receiving a rating of "unsatisfactory" from the AMA in 1906 and after the Flexner Report on American medical schools (which described the college as "a hopeless affair"), Flint's fate was all but sealed. The college had one year to make sufficient changes to bring it up to code; those changes amounted to some $100,000 the college did not have.[39] Eventually Flint suffered the same fate as nearly all Black medical colleges in the early 1910s and closed down. Nevertheless, Marmillion was able to earn his medical degree in the short time the college was open, and he moved to Lake Charles, Louisiana, where he owned and operated the Marmillion Sanatorium for Women until he moved to Los Angeles in 1923.

By the time that Marmillion moved to Los Angeles, he was moving into a city that was "half-free."[40] While the West offered Blacks the opportunity to live a comfortable life, their skin color did limit their options. Migrants from all over the country brought their prejudices to Los Angeles at the same time that the Ku Klux Klan was experiencing a rebirth throughout the country.[41] Nevertheless, to many Blacks the West represented freedom from *explicit* repression. By 1926 Marmillion was using Black labor to construct the Marmillion Building, at a cost of over $30,000, and he had found a suitable location for his business in the segregated, yet thriving, Central Avenue district as the hub of Black life in Los Angeles moved further south alongside increasing racial segregation.[42] It must have seemed like an exciting moment when Marmillion began establishing himself in Los Angeles, and indeed it was an exciting time for many professional and middle-class Blacks in the city. However, that excitement, and the successes of these professionals, would be short-lived.

The 1930s proved to be a difficult time for the Black community in Los Angeles as the Great Depression sank its teeth into the city. Though the Depression affected everyone in California, its effects were especially felt within the Black community. During the Depression Black unemployment rose significantly—from 8 percent of Black men in 1930 to 30 percent of Black men in 1931 and nearly 40 percent of Black women that same year; by 1933 nearly half of Black Los Angeles was out of work.[43] The tenuous position of Blacks "in half-free" Los Angeles meant that most of them lacked the resources to ride the wave of the Depression. Because of race prejudice—which also affected the types of jobs that most Blacks could have—they lacked job security, and the lack of revenue impacted professional Blacks' businesses as well. Employers cut back on workers or went out of business, while some companies fired Black employees in order to keep white ones or hire unemployed whites. Private households were forced to cut back as well, firing maids, yard men, and chauffeurs, positions that were disproportionately held by Blacks.[44] In response to the economic crisis and the failure of the New Deal to make an impact on the Black community, individuals like Charlotta Bass, owner of the Black newspaper *California Eagle*, organized campaigns to promote Black employment. Bass's campaign, which urged Blacks to spend their money only at places where they could work, sought to reinvigorate the Black community by boycotting white businesses in favor of patronizing Black ones.[45] Such actions to support the local Black economy also galvanized and united the community. Black citizens in Los Angles increasingly turned inward to care for and protect their own.

In February 1933 Marmillion was arrested and charged with the murder of Margaret Scott following an illegal operation. Eighteen-year-old Margaret, a young Black girl, died of shock on the operating table after her twenty-seven-year-old boyfriend, Archie Hairston, a medical student at the College of Medical Evangelists in Loma Linda, California, had hired Marmillion to treat her for her condition.[46] Margaret was approximately three months pregnant at the time. Many factors could have compelled the couple to terminate the pregnancy; their religion—they were Seventh-Day Adventists—and class-based concerns about sexual propriety would have made premarital sex taboo, while Hairston's schooling and potential career would have made parenthood impractical at the time—much as it had been in the case of the Keemers. Perhaps Hairston did not want to be tied down so soon, and Margaret was almost a decade his junior. For whatever reason, the couple drove approximately sixty miles from San Bernardino to Los Angeles, where Margaret had an abortion and died. Perhaps Marmillion felt pity for the young couple. It is also possible that the crippling economy compelled him to perform the illicit procedure for the money. For their part, a dearth of Black physicians in the small town of San Bernardino might have compelled Margaret and her boyfriend to make the trip to Los Angeles, and Marmillion might have felt that the young couple had no other options.

Because of the scandal, the medical school expelled Hairston.[47] He had experienced a major setback and stood to serve time in prison. However, he agreed to testify for the prosecution in exchange for immunity. There are two versions of Margaret's encounter with Marmillion. One version suggests that she went to him for a tonsillectomy. When she died on the table, it was discovered that she had hemorrhaged from an attempted abortion. Another version suggests that she sought an abortion, but when it failed, Marmillion attempted to cover it up with a tonsillectomy.

Marmillion initially refused to speak on the matter, but he later relented and stated that Margaret had come to him "in a serious condition: that an operation had already been attempted and that his efforts were to save the girl's life."[48] He claimed that Margaret had experienced complications from an earlier operation but that he knew nothing of it at the time. If he had known about the prior operation, he argued, he "would have sent her to the hospital" and "would not have touched her."[49] Marmillion's defense suggested that Hairston, the medical student, had performed the initial operation before bringing Margaret to Marmillion, though Hairston vehemently denied those accusations and claimed that Marmillion alone had botched the procedure.[50]

Unlike coverage in the *Los Angeles Times* for the Delphine Walsh and Vera Nelson abortion cases, the *Los Angeles Sentinel* and the *California Eagle*, both newspapers with a primarily Black readership, did not write about Margaret Scott's life or the details of her family. Consequently we know very little about this young woman before her private life became public spectacle. This difference in media portrayals, however, should not be dismissed. It was intentional. When newspapers with a primarily white readership described the abortion-related deaths of Black women, the coverage did not differ drastically from when these newspapers covered the abortion-related deaths of white women. The abortion-related deaths of Black women did generate stories. The journalists gathered and presented the information in a manner that was analogous to the way they reported on white women's abortion deaths. Nevertheless, there was a certain elusive, impalpable distinction that one can sense when comparing the two approaches. In the case of Black women, not only did the journalists include descriptors such as "negro" or "colored," but there also seems to have been a lack of urgency in determining culpability. While coverage of Delphine's and Vera's abortions included series of articles dedicated to uncovering the identity of the Vancouver millionaire or "Mac," little fanfare was made over the men responsible for the pregnancies of Black women who died from criminal abortions. Perhaps these sentences from an article related to another Black abortion case will serve to illustrate the point: "Dr. Campbell, autopsy surgeon for the coroner's office, who had made a post mortem examination of the body, testified that death was due to septicaemia. The jury found a verdict that Minnie LaRue had died of blood poisoning, following a criminal operation, *but did not attempt to cast the blame on any one*."[51] It is possible that the disparity in coverage in newspapers with a primarily white readership can be reduced to the disproportionately low reporting of violent crimes against women of color generally.[52] Were the *Los Angeles Sentinel* or *California Eagle* to humanize Margaret, to portray her as kind, sweet, innocent, naïve, or even the girl next door, it would be the same as making her a victim. Had they done so, these organs of the Black community would have sabotaged their ability to save Marmillion, an otherwise respectable professional and community pillar in the segregated, insular, and protective Central Avenue district.

In June 1933 a jury of six white men and six white women found the sixty-two-year-old Black physician guilty of second-degree murder and sentenced him to five years to life in prison. Marmillion changed attorneys and filed an appeal while the Black Los Angeles community and the *Los Angeles Sentinel* rallied behind him. Like Fiske, Marmillion was hospitalized for his deteriorating health, and it compelled others to ask that he be allowed to return home—but to no avail. He was denied an appeal. The reason: "The woman died while lying upon an operating table in the office of the defendant.... There is an abundance of evidence of circumstances connecting [the] defendant with the commission of the offense. We are unable to discover so much as an excuse for this appeal."[53]

While serving his sentence in San Quentin, Marmillion received the support of some twenty thousand petitioners who demanded the governor release him. The petitioners emphasized Marmillion's accomplishments and his character, describing him as a charitable, religious man of integrity. They believed Marmillion to be an honest man and trusted his account of the incident. The *Sentinel* urged the governor to give Marmillion back to his community, if only for him to spend "the sunset of his well-spent life" at home.[54] This case even prompted some Black journalists to "raise questions about abortion laws."[55] Clearly the case had galvanized the community, and Black Los Angeles mobilized behind Marmillion.

Black physicians may have been able to claim some stature within their own community. However, within the medical field their race often influenced the patients they received. In some instances whites went to Black physicians because of emergencies or because they were too embarrassed or ashamed to visit their regular doctors. Consequently Black physicians sometimes treated whites when it came to epidemics, outbreaks, or conditions like venereal disease, pregnancy, or abortion.[56] Furthermore, unable to work in white institutions under most circumstances, non-white physicians often catered to patients who were also unable to access these institutions. Margaret Scott and her boyfriend traveled to Los Angeles in order to find a physician they knew wouldn't turn them away. Given such circumstances, physicians of color were often in a predicament. Their resources and energies were spread out thinly over a large geographic area.

The case of Vera Nelson is an interesting counterpoint to the case of Margaret Scott. The cases had very similar circumstances but different outcomes. Both of the doctors involved, Fiske and Marmillion, were of an advanced age, both were Southern California physicians, both were accused of performing illegal abortions on eighteen-year-old women, both women were found deceased on the operating tables of the accused physicians, the trials took their tolls on the two men's health, and both men argued that they had simply performed their legitimate duties as physicians. Yet one man, Fiske, was able to return to his family right away, while the other, Marmillion, would have to wait years for that opportunity. And one physician was white, and the other was Black.

Fiske's trial and arrest did not mobilize the Los Angeles medical community in the same way that Marmillion's arrest mobilized the Black Los Angeles community. Fiske's ill health generated sympathy from the judge and jury, yet Marmillion's did not. Fiske argued that he had performed legitimate duties in his role as physician. Was Dr. Marmillion, a Black physician from a medical school that had failed to earn AMA recognition, even able to claim that he *was* a legitimate physician?

In the spring of 1937 Marmillion was paroled, and efforts continued into 1939 to secure a formal pardon for him. He was fully and officially free in 1940. He died on March 17, 1950, in his home in Los Angeles after a year-long bout of illness. The Marmillion case shows us that when a Black *physician* was accused of performing a criminal operation, the local Black community tended to rally to his aid.[57] In Washington, for example, Dr. J. H. Tompkins was arrested for the murder of Miss Jean Maxwell after an alleged abortion. The $8,000 to secure his release was acquired through security "furnished by colored citizens."[58] Tompkins's arrest occurred at a different time (around 1905), thus showing that the proclivity among African American communities to protect their most respectable citizens was not limited to the Great Depression; rather it was a hallmark of their existence that transcended place and time. Marmillion was part of the backbone of the Black Los Angeles community. If even the community's most educated and elite members could not have equality in the American judicial system, then, in the midst of ongoing segregation and discrimination, what options were there for the rest of them?

In the next chapter we will explore female providers of illegal abortions. Like their Black counterparts, these women faced unique obstacles in this line of work. The AMA's anti-abortion campaign and the creation of obstetric and gynecological specialties were efforts to establish male authority over women and marginalize midwives. Medical men, obstetricians, and gynecologists deliberately sought to legitimate their specialties in order to pull their practices away from midwives. Some male obstetricians even went so far as to say that "midwife" and "abortionist" were "synonymous terms."[59] As a result, female providers of illegal abortions were doubly degenerate in the eyes of the organized medical field. They were not only subverting the medical profession, but they were also helping women to shirk their natural responsibilities of motherhood.

"The Mid-Wife Type"   4
Wicked Women Abortionists

> There are mills operating in our City of Los Angeles, for instances where the price runs very high. These people may have had medical training but I don't know if you could call them doctors. I think most abortions fall into that category.... The mid-wife type of thing.
>
> —Testimony from AB 2614 Abortion Hearing, 1962

In a meeting of the Maternity and Child Welfare Group in October 1937, doctors Violet Russell and Joan Malleson asserted that physicians needed to support more lenient abortion laws. Arguing that women faced greater danger in the absence of legal access to abortions, Russell and Malleson expressed that expanding the grounds for legal abortion would promote women's safety. Their endorsement of more lenient abortion laws would have been inconceivable in the late nineteenth century—not just because of mainline AMA beliefs about abortion, but also because Russell and Malleson were women. Because women physicians tried desperately to distance themselves from midwives after the professionalization of medicine, many took a staunchly conservative anti-abortion stance. Female physicians often spearheaded anti-abortion and anti-midwife campaigns so that they would not appear tolerant, weak, or unprofessional. Dr. Emma Drake, for example, wrote in 1908: "No thwarting of nature has any ground for excuse, and the so-called physician who peddles any theory or device for so doing has no right to the name and has no recognition among the ranks of the reputable men and women in the honored profession of medicine. His work is done in the dark and under the pledge of secrecy, and so he marks himself of the abode of Satan."[1]

Drake's writings were a scathing indictment of "antenatal infanticide." At the same time, however, they were upholding the mainline AMA anti-abortion stance and defending women's position in the professional medical field. Russell and Malleson's outspokenness *for* legal abortion in the 1930s suggests that female physicians had by then established themselves as medical professionals and that midwives were no longer as much of a professional threat or concern.[2] Nevertheless, Russell and Malleson's position was unique. While women were beginning to gain professional legitimacy in the medical field, the conflation of female physicians with midwives and abortionists remained and was hard to shake off.

Until the middle of the nineteenth century pregnancy and childbirth were understood as women-centered events. Midwives and family members helped with delivery, and delivery took place in the home since childbirth was considered a normal function—not a disease or condition. Part of the efforts to legitimate gynecology and obstetrics as specialties relied upon pushing the idea that childbirth required medical intervention. Physicians argued that childbirth was not a simple function to be left to sisters, mothers, neighbors, or ignorant, untrained midwives; rather it was a technical, potentially dangerous occurrence that required medical supervision.[3] As physicians gradually took the place of midwives in labor and delivery and moved their work into medical offices and hospitals, they delineated a clear line between "regular" and "irregular" medicine and "legitimate" and "illegitimate" practitioners.

In the nineteenth century physicians in the AMA worked tirelessly to legitimate the medical field, and much of that work revolved around censuring "quacks" and practitioners of irregular medicine. Abortion was a practical platform upon which to build their professional status because "irregulars" and midwives were thought to be the ones who performed these procedures most often. By arguing vehemently against abortions—and the people who performed them—physicians presented themselves as legitimate practitioners of medicine and guardians of health and life. While there was a consumer safety aspect to this campaign, the reality was that the vast majority of those the

AMA considered quacks or irregulars were people of color and midwives. Regular physicians used their professional campaign to position themselves as the ethical medical vanguards of society and to effectively remove and discredit their opposition.

Physicians did not just resort to science and medicine to speak out against abortion; they used a moral language as well. Such language may have been used as an attempt to drive public sentiment against abortion because of the effects many believed it had on traditional gender norms. This attempt was particularly aimed against white women in the middle and upper classes during the nineteenth century. Many were choosing to delay childbirth until later years, have fewer children, or even forgo childbearing in order to pursue educational or political goals.[4] Indeed one could argue that the anti-abortion campaign illustrated that women's choices were obvious and that the campaign was a form of backlash against the changes in society. Nevertheless, since physicians hoped to retain as their patients the same white women who might have had, or sought, abortions, they could not call these women depraved. Physicians emphasized their own medical education, training, and increased understanding of the development of fetal life rather than openly vilifying their patients.[5] In 1864, for example, the AMA proposed developing a short tract for women "designed to *enlighten* them upon the criminality and physical evil of forced abortion."[6] Similarly Drake referred to women who wanted abortions as "untaught." It was the job of the physician to undo the improper teachings young women learned from their friends, relatives, and mothers so that they could be instructed to see the errors of their thought.[7] In making abortion an issue of *education*—or the lack thereof—physicians simultaneously confirmed their own prestige and challenged their professional rivals without alienating their patients too much.[8] In her 1908 manual to young women, Drake lamented that young women came to matrimony with more of an interest in preventing conception than concerns about preparing for motherhood. She claimed that women who entered into the marriage contract with plans other than being the "joyful mother of children" committed a "grievous sin."[9] Her words provide an interesting point of view. Her rigid anti-contraception/anti-abortion stance and her own position as a female physician together illustrate her adherence to the AMA's mores, while her gendered primer also worked to prepare young women for their fulfillment of acceptable gendered roles.

As new specialties in gynecology and obstetrics coupled with social ideas like "the domestic sphere," it would appear that the AMA's professionalization efforts were part of a larger "covert battle" that reduced women to their wombs.[10] As French historian Jules Michelet aptly described, the nineteenth century *was* "the age of the womb."[11] It was in the nineteenth century, for example, that physicians discovered "neurasthenia," a disease of the highly evolved caused by "excessive brain work and nervous strain."[12] Neurasthenia led to effeminacy and weakness in men; in women it produced hysteria and other diseases of the womb. For men neurasthenia meant that they needed to return to some kind of masculine primitivism because they had grown too soft and womanly over the course of the nineteenth century. The discovery of neurasthenia contributed to the rise of a more rugged masculinity, and it also explains why things like pugilism, the Boy Scouts, and professional football all emerged at the turn of the century. For women, neurasthenia was the result of trying to become more like men. Women had exhausted their brains and nerves by seeking higher education, getting careers, and limiting childbirth; their bodies were literally shutting down because they were neglecting their supposedly natural and primary obligations. Some physicians also claimed that women's desires to remain unmarried or childless were also unnatural and that higher education and women's involvement in social clubs and organizations invariably led to "grievous maladies" like "amenorrhoea, dysmenorrhoea, chronic and acute ovaritis, prolapsus uteri," and the like.[13] In making the womb central to women's health and national vigor, physicians reaffirmed traditional gender roles and linked modern women's actions to sickness and disease.

Some physicians even claimed that contraceptive use induced "cancer, sterility, insanity, or 'deranged' bladders and rectums."[14] Many physicians from the late nineteenth century through the twentieth conflated birth control and feminism with national decline, as well as physical and moral degeneration—suggesting, for example, not only that it was unnatural to marry and not want children but also that women who used birth control were prostitutes.[15] According to Victorian beliefs, prostitutes were the women who knew of effective birth control as a matter of professional survival. In contrast, chastity until marriage and motherhood were essential to solidifying proper women's positions in society.[16] As a result, birth control became associated with immorality because of its connection to prostitution and the evasion of maternal destiny. Prominent figures in the women's rights movement, like Elizabeth Cady Stanton and Susan B. Anthony, understood the ideological power that motherhood possessed. They also believed that infanticide and abortion were morally depraved. However, they believed that women's inability to secure divorces and their status as second-class citizens sometimes forced them to seek abortions.[17] Stanton and Anthony believed that if women had political equality, they would need fewer abortions. Though Stanton, Anthony, and most early women's rights activists were anti-abortion, they were still often lumped together with others who were thought to be disrupting the fabric of American life: fecund immigrant women, white women who used birth control, women's rights advocates, and female abortionists.

It was quite common for an abortionist to be caricatured as female. In his treatise *On Criminal Abortion in America*, Horatio Storer himself suggested that women were the chief perpetrators of the crime. He not only condemned the women who submitted themselves for abortions, but he also blamed nurses, midwives, female physicians, and female friends who had also had abortions.[18] Storer claimed he did not hope to incite prejudice or hostility toward women physicians; he simply lamented that they were "peculiarly and unfortunately situated" to commit the crime since women who wanted abortions likely felt more comfortable with asking other women first.[19] This point rings particularly true, given earlier scholars' discussions and explorations of intimate female networks and the role of midwives.

Storer wasn't entirely off base. Because of female networks, women who wanted abortions were likely first to ask a friend or relative who may have had an abortion or knew of someone who had. These networks were not silent on the issue of abortion; they often held the keys to its access. Though there were likely just as many men who performed abortions—if not more—the image of a woman abortionist was especially inflammatory. Moreover, since the only abortion cases that came to the public's attention were those that had resulted in death, female abortionists were aberrations of idealized femininity. They were violent criminals and murderesses who helped other women escape motherhood by essentially committing infanticide. In an era when women were defined by their adherence to the gendered ideologies of separate spheres, female abortionists were the antitheses of respectable mothers, who guarded the domestic sphere. They were subversive on multiple fronts, violating sexual norms, the norms of patriarchy, and the law. Women abortionists were threats not only to other women's safety, but also to the community and society in general.

As a society, we continue to have an obsession with female criminals since statistically they're rare. Female criminals go against respectable gender norms—particularly when it comes to the crime of abortion. When combined with gendered stereotypes that expect women to be docile, gentle, and nurturing caregivers, women who kill are often perceived differently from men who kill.[20] Men are thought to be biologically more aggressive, so when men commit violent crimes, it is thought to be a manifestation of their nature. It is not so for women. Consequently women who kill are often pathologized as victims or mentally ill, and if they seem to show agency or willingness to commit a crime, they're described as bad or evil.[21] While men may "kill because they possess the propensity to kill," societal constructs reject that the same propensity even exists in women.[22] When such aberrations became visible in women abortionists, their crime—antenatal infanticide—was a combination of everything women were not supposed to do. They were not acting as gentle, docile caregivers to infants. Instead they were killing them for money—usually at the behest of another woman. It was a crime of two women acting abnor-

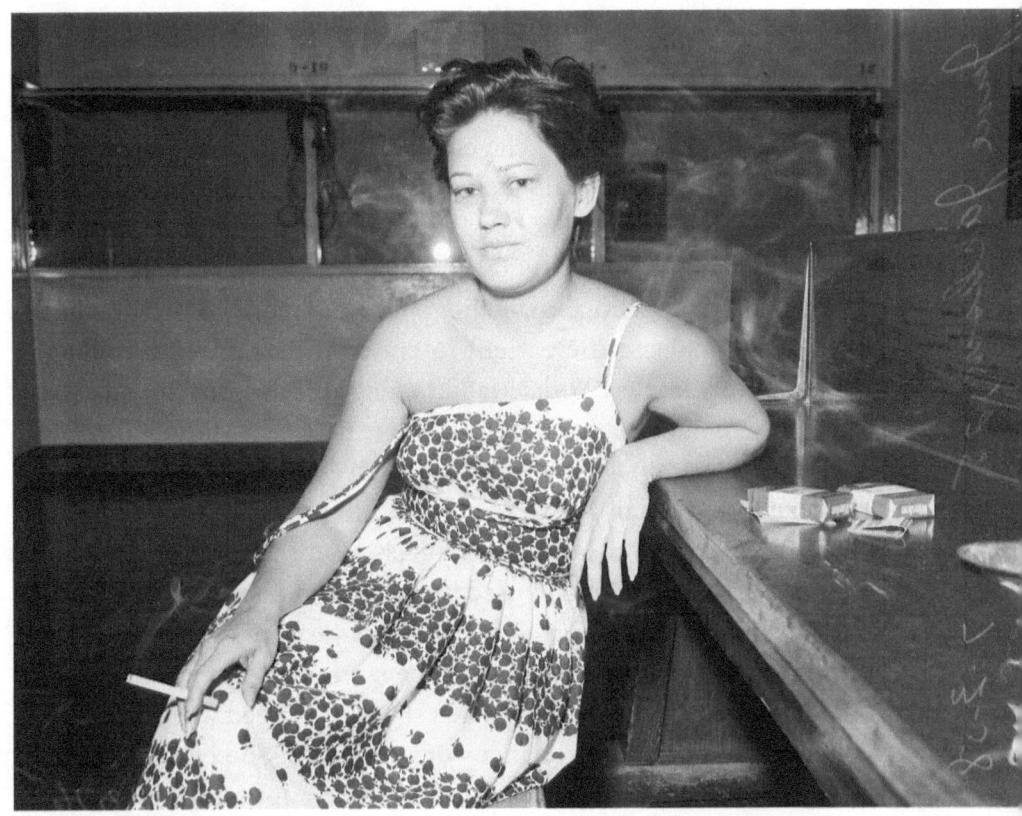

1. Abortion arrest, July 22, 1953. Gloria June Weisbrod, twenty-two years (suspect). Caption slip reads: "Photographer: Brunk. Date: 1953-07-22. Reporter: T. T. Assignment: Abortion arrest. 27–28: Gloria June Weisbrod, 22, suspected of fatal illegal operation on her cousin, shown in Compton Jail." *Los Angeles Examiner* Photographs Collection, 1920–1961. USC Libraries Special Collections.

mally, each woman murderous and culpable. Women abortionists—and the women requesting abortions—weren't murdering abusive husbands. They were killing a life they had created and that they were supposed to protect.

Regardless of these negative views of women abortionists, many women became specialists in the procedure for a variety of reasons. In the late nineteenth and early twentieth centuries figures like Dr. Lucy Hagenow of Chicago and "Madame Restell" of New York became the faces of female abortionists in America. Following her arrest for an illegal operation she had performed, Hagenow told the authorities that business was "booming"—not only for herself but also for a whole host of abortionists, whose alliances with hushed officials allowed them to thrive.[23] Hagenow claimed that some abortionists in Chicago were so skilled that it would be nearly impossible to catch them. On the other hand, she described an industry rife with greedy villains and disreputable practitioners when she told the story of one midwife who allowed her patient to die of blood poisoning when she realized the patient intended to pay only $2.50 for the procedure.[24] In New York "Madame Restell"—whose real name was Ann Lohmann—had amassed a fortune from 1836 through 1878. Her career as a criminal abortionist—which earned her the title of "the Wickedest Woman in the City"—began after her foray in contraceptives.[25] In 1836 she married a quack doctor who created patented female contraceptives and used the name and title "Madame Restell, female physician and professor of midwifery," to market and brand them.[26] Eventually Restell herself began to perform abortions. Her first known trial was in 1841, when she was charged with performing an abortion that resulted in a woman's death. She had several subsequent trials and brushes with the law. In another trial she simply settled out of court. Some of her critics cited her political campaign contributions as the reason why she always seemed to get off easily. She was believed to have had the superintendent of the New York City police on her payroll. After the one trial for which she did have to serve time in prison, she received such special treatment and luxurious accommodations that the city council opened an investigation into the matter and fired the prison warden. Madame Restell was so successful and her business so profitable that when her daughter married in 1854, her present to the young couple was $50,000 and a lengthy European honeymoon.

In 1878 Anthony Comstock disguised himself as a potential customer and approached Madame Restell about purchasing contraceptive materials. After making the purchase, he acquired a search warrant and collected enough evidence to bring Madame Restell to trial for violating the Comstock Act. Though Madame Restell hired an attorney who did his best to maneuver her out of the charges, it was to no avail. Rather than face trial, she committed suicide on April 1, 1878, by slitting her throat with a carving knife in her bathtub. At the time of her death her estate was valued at nearly $1,000,000. Though some criticized Comstock for his entrapment, he found her bloody death fitting given the way she had earned a living. Others felt similarly. The *National Police Gazette*, for example, described in detail her "bloody empire," which warranted "public indignation." Nevertheless, her "wholesale bloodshed" earned her a living.[27]

Madame Restell was not the only high-profile female abortionist. Other women came into the world of illegal abortion perhaps because of their social networks and connections. In late November 1932, when Margaret Browning, a well-known and prominent clubwoman of Madera County, California, was arrested for second-degree murder and for performing illegal abortions, she became the talk of the town. After three illegal abortion deaths in the area sheriff's officers and the district attorney began to link evidence connecting these operations to the Brownings' farm in Chowchilla, California. Apparently it had been widely suspected for the past decade that Browning performed abortions there, and her farm had been "credited [to] some 25 to 30 deaths."[28] An investigation into the farm yielded "surgical instruments and a small note book said to contain names, addresses and amounts paid by several hundred women over a period of ten years."[29] After Browning was freed on $15,000 bail, jury selection began.[30] Browning's trial generated much attention and publicity. Several California newspapers covered her story daily, and the opening day of the trial witnessed "a crowded court room of the curious, with a large percentage of women present."[31] In fact interest was so great that newspapers frequently referenced the full and crowded courtroom—full of both men and women. After hearing all the evidence and witness testimony, the jury began deliberations on January 12, 1933. Browning expected a quick acquittal but was surprised that the jury did not reach a verdict within a couple of hours. She nervously waited in the courtroom until 11 p.m. the first day before she was told to leave and return the next day. On January 14 the jury announced that it was deadlocked and unable to reach a verdict. The district attorney immediately moved for a retrial.

Browning's second trial began on February 27.[32] Unlike the first trial, however, the jury found her guilty on March 3, 1933. In a strange turn of events, though, Browning's defense attorney moved to have the verdict set aside since Governor James Rolph had declared a holiday for an emergency banking measure on March 1. According to her attorney, "holding a court session on a legal holiday constituted a mistrial."[33] The judge issued a writ of habeas corpus for Browning and demanded that she be present for sentencing on Tuesday, March 7. However, the defense sought a continuance in order to request a new trial.[34] On March 7 Browning was sentenced to a term of two to five years in San Quentin for performing an illegal abortion. On March 11 a jury venire was called together for Browning's murder trial, which was slated to begin on April 4.

The murder trial began on April 6, 1933. Allegedly Browning had performed an illegal operation upon Helen Ruth Ostergaard of El Cerrito, California, in early November 1931. Ostergaard became ill and returned to the Browning farm, where she remained for several days. Browning continued to administer treatment to her, but when it became clear her health was not improving, Ostergaard was "taken to the hospital where she lingered on until the time of her death, February 26, 1932."[35] While Ostergaard remained on the Browning property, her husband visited her several times, even eating dinner at the residence, though he claimed to have no knowledge of the purpose of his wife's stay. By April 8 the jury of twelve men was deadlocked, evenly split and unable to come to a verdict. The murder case was dismissed.

While Browning may have had a stroke of luck with the murder case dismissal, her appeal against the initial abortion charge was still up in the air. On May 20, 1933, Browning's conviction on the charge of performing an illegal abortion was upheld. Though the case had been tried, and the verdict declared, on a bank holiday, the appellate court argued that since her attorney had failed to raise any objections at the time, there was no need to invalidate the trial or verdict.[36] The failure to object, in essence, was seen as tacit approval of the trial's continuation. Browning and her attorney continued to fight the conviction, but the state Supreme Court denied any further appeals.[37] Browning began to serve her sentence on June 27, 1933, and on December 1, 1933, she requested a pardon or commutation of her sentence from Governor Rolph. She did not appear to receive any word from the governor; even worse, on February 21, 1934, her indeterminate sentence of two to five years was fixed at five years. Though Browning was eligible for parole after one year, and despite a petition in favor of it signed by the mayor, city council, and over three hundred residents of Chowchilla, the parole board refused to release her.[38] It wasn't until December 19, 1934, that Browning was finally paroled—with sixty other inmates and in time for Christmas.[39] Her release after serving only eighteen months of a five-year sentence, however, generated controversy. One journalist wrote the following:

> There is something decidedly wrong in this release, from the manner in which it was done right up to the reason why it was done. Mrs. Browning was released December 19, but her name was not included in the list of "Christmas Gift" paroles granted at that time. . . . Why was Mrs. Browning's name not given with the list of those receiving Christmas paroles? Why was this woman only made to serve 18 months of a two to five year sentence? The parole board, at the time of her incarceration, set her sentence at five years—now they say her sentence was 'secretly understood' to be 18 months. Why? There was no recommendation of leniency at the time of Mrs. Browning's trial. Now why is the Prison Board so big hearted? According to Prison Board procedure, a person sentenced from two to five years must serve a year and nine months as a minimum to be eligible for a parole. Why was an exception made in Mrs. Browning's case? These are questions that every law abiding citizens has a right to know. Secret pardons, special paroles and favoritism make the public suspicious of the Prison Board.[40]

Thus ended the saga of Browning's "death farm." Despite the protestations of some, her name faded away from the front page and crime sections of the *Madera Daily Tribune* and shifted back to the social events and gossip pages, where her name was afterward listed only as a guest at the birthday parties, soirees, and club meetings of the local elite.[41]

Madame Restell and Margaret Browning were both prominent women of means, yet they had widely divergent experiences. In reality few women abortionists were as wealthy or carried as much pull as these two. While Restell and Browning are exceptional examples, the reality was that they, like their Black counterparts, had little social or political clout in the event of an indictment. While the BME and law enforcement may have been slow or reluctant to act when dealing with male physicians, female abortionists were promptly indicted. For example, a certain Dr. Raye Everett, a female physician in Detroit, was accused of malpractice and of performing an illegal operation on a young married woman who died of peritonitis.[42] The victim's father was a very prominent man in the neighboring Grayling area, and it likely had something to do with Everett's swift indictment. However, the father also claimed that Everett must have coerced his daughter into having the operation because she would never have agreed to it on her own. Because of the particularly negative view that the public held of women abortionists, this sentiment was widely accepted, and thus female abortionists had little recourse when caught. Elsewhere the arrest and indictment of midwife Rachael Schumacher were swift after she performed an illegal abortion upon the wife of a prominent local oil man in Healdsburg, California.[43] While professional women—whether physicians or midwives—could claim a certain degree of authority or expertise when it came to medical practice, they could not escape the patriarchal structures that still governed their lives outside of their professional world. If they provided abortions to the wrong women or if things went poorly for wealthy, well-connected women, they could expect retribution.

For some female abortionists the prospect of incarceration, or even a trial, was too much. When the police arrived at Margaret Sloman's house and asked the woman to accompany them to the police station to speak about an abortion, she attempted suicide by ingesting four tablets of bichloride of mercury.[44] Sixty-eight-year-old Emma Schulz

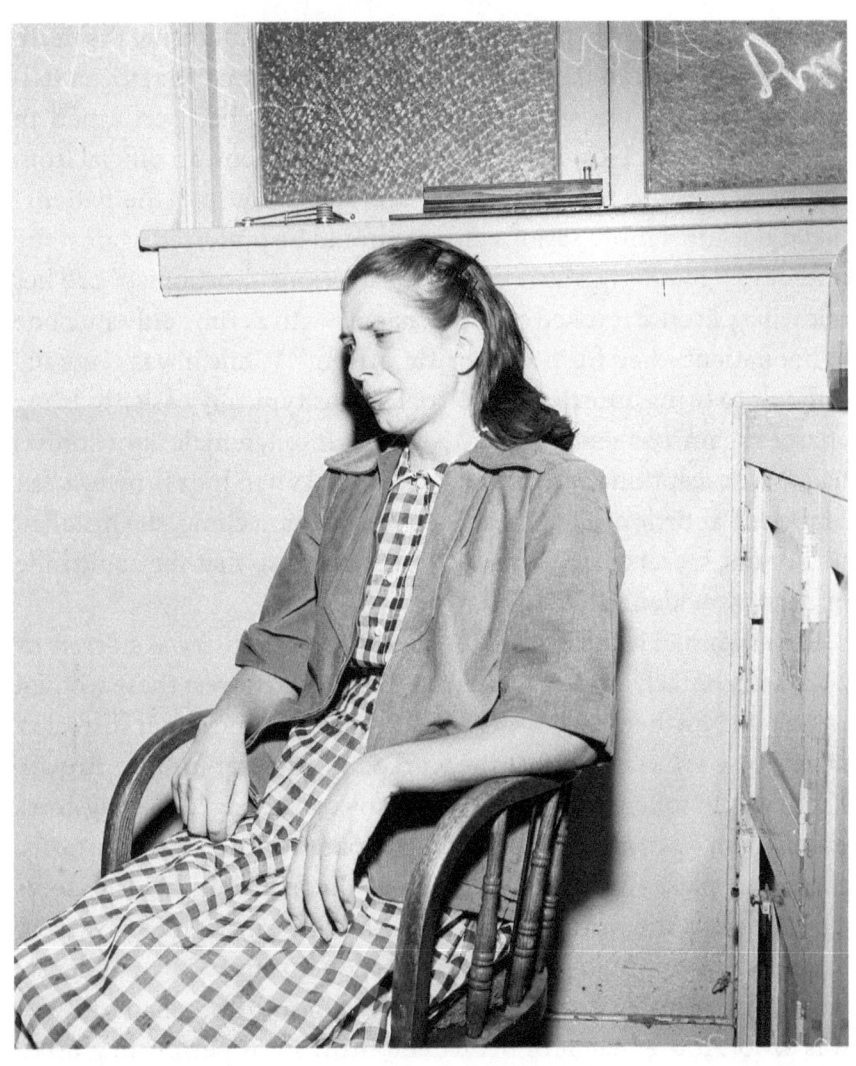

2. Abortion suspect, July 3, 1958. June Jackson, twenty-five years (in jail). Caption slip reads: "Photographer: Miller. Date: 1958-06-03. Reporter: Waymire. Assignment: Abortion suspect. 17/18: June Jackson, 25, at Lincoln Heights jail." *Los Angeles Examiner* Photographs Collection, 1920–1961. USC Libraries Special Collections.

attempted suicide when she was faced with arrest following the death of a woman from an illegal operation.[45] When Elena Rinetti, an Italian midwife, was arrested, she admitted that she had performed an illegal operation. However, during her arraignment, an official from the BME ran into the courtroom "and declared that [the patient] had died, and a more serious charge should be preferred against the midwife."[46] Similarly Maria Caron, a "notorious abortionist," had her midwifery license revoked and was charged with a crime only after one of her patients died from an illegal abortion.[47] While it was generally difficult to bring abortionists to trial, it was typically easier to bring charges against a female abortionist. As a result, female abortionists had to be exceptionally savvy and prepared. When Inez Brown, a San Francisco abortionist, opened her own abortion clinic, she installed trap doors, secret compartments, and furnaces so that she could hide or destroy evidence if needed.[48]

Some women were involved in the abortion industry as steerers or points of contact, and the police did their best to arrest these women as well. In Northern California Marjorie Krebs came under suspicion when the BME realized that she worked as a steerer for Inez Brown. Krebs would solicit business for Brown by contacting local drugstores to let them know that if they had patrons who needed abortions, there were places nearby that could help them. Ideally the drugstores would spread the word or would relay the information when asked. For $60 Brown would perform an abortion on any woman under six weeks gestation. If the woman was three months pregnant, the fee was $100. At the height of her career, Brown was performing up to thirty abortions per day and earning approximately $50,000 a month. We will mention her in slightly more detail later.

When interrogated, Krebs claimed that she had sought a job from Brown when her husband abandoned her and their two children. Interrogators—hoping to get Krebs to flip on Brown—warned her that she could be charged as an accessory to murder in the event of a patient's death. However, Krebs didn't seem too worried. Rather she told the officers that there was not a "better operator in the State" than Brown. Krebs, who had had several abortions of her own, seemed defiant at the interrogation. While she probably despised the law and the fact that these officers were interrogating her, she was also keenly aware that she was helping women access a service that they needed and with a provider she personally trusted. Krebs's wit obviously struck a chord with the interrogators, who told her that she was too intelligent to be mixed up with an illegal abortionist. Her terse response—"Well, it might seem such"—hinted at her frustration with law enforcement, perhaps with a touch of sarcasm for added value.[49] Despite the harassment, women continued to provide illegal abortions. It is possible that some of these women had personally known fears associated with pregnancy and motherhood. Others may have undergone their own illegal abortions, propelling them into a career of helping other women. In a society that explicitly stated female abortionists were "not fit for decent society," at the same time it said that it was "the duty of any healthy married woman to bear children," these female abortionists were rebels.[50] These were the women that the anti-abortion campaign caricatured relentlessly.

The female abortionists discussed previously were exceptional in the sense that they operated their own businesses and performed abortions themselves. Frequently women served in auxiliary roles—as nurses, staff, or steerers, like Krebs. In San Diego Laura Miner made a name for herself as one of the most skilled and proficient abortionists in the industry. While she began her career independently, she would soon join a racket that would take over the Pacific Coast.

Laura Kershaw was born in 1898.[51] She did not have a happy childhood. In fact her own mother had nearly died from a back-alley abortion. Instead she died when Laura was nine years old, exhausted from bearing eight children within a twelve-year span. Laura went through a series of orphan asylums, foster homes, and stepmothers before reaching adulthood. On October 18, 1924, Laura married Glen Miner in Chicago. Shortly thereafter Glen and their two children, Donald and newborn Lorraine, became ill with different conditions. Donald had developed infantile paralysis, and Lorraine had caught tuberculosis from her father. Unfortunately both children died. Glen failed to make a full recovery, and his physician urged him to seek treatment at a hospital in Prescott, Arizona. Glen was not interested in going to Arizona, but when he realized that Laura was pregnant again, he decided to seek treatment before the birth of their daughter, Joyce. When Joyce was six months old, Laura moved with the infant to Arizona as well. Glen and Laura lived mostly separate lives. Glen had to stay in the hospital for treatment, though he tried to visit Laura and Joyce periodically. Laura lived on a tight budget while Glen was hospitalized, and in the three years that they lived in Arizona, Laura became pregnant twice. Due to his condition and their finances, Glen did not think it was the best time for them to have more children, so he performed two abortions on his wife.[52]

In late 1931 Laura became pregnant again and was determined to keep the baby. Their son Jerry was born in May 1932. The following fall Glen left the hospital because he believed that he was well enough. However, Jerry soon fell ill. He began to lose weight, and they discovered that he had contracted tuberculosis as well. The doctor told Laura she needed to move her children to another state. Laura borrowed money from family in Chicago, and she took her children, and what few belongings she could, to San Diego, California. Glen remained in the hospital in Arizona, and Jerry was able to make a full recovery. However, Glen soon got a job at the Governor's Office in Arizona, where he stayed, while Laura struggled to provide for their two children in San Diego.[53]

In order to support her family Laura started a bridge club. She would offer private and group lessons in bridge so that she could stay home with her children. In the middle of 1934 one of Laura's bridge students confided that she was pregnant and begged for advice. Laura explained that she had some experience in that department. In fact she had the instruments Glen had used for her abortions in her possession, but she worried that even if she could start the procedure, she might need a doctor to help her finish it. Laura found a doctor who said he would be willing to help her if necessary. Laura then felt secure. Everything went smoothly, and Laura began to work for a doctor who performed abortions exclusively.[54] Laura did not choose the abortion industry first; rather she came to it as part of a female network in which women trusted each other for advice. Her personal experiences—with her mother and her own abortions—made her empathetic. She knew from both sides why women wanted to procure abortions.

Scholars have explained how the contraceptive industry provided women with a greater degree of freedom. Furthermore, women in this industry also had another advantage that made them more likely to succeed: their sex. Andrea Tone states, "At a time when almost all doctors, druggists, sales agents, and vendors were men, women contraceptive entrepreneurs made biological difference a marketing advantage, urging women to place their confidence in products designed by those with firsthand knowledge of childbearing and its prevention."[55] The same was true for women who provided illegal abortions. In the abortion industry Laura found independence. She earned a steady income and was able to support herself and her children. She eventually earned enough to be able to tell Glen that they didn't need his money anymore.[56] Laura hired a housekeeper, bought a new car, and put a down payment on a three-bedroom, two-bathroom house with a double garage. Laura not only helped women exercise their own reproductive choices, but she also gained financial independence, stability, and the ability to provide a comfortable life for herself and her two children. As part of extended female networks, female abortionists may have been more accessible to women, and women may have felt more comfortable approaching them about their situations. On a more personal level many female abortionists understood their patients' predicaments and attempted to help them as someone had possibly helped them before.

Laura Miner established herself and would become absorbed into the Pacific Coast Abortion Ring (PCAR) when it spread to San Diego. PCAR's San Diego facility had nine rooms, and Laura initially began as the office receptionist and nurse. Eventually she was trusted to perform all of the procedures at the San Diego location. She soon hired her own nurse and receptionist. Women would go to the San Diego location and ask for Laura Miner by name. Laura Miner would soon run the San Diego location on her own.

Over time PCAR would become a large, coastwide abortion mill that provided safe abortions to hundreds—if not thousands—of women in California, Washington, and Oregon. The following chapter outlines this extensive abortion mill, its rise and fall, why it was unique, and how its success—specifically its ability to provide safe, illegal abortions without injury or death—contributed to a shift in the ways law enforcement tackled illegal abortions in California.

The Pacific Coast Abortion Ring   5
Organized Crime and Criminal Ambitions

> The story . . . told revealed the most amazing and revolting criminal conspiracy in the history of medical science. It revealed the unbelievable scale on which the meanest and filthiest of all rackets—the abortion racket—is carried on. It was a story of shame, blood, pain, disgrace, greed, and death; of how the red-gloved abortion quacks, dominated by master criminal brains, fatten on the profits from the murder of the unborn.
>
> —Edward S. Sullivan, 1937

In 1934 Reginald Rankin went to Portland, Oregon, to recruit Dr. George E. Watts into his abortion syndicate. Rankin sought Watts specifically. The aging physician had been practicing abortions for some forty years in Portland and was an abortion specialist. Over the course of his career Watts had developed a "vacuum aspiration technique" to perform abortions. This innovation was significant because it reduced the risk of infection or sepsis by ensuring the removal of all fetal tissue from the uterus; and, perhaps more important to Rankin, this method had proved safe and effective enough to keep Watts under the radar and out of the eye of law enforcement. Rankin knew that abortion's illegal status meant he could amass a small fortune by offering it, so when he met with Watts, he described his plans for an organized criminal abortion syndicate that would span the entire West Coast—from Seattle to the U.S.-Mexico border. Rankin's syndicate was a testament to his character. He had a big personality, he thought he was above the law, and he wanted his massive abortion racket to represent that.

The idea for an organized abortion syndicate wasn't new. There had been other abortion rackets in the United States before, and they had certainly come to the attention of law enforcement, but they had been more restrained. In New York, for example, the health commissioner estimated that some 100,000 women per year went through the city's most prominent abortion mill, while another New York physician put that number at closer to 250,000 per year and called it "one of the safest, best protected, as well as one of the most vicious rackets in the city."[1] Leslie Reagan described another such racket in New Jersey—the so-called Birth Control Club—that allowed the approximately 800 card-carrying members to get as many abortions as they needed—so long as they paid their club fees. These members, many of them clerks in Newark offices, used membership in the club as a form of health insurance; they expected they would have an abortion in the future. Much smaller rings also existed. For example, near Park Avenue in New York three or four physicians would ally and perform abortions for the elite women of the city, charging between $1,000 and $3,000 per procedure. In the event that the police arrested one of the physicians for performing an abortion, the others would immediately testify that the arrested physician had consulted with them and that they had all agreed the abortion had been medically necessary.[2] Thus these physicians were also members of a criminal syndicate, even if a relatively small one.

Rankin, the Birth Control Club, and these Park Avenue physicians were immediately influenced by changes of the Prohibition era. Just days after the Volstead Act and the Eighteenth Amendment passed, police in Chicago were indicted for accepting bribes and selling confiscated liquor. Law enforcement colluded with bootleggers, and there was a vast contempt for the law. Under Prohibition those who were willing to break the law by selling and producing alcohol were merely catering to the demands of consumers who didn't really believe that drinking was a crime—even if it had been criminalized.

Crimes such as alcohol consumption, prostitution, bootlegging, and abortion—*mala prohibita* crimes—are considered wrong because they're illegal. These crimes are less clearly defined in contrast to *mala in se* crimes, such as murder and theft, and there is less moral consensus about the action the law is criminalizing. *Mala prohibita* crimes have historically posed a challenge to law enforcement because they are proliferative, highly profitable, connected to black markets, and expensive and difficult to prosecute. They are often crimes in which the middle class is the primary consumer, and this class expresses a desire to continue partaking in the behavior regardless of its legality.[3] There have been discussions about whether or not abortion is a "vice" crime. While vice crimes involve willing participants, their association with pleasure and repeated behavior differentiates them from abortions.[4] Women seeking illegal abortions are not chasing a high (as are drug users, gamblers, or johns), nor are they addicted or habitual abortion patients.

Nevertheless, because of the steady middle-class demand for commodities such as prostitution, alcohol, and abortion, organizations stand to profit if they can supply where there is demand. When such a commodity becomes illegal, its value increases, creating an opportunity for organized crime to step in. Moreover, since such crimes are more difficult to regulate, they are often brought to the public's attention through sporadic and selective crackdowns—a method of law enforcement that would be unacceptable or inconceivable for crimes like murder.[5]

Criminal organizations share some features: an organized hierarchy, long-term goals, profit through illegal activities, neutralization of public officers, and the provision of illegal goods or services. The Pacific Coast Abortion Ring—or the Watts-Rankin outfit—had these features. Rankin, Watts, and Joseph Shinn, their accountant, were at the top of the organization. They hired abortion specialists at will and moved them around at their discretion to deprive them of any sense of comfort or control. In order to extend the business along the entire West Coast, Rankin and his cohorts were methodical in planning and managing their enterprise. They paid off members of law enforcement and the BME to avoid prosecution. (For these people the opportunity to earn supplemental income in exchange for turning a blind eye to illegal activity was simple enough.) Most important,

Rankin, Watts, and Shinn made illegal operations accessible to the public and relatively easy to acquire, and they profited as a result.

In 1954 Jerome E. Bates, assistant superintendent of Children's Institutions in New York City, described the criteria for distinguishing abortion rings from abortion mills. Bates defined an "abortion mill" as one in which "an abortionist or several abortionists [were] working steadily in a fairly permanent location and aborting a dozen or so women daily." He later stated that a ring changes "the location of its mill or mills fairly frequently while the true mill has a reasonability stable location month after month." At times PCAR embodied both of these characteristics. Bates further stated that abortion mills and rings are more accurately described "as deviant types of crescive institutions."[6] However, "mill," "racket," and "ring" carry with them seedy connotations that detract from the generally high quality of care that Rankin and his associates provided. The terms may accurately describe some of the behind-the-scenes bribery, corruption, and illegal activities, but they do not accurately convey the medical care that was offered. Since BME records refer to PCAR as a ring, racket, or mill interchangeably, I will do the same.

When Rankin proposed his idea for a coastwide syndicate to Watts, he fed into the ego of an aging doctor who, until recently, had been planning to retire. Prior to organizing the syndicate, Rankin had been successful in tax and real estate ventures in Los Angeles until the Great Depression, so perhaps he already knew how to bribe officials and avoid the law. It is not clear whether Rankin was genuinely concerned about providing women with access to safe abortions or if his interest was limited to what their misfortunes could bring to his pocketbook. Watts believed Rankin was a humanitarian with a noble goal, though the court would later say the men "knowingly, willfully, unlawfully, and feloniously conspired, combined, confederated and agreed" to provide abortions to women whose conditions did not warrant such procedures.[7] In any case, the two men came to an agreement: Watts would turn over 50 percent of his net profits to Rankin in exchange for Rankin's business, financial, and tax expertise. Watts moved south to Los Angeles, where he and Rankin established their headquarters (Dr. Harry Houston, a friend of Watts, took over Watts's Portland clinic.)

Between 1934 and 1936 Rankin brought several more abortion specialists into his syndicate and bought up the businesses of other doctors. In 1934 he hired Dr. Jesse C. Ross, who had previously operated a clinic on Hollywood Boulevard. Rankin moved Ross to San Diego and placed another abortionist in Ross's former office. He hired Dr. James Beggs, and a female steerer.[8] In 1935 he hired Dr. J. E. Folsom and moved Beggs into Folsom's Oakland office. In March of that same year he bought Folsom's private cottage outside of Oakland to use for women who needed additional treatment. Later in 1935 Rankin bought an office in San Francisco and the office of Dr. Lawrence Guibbini in San Jose. He hired two more abortionists in the middle of 1935: Dr. Eric Wilson and Dr. W. Norman Powers, both from Seattle. Rankin placed Powers in his new Long Beach office and Wilson in San Francisco. (Rankin was so busy in San Francisco that he had two offices in the Elkin-Gunst Building.) This synopsis is by no means exhaustive, and it does not include all of the nurses and steerers who solicited business for the racket. However, it illustrates a pattern, as already indicated: as Rankin hired a new abortionist, he shuffled those already working for him and immediately removed his new abortionist from the clinic in which he had been working. By 1936 the Watts-Rankin outfit spanned three states—California, Washington, and Oregon—and had offices in many of the major cities: San Diego, Long Beach, Hollywood, Los Angeles, San Francisco, Oakland, San Jose, Portland, and Seattle. By the time of the ring's demise Rankin had more than thirty people in his organization.

Rankin wanted his clinics, doctors, and nurses to be interchangeable; he wanted all to have the same equipment and procedures and to be headed by licensed physicians or abortion specialists, all of whom would still receive a crash course from Watts so that they would all perform abortions his way. But Rankin also wanted uniformity for practical reasons. If all of the offices had the same office layout, when an abortionist was moved, he could immediately get to work, already knowing the standard room layout, cabinet organization, and procedures. The uniformity made moving abortionists easy and also provided a measure of protection.[9] As noted previously, when Rankin hired a new abortionist, he made sure to separate him from his former office.[10] Part of this was psychological. Rankin wanted to remind his new specialist that he worked for him and that these were Rankin's offices. The immediate move was the new doctor's first reminder to not get too comfortable. Rankin also moved his abortionists around for extra security. If Rankin suspected that an abortionist's procedure had gone poorly, that doctor would immediately be transferred to another location. If there was an investigation about the procedure, the abortionist who had performed it would no longer be at the location under investigation, and there would be no one practicing in that office by the name under suspicion. In order to ensure such mobility Rankin owned his own planes and had landing fields in Oregon and in an isolated mountain region of Northern California.[11] Folsom's cottage, "the Ranch," could also function as a hideout if necessary.

Rankin wanted his entire enterprise to be unassuming so that every clinic appeared to be a legitimate doctor's office. When a woman arrived for treatment, she would tell the nurse or receptionist how far along she was in her pregnancy. The further along she was, the more the procedure would cost. The clinic would charge between $35 and $50 per procedure, though charges could vary.[12] The $35–$50 price applied only if a woman was in her first six to eight weeks of pregnancy. If she was about ten to twelve weeks along, Rankin told his clinics to charge between $50 and $75 or even $100. Beyond twelve weeks women were charged as much as possible—$200, $250, or even $300. Rankin urged his clinics to take as many cases as they could and to extract as much money from each client as possible—with the exception of clients that the staff didn't care to accept. For their own protection Rankin told his staff to refuse service to any woman who appeared to have attempted her own abortion and to any who appeared to be on the verge of an infection.[13] The goal was profit but not at the expense of security.

Once a woman agreed to a price, a nurse would gather information, including the date of the woman's last menstrual period and her steerer's name. Then the patient signed a blank consent form wherein she agreed to submit to treatment by a doctor whose name was left blank on the form. For example, if Watts had performed a procedure and it hadn't gone well, the nurse or Rankin would write in the name of another abortionist in the syndicate—say, De Gaston, or Ross. If an investigation was started, the woman would then be asked to identify De Gaston or Ross, but she would be unable to identify the man she had consented to treat her. The official form read: "I hereby declare that I am at this time freely and voluntarily applying to Dr. _____ for treatment. I believe my condition demands immediate medical and surgical attention and therefore give consent to such treatment as the doctor may determine in the premises; that I have read the above statements and am fully aware of the contents thereof, and state that I believe that same contains a true statement of my physical condition."[14] The same document also had spaces marked "condition" and "treatment"; these were also left blank for the same reason. Once the office staff collected fees and forms, the nurse would escort the patient to the operating room and prepare her for the procedure. The doctor would come in at the last minute. To most women a visit to a PCAR physician would resemble a visit to any other physician—with a few exceptions. She might have been blindfolded before or during the procedure, had multiple doctors in the room at the time of the procedure, or might never have seen the doctor's face at all, just a surgical mask, so that she could not ascertain who had *actually* performed the procedure.

When Dorothy Woods needed to go to the hospital after her abortion with Watts, Rankin deliberately sent two other physicians to her bedside so that she would be unable to make a positive identification.[15] When the police investigator asked if Woods recognized whether either of the men had performed her procedure, she said she did not and signed a document stating she did not recognize the man who had performed it.[16] Unable to identify her abortionist, Dorothy Woods hired an attorney to establish a case against Watts. After realizing she would not let it go, Rankin tried to silence her with $100. When she turned it down, he upped his offer to $110. Dorothy's mother, Margaret

Nichols, grew frustrated and argued that $110 did not even cover the medical bills and hospital stay that Dorothy required. Rankin didn't need to hear any more. He sent money via Western Union to the Seaside Hospital in Long Beach, where Dorothy was staying, and he also sent payment to the doctor at the hospital who had taken Dorothy into his care—over $300 in total. Dorothy and her mother did not pursue any further action against Rankin, and they remained quiet until they were later subpoenaed to testify against him.

Similarly when Mrs. Josephine Perat experienced complications from her late-term abortion by Watts, she sought outside help at a lying-in hospital. The nurse there phoned Watts to inform him his patient was at the hospital. Rather than acknowledge Perat, Watts feigned ignorance and claimed he had no patient by that name. He went even further, pretending to be offended that his name had come up and threatening the nurse that he would call the BME to investigate the facility. Of course the nurse was not aware that the local BME agent, William Byrne, was already on Rankin's payroll.

The California BME knew of the Watts-Rankin syndicate from nearly the beginning. In 1934 Dr. Charles Pinkham, the secretary-treasurer of the BME, responded to a letter from Verne L. Ferguson, the chief complaint deputy to the Los Angeles County district attorney, Buron Fitts. Ferguson had written Pinkham inquiring specifically about Watts, asking if Watts was licensed to practice medicine in California and what the BME knew about him. Pinkham responded: "Our files indicate that George E. Watts, M.D. was licensed to practice in this state in 1899 on presentation of his medical diploma, and that he thereafter located in Portland, Oregon, where, according to reports, his practice has been largely abortions."[17] Pinkham also explained that Watts had moved back to California recently and had established his office at the Signal Oil Building at 811 West Seventh Street in Los Angeles "for the asserted purpose of inaugurating a chain of abortion offices along the Pacific Coast."[18] In November 1934, responding to BME claims that he was operating a chain of abortion clinics, Rankin even met with Pinkham to explain that he merely handled taxes for nearby abortionists, that he had no interest in the business, and that

Watts was just an acquaintance.[19] Given the board's awareness, or suspicions, of Watts and Rankin, it is not surprising that the BME had the office on Seventh Street under regular surveillance. BME investigators claimed the office was busy from 8 a.m. through 6:30 p.m., particularly at noon, when women presumably would get the procedure during their lunch breaks.[20]

Someone in Portland had apparently tipped off the BME as to Watts's intentions. Shortly after Watts left Oregon, the anonymous tipster mailed a letter to the BME. At the front of the letter was Watts's professional announcement that he was leaving Portland, and on the back the tipster wrote: "Dr. Watts is located permently [sic] in Los Angeles Calif. Office in Signal Oil Bldg. It is his intentsions [sic] to open up a chain of abortion offices in Washington, Calif, and Oregon. Look him up."[21] The BME was also aware that the syndicate bought protection. According to Pinkham, agents for the syndicate would approach law enforcement officers they felt might "menace" the syndicate's business. These agents would offer the names of *other abortionists*—that is, abortionists who were unwilling to join the syndicate—so that the police would arrest the syndicate's competition. These agents even offered to pay several law enforcement officers off each month in order to protect their business.

To secure a steady stream of clients Rankin hired steerers. These could be young women or individuals like Marvin Raithel, Rankin's brother-in-law. For a salary of $300 per month Raithel, a regular druggist in San Jose, solicited business for the syndicate. He would contact medical supply houses, doctors, and pharmacists to encourage them to refer women to one of PCAR's clinics. The syndicate paid the referrers a commission of between 30–50 percent to encourage them to continue referring more clients. Raithel recruited mostly for the clinics in San Francisco and Oakland, though Rankin had other steerers up and down the Pacific Coast.[22] While Raithel worked with pharmacists, other steerers, particularly young females, might use their connections to spread the word, or they might frequent places of interest to other young women, their potential clientele.

By 1935 the PCAR racket was doing well, but Rankin and Shinn, the

3. Signal Oil Building, 1920. Security Pacific National Bank Collection. Los Angeles Public Library.

primary financial decision makers, wanted to find a way to maximize profits. They had already established a system wherein office nurses would make daily deposits into an account held in Rankin's name. Shinn also requested copies of all deposit slips. By the fall the two decided to incorporate a "credit arm" into their racket—the Medical Acceptance Corporation (MAC). Although MAC was a financial arm of PCAR, it represented itself as a separate entity—a supposed third-party company that financed medical procedures. (Coincidentally there were soon MAC offices near almost every PCAR clinic.) Specifically MAC allowed PCAR to make more money from women who did not have the money to pay for their abortions up front. If a woman wanted an abortion but did not have the money, the PCAR office nurse would send her to MAC. The woman would show the MAC office a note indicating the agreed price for the procedure. For example, if the agreed price was $50, the MAC manager would finance the woman for $75. The manager would convince the woman that the additional $25 was for MAC to finance the bill. Once the woman agreed to the new price, MAC would take collateral—often jewelry or fur coats—call the PCAR office, and send the woman back for the procedure.

Rankin's abortionists used a standard dilation and curettement (D&C) if the woman was in her first twelve weeks of pregnancy.[23] The physician would administer a local anesthetic and use a speculum to open, or dilate, the woman's cervix. If the fetus was too large, the doctor would use a set of forceps or an "obstetrician's guillotine hook" to dismember the fetus and remove it.[24] After removing the fetus, the doctor would use a curette—a spoonlike medical instrument—to scrape her uterus and remove any large fragments of material. As a final measure the doctor would perform a suction of the uterus with a metal catheter attached to a hose: Watts's vacuum aspiration method.

If a woman was beyond the twelfth week of pregnancy, she was a "packed case."[25] For packed cases the doctor would dilate the cervix and fill the patient's uterus with gauze. This would induce premature labor. After the woman had been packed in the clinic, she would be transported to another location where she would miscarry. Paul De Gaston, who would become Rankin's right hand, claimed he never witnessed an abortion where the woman was beyond five months pregnant; however, one of the nurses suggested that PCAR took cases as late as seven and eight months and ran the dismembered fetuses through a sewer.[26] Most women who received standard D&Cs were able to leave the same day as their procedures. Others—particularly packed cases, women who experienced complications, or women who paid for additional time—lay in a room until they were well enough to leave.

Rankin's previous work as a "tax factor" had taught him much about bribery, allies, and protection. When it came to PCAR, he was able to profit from the tenuous position of his doctors. They needed a steady source of work during the Depression, and abortions remained profitable, particularly since the economic conditions meant few women could afford to bear more children—whether out of fear of losing their jobs, fear of being unable to provide for an additional child, or simply because they did not want a child. Through his steerers Rankin secured a steady clientele for his doctors and provided them with a cut of the profits. Rankin's main job was to "neutralize" the law, and he found a well-placed ally early on. William Byrne was a special agent in Los Angeles for the California BME. Byrne first appeared in the BME directory in January 1928, and his primary job was to investigate individuals accused of violating the state's Medical Practice Act—specifically irregular practitioners of medicine and abortionists. It's clear no one suspected Byrne of colluding with Rankin. In fact in a letter to Pinkham from BME special agent Albert Carter, Carter asks for more funds for Byrne to carry out his investigations. Carter was frustrated at the BME's inability to target "some of the more prominent abortionists" and specifically mentioned "a well-known abortionist in the Signal Oil Building."[27] Byrne had been in the BME's employ for approximately six or seven years when Rankin first approached him. Perhaps he was bored, perhaps he wanted a bigger salary, or maybe Rankin just made him an offer he couldn't refuse.

Rankin's first job for Byrne was to get rid of evidence in the murder case against Paul De Gaston.[28] In 1934 De Gaston, a Hollywood concert violinist, was charged with the murder of Irene Eilert, a "dazzling blond 'butterfly' divorcee of the film colony."[29] The police charged De Gaston when they found Eilert's body in his house after "a crudely performed abortion."[30] De Gaston had rare qualities, and perhaps that's why Rankin was drawn to him. He was born and studied in China before studying in England and Germany. Eventually he went to medical school in France. De Gaston never actually practiced professional medicine though. Shortly after receiving his Doctor of Medicine from the Sorbonne in 1916, he volunteered for the French Army during the Great War and subsequently moved to the United States. De Gaston moved throughout the states, failing at numerous sales ventures. When he finally arrived in Hollywood in 1925, he had hopes of becoming a film star. Some directors were initially intrigued with De Gaston's exotic, foreign, jet-setter lifestyle and history, but De Gaston had no talent—at least not enough to get him beyond some minor roles here and there. In order to make ends meet De Gaston supported himself by performing the occasional abortion. Rankin became aware of De Gaston through his network in Los Angeles. Just days after the two discussed going into business together, De Gaston's run-in with Eilert happened.

Ilene Eilert worked in a beauty parlor and had been estranged from her husband, George, for a short period.[31] Eilert's friend Louise Eldridge introduced her to De Gaston. Eldridge accompanied Eilert to De Gaston's house and left. According to reports, De Gaston later called Eldridge to tell her that Eilert was unwell but appeared to be improving. Prosecutors claimed that De Gaston had administered an anesthetic and performed an illegal procedure on Eilert. The court even hired chemists to testify that rouge stains on a face mask in De Gaston's house were a chemical match to Eilert's rouge. De Gaston denied performing an abortion on Eilert. Instead he claimed she was a casual acquaintance. He claimed that she asked for a drink of water and died suddenly before he could administer medical aid.[32] He even suggested that she had probably ingested drugs to induce an abortion before her visit.

While Byrne was working for the BME to build a case against De Gaston, he was simultaneously destroying evidence for the same case for Rankin. Rankin visited De Gaston while he was in jail. The calculating man he was, Rankin asked De Gaston whether he was having financial troubles; if he loaned him money, De Gaston would be in his debt, at his beck and call. Rankin assured De Gaston that if he gave him the names of the druggists and physicians who had referred their clients, he would take care of the patients and send part of the profits to help him out.[33] The court had charged De Gaston with murder, abortion, and practicing medicine without a license. De Gaston spent approximately five months in jail, and when he was released in January 1935, Rankin asked him to visit him at his office in the Signal Oil Building. Because of Byrne's intervention at Rankin's bidding, De Gaston was acquitted of the abortion and murder charges. De Gaston wanted to fight the third charge—practicing medicine without a license—but Rankin said it would be in bad taste. Either way Rankin now felt that he had bought De Gaston's loyalty and services rather cheaply. Upon his release De Gaston met with Rankin, who introduced him to Watts. Watts asked De Gaston about his medical training and his familiarity with gynecological procedures. Rankin give De Gaston $50 and asked him to come on board, bragging about Watt's aspirator, a contraption he haughtily referred to as "the sucker." Perhaps De Gaston had nowhere else to go, perhaps he felt he owed Rankin, or perhaps PCAR seemed like a lucrative opportunity. De Gaston joined PCAR, but at the beginning he was too shy to solicit clients. In his first month of employ he failed to perform a single abortion. Rankin grew impatient. He told De Gaston to find a woman who needed an abortion—regardless of whether or not she could pay—so he could perform an abortion under Watts's guidance. With his new orders De Gaston "passed word along Hollywood Boulevard and got [a client]."[34] He brought the woman to the Signal Oil Building and finally performed his first abortion as a member of the syndicate; Watts described it as "very clean."[35]

De Gaston's ability to perform flawless abortions, coupled with his formal medical training and experience, paved the way for him to become Rankin's protégé and right-hand man. Rankin knew he had De Gaston on a leash. Before De Gaston would be able to earn a salary from PCAR, Rankin told him that he would first have to pay back the money loaned to him while he had been in jail. Then Rankin promised he would pay him $300 for the first month, $500 per month for the next two months, and $750 per month thereafter. De Gaston agreed to this arrangement.

Believing De Gaston's name was "too hot," Rankin secured a fake license for him to practice medicine from a defunct medical school and put him to work in the Signal Oil Building. With the assistance of another BME agent on PCAR's payroll, De Gaston began to operate under the name of Dr. J. F. Harsh, a licensed Oregon physician. In his first two weeks of work De Gaston claimed to have performed approximately forty abortions.[36] Eventually Rankin would transfer De Gaston to San Francisco. Then De Gaston became Rankin's errand boy. Since De Gaston did so well, Rankin would frequently send him out to teach Watts's technique to the syndicate's new abortionists; Rankin may have also used De Gaston for this task since the elderly Watts could not keep up. Because of De Gaston's debt to him, Rankin likely felt that he owned him. He felt the same way about Byrne.

When Byrne was not fixing Rankin's legal troubles, he was offering another service to the syndicate. Since part of his job at the BME was to find abortionists and build cases against them, Byrne knew where he could find all of the syndicate's competition. On one hand, in visiting these abortionists, Byrne could claim that Rankin was interested in purchasing their business and that it would be in their interest to fall in line. If they refused, Byrne could strong-arm them and make their lives difficult as an officer of the BME. For many of these small abortionists joining the syndicate may have seemed like a worthwhile opportunity and a source of stability and security. Byrne offered salaries of up to $1,000 per month and police protection, neither of which most abortionists were likely to have. The abortionists who joined the syndicate became members of something bigger than themselves, and they were protected from the economic undulations of the Great Depression.

However, some abortionists refused. When they did, they faced harassment. On one occasion Rankin tried to coerce a Long Beach abortionist to join his empire. When the abortionist refused, Rankin staged a fake arrest of the office nurse—essentially kidnapping her until the abortionist relented. In another incident, when Rankin and Byrne approached Dr. Blanche Ramer of San Diego, she refused. BME agent Byrne apparently "balled on her and 'bawled her out' for doing abortions."[37] After yelling at her, though, PCAR agent Byrne gave her Dr. Watts's card and told her she would be better off referring her clients to him. The following day Rankin followed up with Ramer and explained that if she referred her patients to Watts, they would extort all the money from her clients that they could and would send her half the profits. It appears Ramer never gave in and that Rankin did not pursue the matter further. By this time Laura Miner was already working well for Rankin in San Diego, and Rankin was more preoccupied with expanding his clinics in the north. Perhaps Rankin may have felt Ramer was too strong-willed and had second thoughts about working with someone he deemed too difficult.

Rankin consistently recruited for his empire. He cared less about the skill of the abortionists he hired since he believed Watts or De Gaston could retrain them; he cared more about new connections or locations to gain new patrons. For example, in 1935 Rankin bought out the Heddens' clinic in San Francisco at 2240 Van Ness Avenue. In this context "clinic" was really an aggrandizement. In contrast to the medical offices Rankin purchased and transformed with elegant furnishings and sterile conditions, Harley and Rose Marie Heddens performed abortions in their apartment. Harley Heddens was an engineer with no medical training, and his abortions were notoriously crude. Instead of using a surgical table, Heddens performed his operations on a board laid across his bathroom tub. Of course the Hickok and Mottard cases previously discussed demonstrate that a poor reputation or track record did not put an abortionist out of business, so it didn't matter that the Heddens were not up to Rankin's standards. When Rankin purchased their business, the Heddens were on trial for murder in the abortion-related death of sixteen-year-old Ruth Attaway. Rankin took advantage of their legal troubles and purchased their location and phone number (so that existing networks and referrers could continue to direct patients without interruption) at a rock bottom price.[38]

Rankin had De Gaston move into the Van Ness location while he searched for new practices to purchase further north. By the middle of 1935 Rankin had bought the practice of a Dr. Hart in the Joshua

4. Jewel Inez Joseph (mother of Ruth Attaway, who died after an abortion) in court, Los Angeles, 1935. *Los Angeles Times* Photographic Archive. Department of Special Collections, Charles E. Young Research Library, UCLA.

Green Building in Seattle. This office, however, did poorly. While other PCAR clinics were charging $50 and up for an abortion, this office struggled to get between $20 and $40. Dissatisfied with how his only Seattle office was performing, Rankin bought the office of a Dr. Powers in the Securities Building. Shortly thereafter Rankin moved De Gaston to Seattle under the new alias of Dr. F. T. Read, a graduate of the now defunct Bennett University in Chicago. Once a university was closed, it was difficult to ascertain whether someone had actually graduated from it. As a result, fraudulent diplomas associated with closed medical schools were often associated not only with PCAR associates, but also with other quacks outside of the abortion industry. De Gaston trained Drs. Powers and Wilson in Seattle, and Rankin informed him that he would stay in the city for the immediate future.

From the very beginning Rankin suspected that Wilson would give him trouble. He accused Wilson of misreporting numbers, hiding receipts, and pocketing money for himself. Perhaps more significant, Rankin suspected that Wilson was pulling De Gaston away from him.[39] Rankin's concerns were appropriate. With the autonomy Wilson and De Gaston had in Seattle—far from Los Angeles—they thrived. Wilson began to think they didn't need Rankin at all and often wondered why they were sending half of their profits to him. Wilson began to complain regularly and often mused that they were better off without Rankin. Wilson told Rankin they didn't need him and that if Rankin wanted them to stick around, he needed to fix his management style, promptly settle MAC accounts, and streamline the paperwork process. Rankin tried to propitiate Wilson. He even allowed Wilson to purchase a share of the business in the office. But it was not enough. Wilson continued to push until Rankin finally relented. On November 20, 1935, Rankin sold Wilson all of his interest in the office in the Securities Building, and—perhaps worst of all—he ceded De Gaston's services to Wilson as part of that sale.

Rankin regretted the sale immediately. He despised Wilson's independence and thought of all the money they were making without him. He wanted De Gaston back. For the next month Rankin wrote De Gaston tirelessly. He told De Gaston he would have him back and that Wilson's actions were going to get them in trouble. Even though Rankin had tried to prevent his abortionists from claiming ownership of their clinics, he had failed to do so with Wilson. Moreover, Wilson had taken De Gaston—the man in whom Rankin had invested—with him.

By April 1936 Rankin used his connections to act on his threats against Wilson and De Gaston and had them both arrested. De Gaston and Wilson's attorney made the arrest a spectacle and claimed that his clients had been "framed" for defying Rankin's "coastwide abortion syndicate."[40] This claim garnered wide publicity. It was the first time many in law enforcement had heard about the expansive syndicate. Rankin's efforts to exact revenge ultimately backfired: they piqued the interests of Captain Charles Dullea and Inspectors George Engler and Harry Husted of the San Francisco Police Department (SFPD) and brought about the ring's demise.

At the end of a routine investigation into another abortion-related death in San Francisco, the SFPD investigators asked BME secretary-treasurer Pinkham if the "sensational stories about a hundred-million-dollar abortion syndicate on the Pacific Coast" were true.[41] Pinkham claimed they were but that there was little his office could do about the syndicate because of the way that its abortionists moved around and how well it paid off some doctors and law enforcement officers. This was a sort of dare that compelled the San Francisco investigators to look into PCAR. When Dullea, Engler, and Husted told Pinkham they were going to investigate the matter and arrest the syndicate members, Pinkham seemed to shrug it off, told them where the syndicate's headquarters were, and wished them luck.[42]

With Pinkham's blessing Captain Dullea urged Engler and Husted to exclusively focus on the syndicate. On June 2, 1936, they started their investigation at the MAC office in the Elkan-Gunst Building in San Francisco. When the investigators asked Mr. J. Clinton Perry, the local MAC manager, about the nature of his company's business, Perry responded that it provided loans for patients who could not afford medical treatment. Engler and Husted asked which physicians MAC worked with, but Perry refused to answer. When asked if it did business with a Dr. Ross—one of Rankin's men in an office upstairs in the building—Perry responded that it did on occasion. The investigators left MAC, went to Ross's office, and asked for him. Though Ross was not in the office, the investigators got more than they had bargained for when they found Marvin Raithel—Rankin's brother-in-law—and escorted him to the Hall of Justice.

The investigators interrogated Raithel, and he cracked. He explained the ring's beginnings, its organization, its structure, and its profits. He spoke to the investigators for hours, and he gave district attorneys in San Francisco and Los Angeles sufficient information to acquire search warrants. The following day Assistant District Attorney John McMahon; Captain Dullea; Inspectors Harry Majors, Frank Lucey, Engler, and Husted; and Assistant District Attorney Frank Coakley of Alameda County conducted a raid. They began at the Van Ness location (the former Heddens clinic) and the neighboring apartment where Rankin was living at the time. When investigators descended upon Rankin's apartment, no one was home; however, they found the apartment equipped for abortions: cots, surgical tables, and other medical equipment. The investigators found case cards with patient names and commission slips. As the police ransacked the apartment, Violet Rankin, Reginald's wife, returned home and was immediately taken into custody.

The investigators went back to the Elkan-Gunst Building to further investigate Dr. Ross's clinic and MAC. Inside the clinic they found lavishly furnished offices with rich walnut desks and elegant paintings. They arrested J. C. Perry and nurse Leola Habel. The investigators gathered the plethora of abortion tools and the massive collection of medical records. When they returned to MAC, they broke open a safe and found the syndicate's books listing profits and losses.[43] The last entry in those books—for the month of February—indicated that the Signal Oil office alone had generated a net profit of $5,000; the Long Beach office, $1,000; and Hollywood, $1,800.[44] From the Elkan-Gunst Building the investigators moved quickly to Beggs's office in Oakland, where they found similar evidence.

As the investigators poured over the patient cards they had recovered from the Elkan-Gunst and Van Ness locations, they realized that most were dead ends. The patients had provided the clinic with fake names or phone numbers that effectively rendered most of the women invisible. However, when under arrest, Perry had said that he shipped his records to the Los Angeles location every month, so it became clear that a raid of the Los Angeles office was necessary. Engler flew down to Los Angeles and contacted Buron Fitts, the district attorney. Despite their attempts to move quickly and quietly, when they raided the Los Angeles office, it was clear that it had already been tipped off. Nevertheless, from the Signal Oil Building, the Hollywood office, and the Long Beach office, the investigators were able to gather two truckloads of evidence, items that had been collected as collateral for payment; the most surprising of these were furs and jewels, including wedding and engagement rings.[45]

In the southern California raids the investigators found more patient cards and set out to question the women whose names appeared on them. Detectives posed as switchboard operators and took the names and addresses of the women who continued to call seeking appointments. After the offices had been raided, two Los Angeles Police Department (LAPD) detectives remained in the Signal Oil Building posing as doctors.[46] Though the San Jose office had been cleaned out before the detectives got there, the joint task force believed it had enough evidence to mount a case against PCAR.

News of the syndicate spread throughout the region and then the country. Wilson began distributing pamphlets urging physicians to be mindful of their referrals.[47] The pamphlet described the history of the syndicate and stressed the syndicate's dealings with the underworld. In addition, another abortion death in Washington generated attention toward the syndicate: a beautiful young woman's body was discovered in a river; it had bled out from a botched abortion. Though the woman had died at the hands of a traveling chiropractor and not one of the syndicate's own, the public created an equivalency. Such news gave prosecutors additional incentive to charge the syndicate members to the fullest extent of the law.[48] Reportedly Rankin remained confident even up until the morning of the trial, treating the indictment as a "joke" and even telling Laura Miner that the trial would be a good test to see whom the syndicate could trust so that "in the future ... [it could] build on a solid foundation."[49]

Court reporters and newspaper journalists crowded the courtroom to get the latest details. Witnesses suggested that fetuses had been discarded in sewer lines or burned at the cottage; patients described their late-term abortions; nurses like Bernice Tieman testified that premature babies had been delivered with bruises and indented skulls or had been dismembered after dying; and doctors and nurses from rival abortion clinics described how Rankin had threatened them.

One of the witnesses, Josephine Perat, had a late-term abortion for reasons unspecified. She told Watts that she was approximately five months pregnant—probably so that she would have to pay less for her procedure. But she was a packed case. She fell ill and went to a nearby lying-in hospital, where she went into premature labor and delivered a 3 pound, 8 ounce boy who died within twenty-four hours. According to the nurse from the lying-in hospital, Perat was probably seven to seven-and-a-half months pregnant at the time. The nurse described an indentation on the left side of the infant's skull and dark blue and reddish-blue discolorations as well. The nurse claimed she had put the baby in an incubator, but it did not live.

Several stories also ran in various newspapers about Rankin threatening witnesses. Most of these allegations surrounded Bernice Tieman, a twenty-five-year-old nurse who worked for the syndicate. According to the *Reading Eagle*, Tieman was in protective custody during the trial because Rankin threatened to "get rid of her." Fearing reprisal, she temporarily fled but later "regained [her] courage and decided to testify" that she had witnessed the disposal of two babies delivered through abortion. The testimony was damning, it heightened the drama in the courtroom, and it portrayed the syndicate as villainous and criminal.[50] Unable to parade a series of abortion fatality stories, prosecutors still attempted to show how malevolent these abortionists were by suggesting how devastated the women were, by describing the abortion procedures with as much detail as possible, or by discussing fetal viability with the women who had terminated their pregnancies. Recognizing how incriminating Tieman's testimony was, Rankin's attorneys attempted to paint Tieman as a psychopathic, hysterical woman by bringing in documents to show that she had been a patient at Patton Asylum in 1932. Nevertheless, the judge ruled that her testimony was admissible.

The case was sensational for all the obvious reasons—abortion, sex, and the criminal underworld. However, the case was also significant. In contrast to almost all previous abortion cases, none of the women died. This case would not be decided because of a dying declaration. Though other young women were dying from crudely performed abortions, they were not receiving their abortions from *this* syndicate. The syndicate's abortions were the antithesis of the botched procedures that had become synonymous with criminal abortions. Ironically the ability of the detectives to bring in witnesses and patients was possible only because PCAR's abortions were comparatively safe. However, the attorneys made little effort to ask these women why they had attempted to procure abortions. They asked only if they had some illness or defect that would render them incapable of bearing children; most women replied "no." They said that they had previously had difficult pregnancies or they were tired. The women were not asked if they were struggling financially, if they had stable relationships with their partners, or if they wanted to be parents at all. Though the attorneys hardly indulged these women with the opportunity to explain themselves, some women were able to state their own opinions, and several indicated that they appreciated what Rankin and his doctors had done for them.

The trial lasted from October 1 to October 23, 1936. Then the case went to the jury for deliberation. After twenty-four hours a jury of six men and six women found eleven of the PCAR defendants guilty. The jury found Rankin, Watts, Ross, Shinn, Byrne, Grace Moore, Beggs, and Lillian Wilson guilty of conspiracy and four counts each of performing an illegal abortion. Drs. Valentine St. John and John Creeth were found guilty of conspiracy and one count of abortion, and Violet Pellegrini was found guilty of conspiracy and two counts of abortion. Rankin, Byrne, Beggs, Ross, and Watts were sentenced to ten to twenty-five years each in San Quentin. St. John was sentenced to four to ten years in San Quentin. The others were allowed to file for probation. Powers, who had pled guilty, begged for probation but was sentenced to six months in county jail and three years of probation. Some of the other defendants were tried in San Francisco: Mary Wilson, Leola Habel, Dr. Harry Houston, Ruth Hanson, Viola Warner, Bessie McCarthy, and Beatrice Bole. Of these only Wilson and Habel were allowed to plead guilty to a misdemeanor, for which they were just placed on probation. The remainder fled, and eventually their charges were dropped for lack of evidence. After years of successfully providing women safe abortions, PCAR was finally broken.

It is important to note that this was one of the first times that a bevy of women had spoken about their abortions outside of private or intimate spheres. The legislative process of criminalizing and penalizing abortion—in the context of a comparatively safe abortion mill with specialization—forced women to speak openly instead of having journalists speculate about them post-mortem. From 1936 through the early 1950s decreasing mortality rates and increasing surveillance pulled these women from their small, intimate networks and thrust them into the courtroom and national press. Subpoenaed to appear in court, these women were unable to hide their names or faces. They acknowledged their complicity, their abortion stories, and their justifications for having the procedure. These women were claiming ownership over their bodies and over their decisions. Some women were defiant on the stand. Others were deliberately vague and terse. Nevertheless, for a brief moment women had the opportunity to explain why they had sought and obtained abortions.

Writing about PCAR nearly a year later, Louis Blanchard Kaley, a *Forum and Century* contributor, attempted to communicate his interpretation of the syndicate and women's desires to obtain abortions illegally.[51] Kaley asked his readers to consider whether it was in the public's interest to widen the scope of legal abortions. Tempering his comments and aware of possible backlash, Kaley claimed that while increased legal access to abortion might give license to greater degrees of sexual freedom, "the fact must be faced that it is . . . not simply the licentious who reap the fruits of unwanted pregnancy today."[52] While Kaley explained that it was easy for society to understand the desire of a young, unmarried women who, driven by shame or fear, sought to escape degradation through an abortion, for every unmarried girl who sought an abortion there were eight to ten married women also in the same waiting room. Citing statistics from the U.S. Department of Labor, Kaley stated that in a two-year study of 7,500 maternal deaths, 89 percent of the women who died from abortions had been married. These women, Kaley argued, wanted to limit family size because they wanted to preserve the livelihoods of their existing children. This was a common theme. The undercover agents posing as a married couple for the Los Angeles district attorney encountered one woman who "confided that she was the wife of a school-teacher and that she had several living children. 'We simply can't afford another one,' she said despairingly. 'This seems to be the only way out.'"[53] Another woman had three abortions with the syndicate. When she went back for her third and brought only $35, the nurse told her to return only when she had $50. The patient exclaimed that was all she had; her husband's salary was meager, they already had two young boys, and the caesarean operation from her second child had resulted in complications.[54] Many women who had abortions were making difficult decisions, often to protect their families. Kaley added, "[If they] choose to destroy an unformed protoplasm jeopardizing the welfare of the already living... how can we then condemn them?"[55]

Kaley went beyond a discussion of PCAR. He also scolded druggists for the open trade in and sale of toxic and ineffective abortifacients. These unregulated potions, he argued, posed more of a risk than surgical abortion because if a reliable abortion drug existed, "it would be used for therapeutic abortions."[56] If these drugs failed, women then had to resort to other methods to terminate their pregnancies—like violent falls or other physical injuries to bring about miscarriages. These actions contributed to the perception of abortion as a violent, dangerous procedure when in reality it was simple. Yet its simplicity posed another potential danger.

Non-specialists, like Heddens, felt that with the right amount of rudimentary training, they could perform the procedure with ease. The procedure was relatively straightforward; the abortionists just opened the cervix and emptied the uterus. This presumed simplicity, coupled with the possibility of lucrative pecuniary gain was attractive "not only [to] the unscrupulous skilled, but to the incompetent failure, the midwife, and even the outright untrained quack eager for an easy dollar."[57] The real crime was that adequate services were out of reach for most women who wanted abortions. Criminalization was not a deterrent. It only made "desperate women easier prey for individuals... without conscience or principle or ability."[58] While Kaley found abortion palpably wrong, he believed the liberalization of existing laws was the lesser of two evils. If women were able to get safe abortions more easily, there would be a reduction in the net number of lives lost.

While some physicians leaned toward liberalization, others held steadfastly to older, more conservative beliefs. In the 1930s one doctor bemoaned society's plummeting morals and worried that changes in social mores would eventually infiltrate the medical field. He wrote, "The physician is not the dispenser of life and death. He is not the arbiter of the universe. Individual cases may evoke his pity and wring his heart, but he should feel no call to ... cure all the ills of society.... 'Have we the right to interfere with a normal pregnancy?' My answer is 'No.'"[59]

Like the women of the eighteenth and nineteenth centuries, most women who wanted abortions in the twentieth century did not feel that the procedure was wrong. Dr. Violet Russell argued that if the state really wanted to do away with the "sinister atmosphere surrounding the present-day illicit abortion—the knitting needle, the crochet hook, the syringe, the shady doctor, and the dirty old woman; in the background, possible blackmail, injury, death," it needed to provide women with alternatives. Specifically Russell believed that if the state wanted to compel women to bear children, it needed to offer them family allowances or more information on contraception.[60] Russell especially felt that women should have the option to abort if they had about five children. She believed that legal abortion should be an alternative but that there should be a widespread knowledge of contraception first. Russell also suggested that in instances where the mother's physical and/or mental states were at risk, she should be allowed to abort and that a physician should perform a sterilization for the most serious cases.

Adding to Russell's comments, Dr. Joan Malleson argued that an increase in restrictive abortion measures would result in greater mortality.[61] She seemed to recognize that women would continue to procure abortions, regardless of how the medical profession regarded them:

> I have come to believe that there may be certain situations in a woman's life in which nothing will deter her from seeking abortion; to increase restrictive measures is absolutely futile, for she is prepared literally to face death rather than carry on with the pregnancy.... Whether we pity the desperate woman or whether we dislike her ... we as medicals have ... [taken] a very strange attitude towards her. In every other aspect of our work, it is our privilege to save life and maintain health and happiness. Yet, when a woman in deepest distress asks our help, we shelter behind the archaic habits of society; when she is ill and dying, we set about repairs and collecting statistics.... Many people dislike the thought of destroying the early fetus, but we have certainly to realize that most women do not value the early fetus as if it were a child.[62]

Malleson defended abortion specialists because increased abortion restrictions, she believed, would only lead to disaster. Russell and Malleson also recognized the complexities of most women's lives and rejected attempts to mischaracterize women who had had abortions. They argued that women who sought abortions were neither bad women nor bad mothers. On the contrary, many women who wanted abortions cared very much for their existing children and wanted to make sure their opportunities or livelihoods weren't jeopardized. Frustrated with their colleagues and with the existing legislation, Russell and Malleson openly called for the liberalization of existing abortion laws in 1938—decades before the liberalization movement would have any real momentum.

Such arguments for the liberalization of abortion laws would come right before a period of increased repression and criminalization. While safer abortions had made convictions more difficult, the *Rankin* case changed that. Because prosecutors were able to convict many of the defendants without a fatality, law enforcement officials were emboldened. Since prosecutors had convicted the defendants without having to rely on the bodies of victims, they had effectively decreased the burden of proof that prosecutors had previously needed in order to bring about successful abortion convictions. The voices of the women who had testified about their own abortions and pleas for liberalization from Kaley, Russell, and Malleson had either come too late or fell on deaf ears.

The next chapter follows Rankin and Laura Miner after the *Rankin* trial as they separately went back to performing abortions in Oakland and Reno, Nevada (Rankin) and San Diego (Miner). As mentioned, the *Rankin* case was unique in that many of the syndicate members were found guilty even though there were no murder charges attached to the abortion charges. This was a significant departure from the cases involving Galen Hickok, Henry Lee Mottard, Delphine Walsh, Vera Nelson, and Margaret Scott. Together Miner and Rankin's abortion endeavors after PCAR illustrate a decreased tolerance for illegal abortions and increased surveillance, restrictions, and punishments. As providers of illegal abortions felt the push of law enforcement against them in the 1940s, they would modify their practices again in order to maintain a steady stream of clients. In addition, as more women realized the possibility of having to take the stand, they searched for other ways to avoid the hassle of police interference.

After PCAR   6

Surveillance, Repression, and Restriction

> Each experience leaves its imprint, some imprints are more like scars. But I can still hold my head up and I respect myself because my conscience is clear. I have helped humanity—someday it will be legal for a doctor to help a woman who will then have a right to decide for herself how many children she shall have, and when.
>
> —Laura Miner, 1950

The results of the *Rankin* ruling were tangible, both for providers of illegal abortions in Southern California and for women seeking abortions. Because prosecutors in Los Angeles were able to try the PCAR defendants without any evidence of a fatality, law enforcement's handling of abortion took a startlingly repressive turn. In this chapter we will revisit Reginald Rankin and Laura Miner, whose arrests in the 1940s illustrate this new suppression. At the same time the ability of prosecutors to coerce women into testifying against their abortionists became a negative consequence of decreased mortality. After the *Rankin* case crackdowns on abortion providers became much more productive, and women and abortionists were left to resurvey their options. This chapter sets the stage to explain why—for white women in California and for innovative providers of illegal abortions—Tijuana abortions became a reasonable choice in the 1950s and 1960s.

Just a few months after the PCAR crackdown, police officers in San Francisco raided Inez Burns's abortion clinic.[1] This initial raid on the clinic in 1936 did not result in formal charges. Burns's employees refused to speak, and—perhaps due to her trap doors and hidden compartments—the police found no evidence. In 1938 her clinic was the focus of yet another raid—this time after one of her patients confessed. When police entered the building, they found ten patients recovering, but the women all denied having received abortions. Unable to get any of the women to testify, the district attorney was able to muster together a tax evasion charge that Burns promptly settled for $10,000.

In 1943, running on a campaign to clean up the city, Pat Brown became the new San Francisco district attorney. With her name known in San Francisco and after collective hours of surveillance on her clinic, Burns's fate was sealed when a tip in 1945 gave police just cause to raid her clinic yet again. Burns finally went to trial for abortion.[2] Burns's business had been wildly successful. An abortionist in the blurry period immediately following the *Rankin* trial, her arrest and conviction were far from certain. In fact, had she stopped practicing abortion following her 1939 tax evasion charge, she probably would have avoided any repercussions during this period of increased restriction, surveillance, and repression. Instead she continued to provide a service to women regardless, and perhaps unaware, of the shifting climate. This was her downfall, and she would not be alone.

In an undercover investigation for the *San Diego Sun* a woman reporter visited local abortionists and described what it was like trying to get the procedure in San Diego. The reporter gathered names and addresses of presumed abortionists from police, court, and medical association records and visited several of them posing as a prospective patient. According to her report, prices for abortions ranged from $50 to $100. When a woman had a letter from a physician, she faced few obstacles. Providing the name of a friend who had had an abortion by the same practitioner usually worked just as well. However, the reporter found that having no references or credentials often resulted in skepticism, hostile interrogation, or even flat-out refusal. She found that it was easier for a married woman to get an appointment than it was for a single woman. She also found that some offices were not clean or hygienic. Since abortionists worked outside of legitimate medicine and since most of the procedures were illegal, few providers thought it necessary to provide clean, safe, or sanitary conditions, while most patients probably felt they were not in a position to demand them. In some cases luxury abortionists catered to the upper classes. In the late 1930s, for example, the BME received word of an abortion ring for the elite of San Diego operating out of the top floor of the El Cortez Hotel, the tallest and most glamorous hotel in San Diego.³ Nevertheless, the fact that these abortions took place outside of hospitals perpetuated their illegitimacy. As mentioned previously, the PCAR case had marked a shift. A woman's death was no longer necessary to bring about an arrest or conviction. After PCAR, providers of illegal abortions grew leery of providing services to women who came without appropriate referrals. Similarly physicians who wanted to provide abortions for their patients increasingly relied upon justifications for formal therapeutic abortions.

Though most states' abortion laws specified that abortions were allowable if they were to preserve the life or health of the mother, medical science had progressed to a point that there were few diseases or illnesses that would prevent a woman from carrying a pregnancy to term.⁴ With fewer medical conditions that would likely result in the death of the mother, more physicians relied on exceptions based in threats to a woman's health or wellbeing. Thus therapeutic abortions became increasingly amorphous. When Dr. Aleck William Bourne, a respected obstetrician in England, was arrested after performing an abortion on a "feeble-minded" fourteen-year-old rape victim, American physicians followed the case intently to see how their British counterparts handled this murky situation.⁵

According to news and court reports, a twenty-two-year-old guardsman of the Royal Horse Guard had raped a fourteen-year-old girl. She became pregnant and sought help to get an abortion, ultimately leading her to cross paths with Bourne. Bourne, who had sought the opportunity for a test case, performed the abortion for free. While the guardsman was sentenced to four years in prison for the rape of the young girl, Bourne faced life in prison for performing the abortion.⁶ At the time English law prohibited all abortions, with no exceptions to save a woman's life. Nevertheless, Bourne argued that by performing the abortion, he had done his job as a physician.⁷ He agreed that the abortion was not necessary to save the girl's life per se, but he believed the abortion "was justified for the sake of her mental condition and future."[8] Bourne would later say that he liked this case as a legal test since it was an opportunity to discuss therapeutic abortions when there was "no real danger to *life* . . . but one . . . might very strongly suspect great danger to health."[9]

Rex v. Bourne sparked debate throughout the international medical community. The case was complicated. Few physicians wanted to openly support motherhood for a fourteen-year-old—particularly since the pregnancy was the result of rape. However, the bulk of the debate centered on whether the prospect of a fourteen-year-old mother's becoming a "mental wreck" justified a therapeutic abortion. Within the medical community this case forced a discussion of mental health as a justification for therapeutic abortion—a justification that most physicians were wary about accepting—and strengthened the validity of therapeutic exceptions when a woman's health, broadly defined, was endangered. When the court found Bourne not guilty, the first liberalization of English abortion law made American physicians reevaluate the tenets of therapeutic abortions as they applied to health and not just to life.[10]

Through the 1930s it was generally accepted that physicians would come to their own conclusions and perform the procedures they believed were necessary for their patients since they often practiced independently. Therapeutic abortions were valuable legal exceptions to physicians and the women who could afford them. They existed to protect pregnant women in the event of legitimate, life-threatening medical conditions. However, the laws did not specify *what* constituted a bona fide medical condition or a proper threat to life or health. Leslie Regan, for example, found that through the 1940s excessive vomiting remained a justifiable reason for therapeutic abortions—though just how much vomiting constituted "excessive" was hotly debated.[11] As a result, the decision was left to the individual physician's discretion. While there were debates within the medical community over what justified a therapeutic abortion, if a woman had a private physician, a legal abortion was relatively easy to obtain.

However, given the methods by which an abortion became therapeutic or legal—that is, by visiting a private physician and paying for a hospital procedure—native-born white women of financial means were the most typical recipients. Therapeutic abortions also created a space wherein physicians and their patients could *negotiate* the terms of an abortion.[12] As noted, a physician's independence allowed some flexibility in determining what justified a therapeutic abortion, and some physicians even willingly performed them on social or personal grounds. In addition, the fee-for-service element of the work may have compelled some physicians to perform "therapeutic" abortions simply to keep their patients' business.

While California's earliest abortion statutes exempted physicians from punishment if they believed a woman needed an abortion, the 1935 abortion statute was markedly different from its predecessors: "Every person who provides, supplies, or administers to any woman, or procures any woman to take any medicine, drug, or substance, or uses or employs any instrument or other means whatever, with intent thereby to procure the miscarriage of such woman, unless the same is necessary to preserve her life, is punishable by imprisonment in the State prison not less than two nor more than five years."[13]

It is notable that the clause in earlier statutes protecting physicians was conspicuously absent and that the prerequisite that abortions be medically necessary took priority over physicians' authority. While the earlier statutes may have implied that physicians could do no wrong, lawmakers had grown increasingly suspicious of the medical community, as evidenced by the change in this statute. As the number of abortions increased in the state, so too did the number of physicians who performed them. By the 1950s and 1960s the perceived exploitation of therapeutic abortions led to their systemic control by hospital abortion committees. The shift in control—from an individual, private physician to a committee—had powerful ramifications. Rather than allowing physicians to practice independently, the committee—often made up of three to five physicians—determined whether an abortion was therapeutically necessary. If a woman went to her regular physician seeking an abortion, it was up to her physician to present her case before the hospital committee. The committee, never having met, seen, or treated the woman, would then deliberate and return a decision. Under this new system therapeutic abortion rates fell drastically.[14] County and state officials recorded the numbers of therapeutic abortions that came before their committees for approval and the numbers that were authorized. This system led some hospitals to employ deliberate, yet unofficial, quotas in order to stay under the radar. Committee members, aware they were being watched, were particularly strict in their interpretations of what they considered acceptable reasons for therapeutic abortions, particularly since "clinic patients were competing for precious slots" with the committee's private patients as well.[15]

This unofficial quota system also left poor women and women of color who were seeking therapeutic abortions in a precarious position. Without a private physician advocate a poor woman with a condition that justified a therapeutic abortion was likely to be sterilized as well. World War II had changed concepts on eugenics in California, and the number of eugenic sterilizations began to level off between 1950 and 1955. Nevertheless, sterilizations continued in California (and other parts of the nation) under the new banner of the "War on Poverty," and sterilizations continued well through the 1970s, funded in part by federal programs. Perhaps it is not surprising that these federally funded sterilization programs disproportionately targeted women of color.

In 1930, when Dr. J. Whitridge Williams spoke before the students and faculty at the University of Washington on indications for therapeutic sterilization, he offered his own practice up for critique. Of 118 patients he had sterilized 15 for mental or psychiatric reasons and 4 for social reasons. In many of his cases abortion was a by-product of the sterilization procedure (though Williams clarified that all his procedures occurred "prior to the viability of the child").[16] Williams's justifications for sterilization are insightful, particularly since sterilization is the most extreme and irreversible method of birth control. It is not simply the termination of one pregnancy; rather it is the prevention of future pregnancies as well. Some of the justifications that Williams provided for sterilizations were feeblemindedness, dementia, psychosis, chorea, insanity, and depression. The social justifications were syphilis, "general worthlessness," low mental age, and "a worthless husband."[17] His justifications shed light on how physicians weighed their options and made reproductive decisions for their patients. These were cases when physicians felt justified in tampering with a woman's ability to reproduce. When other physicians responded to Williams, they acknowledged that a "wide divergence of views exist[ed]" and that it was a physician's job to strike a balance between medicine and humanitarianism.[18] Eugenic-based concerns about social welfare may have compelled some physicians to sterilize or abort. If a woman's heredity or condition justified an abortion for *this* unborn child, then why not for future children as well? Therefore, if a woman from a marginalized community wanted an abortion and wanted to have children in the future, it was likely that her best chances were in the hands of an illegal abortion provider and not with a physician of the party line who had become increasingly strict.

The providers of illegal abortions who continued practicing after the *Rankin* case faced a new challenge: adaptation for survival. The *Rankin* defendants did not simply disappear after the trial. After all, abortion remained a lucrative procedure that women continued to desire. For PCAR defendants Reginald Rankin and Laura Miner the struggle after *Rankin* was in finding new ways to do the same business.

On May 10, 1940, Reginald Rankin was released from San Quentin and paroled to an address in Minersville, California, where he supposedly worked as a foreman on a ranch. Within months he would be beginning a new abortion racket in several cities in California, and in Reno, Nevada, alongside Ruth Barnett.[19] However, Rankin was a little rusty. His new syndicate was not as well developed as PCAR. He had rushed into it. He hadn't taken the precautionary steps he had taken with PCAR, such as bribing law enforcement officials or getting an ally into the local medical association. After a botched abortion nearly ended in a patient's death, Barnett made a confession, and her testimony was used to convict Rankin yet again—this time in *State of Nevada v. Paul Cushing and R. L. Rankin*.

According to Barnett, Rankin returned to San Francisco upon his release. He visited Barnett in Portland and told her that he, Valentine St. John (from PCAR), and Paul Cushing (whose real name was Leslie Von Kempfeldt) were planning to start a new abortion syndicate.[20] Rankin had met Cushing while incarcerated, and the two openly discussed starting an abortion mill on the outside. Cushing had been released before Rankin and laid the groundwork for their new venture by contacting former PCAR associates.[21] There were two locations in this new syndicate: Reno, Nevada, and Oakland, California. Rankin also had locations in Hollywood and Los Angeles in the works, but it doesn't appear that they came to fruition.

In Oakland Rankin and his cohort joined up with St. John, who was performing abortions under the alias of Dr. Hoag. A Dr. Hoag had previously owned the office, but when he sold it, St. John kept the name. St. John had been in that office only since early September 1940. By October Pinkham of the BME had already received about ten anonymous letters regarding illegal abortions in Oakland.[22] Using an undercover decoy, BME agents, alongside the Oakland police, were able to locate Oakland's leading abortionist—St. John. Not too far into the investigation of St. John, Cushing's name was uncovered, as well as that of the Medical Aid Foundation, the new incarnation of the MAC. As the BME put together the pieces of this abortion syndicate, it recognized some of the similarities to PCAR and wondered whether Rankin was involved. When law enforcement was able to secure a warrant for Cushing's apartment, the links among St. John, Cushing, Rankin, and even Barnett became clear.

It seems that the California abortion offices were not Rankin's main focus. Once everyone was out of prison, St. John was supposed to open a health resort and women's clinic near Reno; in the interim Barnett would help by investing in the clinic and working as a naturopath until St. John acquired his license to practice medicine in Nevada. Barnett and Rankin flew to Reno and contacted Norman Biltz, a real estate agent. They found a suitable office in the Lyons Building and signed a lease. After securing the location, St. John contacted Biltz and told him that he was worried he wouldn't get his Nevada medical license since his medical degree was from a foreign university. St. John asked Biltz if he would be willing to vouch for him to the state medical board, and Biltz did. From Biltz, St. John also acquired a list of local physicians that he intended to use to solicit referrals. Rankin ordered a remodeling of the office, and within a couple months it was ready.

But things quickly fell apart. Though Biltz vouched on his behalf, St. John still had trouble acquiring his Nevada license. Antsy and eager to have a façade of legitimacy, Cushing, Rankin, and St. John urged Biltz to find a local physician who would be willing to just post his name on their door so as to provide them with legitimacy, but that task proved more difficult than they had anticipated. Perhaps Biltz sensed something was off or wanted out. Despite the lack of medical credentials, Barnett took charge of the office. In early November 1940 Rankin and his son went to Las Vegas and met with an old friend, Dr. Z. A. D'Amours, a physician with a Nevada license. Rankin offered to pay D'Amours $50 just to put his name on their clinic door. D'Amours agreed, and they were finally in business.

On November 14, 1940, Bernardine Price entered the Lyons Building in Reno in order to get an abortion. Price, a nurse and mother, was nervous, but she wanted the abortion because she could not afford to have more children. Barnett attempted to calm the young woman and told her that she was in good hands. Barnett laid out the prices: $50 if Price was less than two months pregnant or $75 if she was further along. Price agreed to the terms, left the office to borrow money, and said she would return later that afternoon. When Price returned, Barnett performed the abortion. Price rested for approximately twenty minutes before calling a taxi to take her to work at Washoe General Hospital. Price worked throughout the night, but she had fallen ill by daybreak. On Saturday, weak and ill, Price stayed home from work. She called a physician.

Upon examination, the physician realized that Price was suffering from a severe infection. The physician took her to Washoe General Hospital and performed a curettement, noting that she had recently had an abortion. The physician contacted the hospital chief of staff, who then notified the authorities. Since Price had no illnesses that would justify an abortion, the abortion was illegal, and police arrested her abortionists.²³ Cushing, Rankin, and St. John—who were all in California at the time of the abortion—agreed to be extradited to Reno. They likely believed that the case against them was weak since they were in another state. Yet Barnett agreed to testify against the others as a witness for the state, and her testimony secured their conviction. Rankin and Cushing appealed on the grounds that they had nothing to do with the abortion; however, according to Nevada law, it did not matter that the men were in California. Since Barnett had performed the abortion as part of Rankin and Cushing's organization, they were just as guilty.²⁴

Rankin was sentenced on February 21, 1941, to a maximum of five years at the Nevada State Prison in Carson City; he was released on May 3, 1943. By December 1943 he was back in California. Rankin was supposed to return to San Quentin to serve a sentence for violating his parole, but it doesn't appear that he did. Rankin likely returned to Southern California because he felt comfortable there, but it was also away from his last known address—that is, the apartment he owned with his wife on Van Ness Avenue in San Francisco. Upon his return to the Golden State, Rankin wasted no time. According to state BME reports, Rankin was suspected of borrowing money from former PCAR associates and asking other doctors to turn over their offices to him for abortion services. The BME even had reports that Rankin was soliciting doctors to send their abortion cases to the Cottage Hospital in Tijuana, Mexico. The BME had little evidence to corroborate any of these reports; nevertheless, it continued to monitor him.²⁵ Ultimately Rankin's decision to rush into a syndicate in Nevada was a failure. While the group had trouble properly setting up a clinic, the problem was the clinic model itself. Far too visible, the era of the stand-alone clinic had passed. Rankin knew it, and Laura Miner would soon find out.

Even though Laura Miner performed nearly all of the abortions in PCAR's San Diego office, she was listed only as a nurse on the syndicate's internal roster. When she returned home after testifying for the prosecution in the *Rankin* case, she and her children moved to Los

Angeles so that she could finish chiropractic college.[26] Miner received her degree and license in the summer of 1938, and she returned to San Diego, where she resumed business as usual, even opening a new office on Fifth Avenue. Every morning Miner would head to the local soda fountain to read a newspaper at the counter. This was her "front desk." It was understood that Miner's services often required a trip to the soda fountain. There a patient would go to the counter and ask for her. Miner would briefly chat with the potential patient before sending her to the office. Depending on the referral, Laura would have the patient go directly to her office or would have someone pick her up and drop her off without disclosing the location. After PCAR such precautions became common practice. If the patient wasn't trustworthy, the abortionist would sometimes have one of the steerers pick up the patient from a designated location—usually a grocery store, department store, or some other business with a large parking lot. From that designated location the steerer would drive the (sometimes blindfolded) patient around to disorient her before taking her to the office. For example, when Fran Johns needed to get an illegal abortion, she waited patiently in front of a movie theater for the person who was to transport her. A black Buick pulled up to the theater, and the driver sped off as soon as she got in the car, tossing her a bandana, telling her to cover her eyes, and asking her if she had the payment money with her. He drove around for about twenty minutes—through busy streets, neighborhood blocks, and empty fields—before finally pulling up to the carport of a small house.[27]

As an independent business owner, Laura had some flexibility. She scaled prices according to a client's ability to pay, having wealthier women pay a little more to help those who couldn't afford the procedure. She sometimes performed abortions up front for women with no money, or she accepted furs and jewelry in lieu of cash payment from wealthier clients who could tell their husbands, lovers, boyfriends, or fathers that the item had been lost or stolen. Laura was proud of being able to help women get out of trouble and avoid the life that her own mother had experienced. She truly believed that women should have the right to choose whether to have a baby.

Miner was proficient and well known; she was rumored to have helped a few leading ladies from Hollywood with their own procedures since San Diego was far away from the prying eyes of the industry. One of Miner's standing appointments—a woman named Florence Chadwick—would visit every three months because she trusted Miner more than the unreliable methods of birth control available.[28] In San Diego Miner's business was an open secret. She served a long list of politically important people. They utilized her services and were not interested in shutting her down.

In the spring of 1944 Miner closed her office and sold her equipment. She didn't work for two years. Her children were off in boarding school, and she sold her large home in order to fix up a smaller one. When her kids came back home in the fall of 1946, Laura went back to work part time in a new suite of offices at the Hillcrest Security Bank Building on the corner of Fifth and University. Though Miner claimed that some of her work was legitimate chiropractic work, the vast majority of her clients came for illegal abortions. Rumor has it that when the pregnant secretary (and mistress) of a married San Diego district attorney needed an operation, the secretary quoted her lover an inflated price in order to pocket some money for herself. His outrage at the price brought about Miner's fall.

In late September 1948 the San Diego district attorney led police to raid Miner's office. She and her two associates—Dr. Josephine Page and their assistant Nedra Cordon—were placed under arrest. The district attorney subpoenaed Miner's former patients and forced them to testify. Under examination these women were forced to divulge intimate details about their procedures. Prosecutors asked the women about the positions they assumed on the table for the procedure, if they were naked, if they were draped, or if they felt speculums being inserted into their vaginas. If the women did not know what speculums were or were unaware of certain anatomical terms, the male prosecutors had to explain. The prosecutors were unrelenting and often pushed the women until they broke. When Mrs. Grace Peterson took the stand to speak about her abortion, she burst into tears and said, "I told you I had it done. Isn't that enough?"[29]

On the stand many of the women expressed similar reasons for wanting an abortion. Some said they were weak or ill. Mrs. Elizabeth Potter already had a number of children and was concerned about her age. The women also described similar experiences at Miner's office. Some had their husbands drop them off, others went alone, and some met a liaison who transported them. Once they arrived, Nedra greeted them, asked what they were in for, collected medical history, date of last menstrual period, and the fee after confirming they still wanted an abortion. Sometimes the patients were taken to the back right away. In other instances they had to leave and return at another time.

When it was time, the women were taken into a room where they undressed. From there they were escorted to the operating room, where Nedra would help them onto a table and drape them. The nurse would then call in the doctor—either Miner or Page—to perform the procedure. The doctor would insert a speculum to dilate the cervix. Then the doctor would perform a standard curettement followed by water suction. The women frequently described a dull pain or cramping during the procedure. Once the surgery was completed, the woman was instructed to lie down for ten or fifteen minutes. Most of the patients felt well enough after the short rest to continue with their normal routine. If the women did not have rides, the office would call for a taxi. Nedra would schedule a follow-up appointment with the patient a few days to a week later.[30] During the follow up procedure one of the doctors would essentially perform the same operation—dilation and water suction—to ensure that no material had been left behind. This would prevent the development of infection from residual material, ensuring a clean, safe operation.

Though Miner had attempted to modify some of her practices after PCAR, prosecutors continued to successfully convict abortionists in the absence of patient deaths or complications. Any evidence collected from raids—speculums, patient cards with names, an operating table or curette—was sufficient to convict abortion providers. When the San Francisco homicide squad arrested Mrs. Jane Wright, for example, it took the time to make an inventory of all the medical tools it found in her possession, including five speculums, four hollow currettes, two expansion dilators, and two soft rubber catheters.[31] Arrest warrants for raids also resulted from hours of law enforcement surveillance. Investigators' notes detailed when women arrived and left, the license plates of cars that dropped them off, and what the women looked like, as well as an assessment of their conditions once they left. For example:

> Monday—October 25th, 1948—operative on location. . . . At 8:25 a.m., a gray two door sedan Dodge California License No. 77-V-301, drove up to this location and parked at the curb. A woman driver about 40 yrs. of age, 5'7", 120 lbs., buxom, Brunette, wearing a green dress and tan coat, black leather gloves; got out and entered this residence. At 10:15 a.m. a two-tone (Gray-Black) 1948 Buick four door sedan, California License No. 2-S-3653 drove up at this address headed the wrong way, parked and two women got out and entered this residence. No. 1 woman the driver, in her twenties, 5'7", 110 lbs., wearing slacks; No. 2 woman, 45 yrs. 5'6", 128 lbs., wearing light dress and coat, they remained therein until 10:40 a.m. when both came out entered car and drove north.[32]

While the court could technically convict the patients as well, this rarely happened. Prosecutors frequently convinced the women that they would be convicted if they did not testify against the abortionist. Pressure from police investigators, prosecutors, or personal naivety compelled these women to take the stand and describe their abortion experiences in detail. The jury found Miner guilty, and she spent nearly two years at the California Institution for Women at Tehachapi. After her release she never performed abortions again.

Such were the outcomes of the *Rankin* case. Surveilled abortionists and patients endured law enforcement's encroachment into the most intimate parts of their lives. Rather than tolerate invasive lines of questioning after what had already been an invasive abortion, many women chose another route—abortions in Mexico—to escape the torment, shame, and public exposure brought on by a trial, as we will see.

Table 2. Los Angeles County Coroner's Office abortion cases, 1938–54

Fiscal year	Total number of coroner cases	Total number of abortion cases	Self-induced abortions	Abortions by physician or medical professional	Other	Age of recipient: 10-20 / 20-45	Marital status of recipient
1938–39	6,190	19	10	2	1 criminal by unknown person; 2 spontaneous; 1 caused by fall; 3 criminal or self-induced, undetermined	1 / 18	15 married; 2 divorced; 2 single
1939–40	6,282	22	6	5 (4 criminal, 1 therapeutic)	1 criminal by unknown person; 2 criminal by known person; 1 spontaneous; 3 self-induced or criminal, undetermined; 1 self-induced or spontaneous, undetermined; 1 attempted abortion; 1 self-induced or accidental; 1 incomplete abortion	3 / 19	15 married; 2 divorced; 4 single; 1 widowed
1940–41	6,606	12	6	1	1 criminal by unknown person; 2 self-induced or criminal, undetermined; 1 incomplete abortion; 1 unknown cause	3 / 09	6 married; 1 divorced; 5 single
1941–42	6,760	19	4	5	1 accidental, due to fall; 2 spontaneous; 1 therapeutic; 6 unknown cause, criminal or self-induced, undetermined	4 / 15	16 married; 1 divorced; 2 single

1942–43	6,831	23	9	3	1 criminal by unknown person; 2 spontaneous; 4 undetermined whether criminal or self-induced; 4 unknown cause	3 / 19, 1 unknown	21 married; 1 single; 1 widowed
1943–44	6,889	26	8	5 (4 criminal by physician; 1 justifiable by doctor)	2 criminal by unknown person; 6 undetermined whether criminal or self-induced; 3 unknown; 1 accidental due to fall; 1 induced by heavy lifting	1 / 25	22 married; 4 single
1944–45	7,715	10	2	3	5 unknown	3 / 7	7 married; 3 single
1945–46	7,862	12	4	1	3 criminal by unknown person; 3 spontaneous; 1 criminal or self-induced undetermined	1 / 11	9 married; 3 single
1946–47	7,469	11	6	N/A	1 criminal by known person; 1 criminal by unknown person; 3 unknown	5 / 6	7 married; 1 divorced; 2 single; 1 widowed
1947–48	7,789	8	4	N/A	1 criminal by known person; 1 criminal by unknown person; 3 unknown	1 / 7	6 married; 2 single

1948–49	7,539	10	5	2 criminal by known person; 1 spontaneous; 2 unknown	3/7	4 married; 1 divorced; 3 single; 1 widowed; 1 unknown
1949–50	7,770	6	3	N/A	N/A	5 married; 1 single
1950–51	7,774	4	1	1 criminal by known person; 1 undetermined, self-induced or criminal	0/4	4 married
1951–52	8,134	15	7	3 criminal by known person; 1 criminal by unknown person; 2 criminal or self-induced; 1 spontaneous	0/15	7 married; 6 single; 2 divorced
1952–53	8,534	13	8	4 criminal by known person	3/10	7 married; 3 single; 3 divorced
1953–54	8,539	11	8	2 criminal by known person, 1 criminal or self-induced, undetermined	0/11	8 married, 3 single
TOTALS	118,683	221 (.186% of total)	91 (41.2%)	28 (12.7%)	102 (46.1%)	31/189; 1 unknown	159 married; 13 divorced; 44 single; 4 widowed; 1 unknown

Source: Los Angeles County Coroner's Office, annual reports.

In the years after the PCAR trial, Los Angeles saw a decrease in abortion-related deaths (see table 2). Most likely this decrease resulted from fewer women attempting to procure abortions in the stricter environment and not because abortions were necessarily any safer than before. According to data from the Los Angeles County Coroner's Office, there were 221 abortion deaths in Los Angeles County from July 1, 1938, through June 30, 1954. It is notable that the number of deaths over these fifteen years is lower than the 278 abortion deaths the coroner's office reported in the eleven years prior. Moreover, these 221 abortion deaths represented an insignificant percentage of the coroner office's growing caseload, which had more than doubled since the eleven years prior. Abortions represented .186 percent of the coroner's total caseload from 1938 through 1954—much less than the .514 percent that they represented from 1927 through 1938. The data also indicate a shift in the causes of abortion deaths.

The percentage of abortion deaths caused by a physician or other medical professional actually increased—from 10.79 percent to 12.7 percent—a possible result of more women seeking therapeutic abortions. Abortion deaths from "other" causes also increased, from 36.69 percent to 46.1 percent. It is significant that while self-induced abortions represented the major cause of death from 1927 through 1938 (52.52 percent), self-induced abortions represented only 41.2 percent of the cases from 1938 through 1954. Possible explanations for this decline could be that more women took advantage of therapeutic abortion loopholes or liberalizations for health; saw specialized illegal abortionists; resigned themselves to an unwanted pregnancy; or did not wait as long to see a doctor if they experienced complications from a self-induced abortion. Though married women continued to constitute the majority of victims, the number of single women rose significantly—from 13.9 percent of the victims in the earlier data to just under 20 percent in the data from 1938 to 1954. The decline in the percentage of married women could be attributed to the rise in the percentage of divorced and widowed women who died from abortions. It could also be linked to postwar economic success and the baby-boom era—with more couples wanting children, fewer couples wanted abortions. Likewise the increased visibility of single women who died from abortion could be related to a changing dating culture; boyfriends leaving to fight in World War II; and temporary relationships resulting from wartime mobilization, jobs, and migration.

A number of scholars have pointed out that an increase in the number of "white illegitimate pregnancies" in the 1940s and 1950s forced medical and social work professionals to reevaluate their stances and perceptions of illegitimate pregnancy. While these professionals could attribute non-whites' tendency toward disorganized families to racial difference, they attributed single white women's illegitimate pregnancies to "psychological neuroses."[33] They believed that "with the right psychological treatment, [these women] could potentially prevail over past mistakes and resume the roles of normative young womanhood."[34] Part of such rehabilitation required giving up a baby for adoption after a lengthy stay at a home for unwed mothers. According to Ann Fessler, the rate of premarital pregnancies in the United States increased substantially in the first half of the twentieth century. By the mid-1950s approximately 40 percent of first children born to girls aged fifteen to nineteen were conceived out of wedlock.[35] However, ideologies about sexual propriety did not change with shifting norms—particularly for middle-class families—and society continued to stigmatize unwed mothers and their illegitimate children.

Some young couples married quickly after discovering they were pregnant in order to cover an illegitimate birth, but many young women had their decisions made for them. Parents, religious leaders, and social workers told these young women what was best and made arrangements on their behalf. Most of them, believing "they had already brought shame upon the family by becoming pregnant," raised few objections.[36] When the BME interrogated Mr. and Mrs. Jameson about their daughter Shirley's abortion during a routine investigation of a Long Beach abortionist, the parents offered their full cooperation with one exception. They requested that the board wait until August to interrogate Shirley. After her abortion Shirley was "subject to a certain nervous strain which resulted in her being placed in a home."[37] She recovered and was engaged to be married to "a very reputable young man" that June.[38] Her parents believed that she would be more likely to speak to them after she had been married for some time. When the board interviewed Mrs. Raymond about her nineteen-year-old daughter, Mary, she gave a similar account.[39] According to Raymond, Mary had been engaged to a nice young man. While he was away in college, Mary went out with and became pregnant by a "goon." After contacting friends, physicians, acquaintances, and the family doctor with no success, Raymond drove her daughter down to Mexicali in hopes of finding an abortionist. Eventually she found one in Ensenada. Mary and her mother followed the instructions, and Mary had her abortion. "[Mrs. Raymond] stated that she was not sorry that she had Mary aborted and would do it again if it became necessary. She felt that by having the abortion she saved Mary from becoming a social outcast, preserved her engagement to a promising young man, and might possibly have saved Mary's life as Mary was so depressed that she mentioned suicide."[40]

Postwar conditions and increased middle-class conservativism may have also played a role in the reduction of the number of women who sought abortions and may instead have fostered an increase in the number of lying-in homes and adoptions.[41] The period between the 1940s and 1973 is sometimes described as the "Baby Scoop Era," when the rate of premarital pregnancies increased and was accompanied by a higher rate of nonfamilial adoptions of newborns. Scholars of this phenomenon argue that young, white unwed mothers were cast as victims: pregnancy out of wedlock was seen as a sort of catastrophic event, and the young women could reform by giving up the child for adoption. Rather than their illegitimate pregnancies being ascribed to moral degeneracy or racial inferiority, these young white women were psychologically pathologized. In the absence of legal abortion and given existing postwar patriarchal structures, few options existed for single motherhood. Carrying a pregnancy to term and keeping the child might burden a young woman's family or might render future relationships implausible, as a new beau was unlikely to care for another man's child. Therefore these young women were often pressured into adoption in the absence of other options.[42]

Estimates vary for how many children were adopted out during this period. Adoption's legal history is relatively modern, and records were not always kept consistently. In addition, numbers vary when we consider whether the adoption was outside the family or with kin. Most experts estimate that approximately 1.5 million young white women were coerced into giving up their children for adoption, though some estimates are as high as 4 million—but the dates are flexible as well. Most experts agree the Baby Scoop Era ended in 1973 with the *Roe v. Wade* decision, but some believe that it began around 1945, while others believe it started somewhere in the 1950s.[43] This was also the era of Cold War ideology—specifically "containment." In the United States "fighting communism abroad" was linked not only to national security, but it was also "linked to the idealization of motherhood and reproduction and to the sexual regulation of women's bodies."[44] For women who were unable to have children or whose genes made a biological family unwise (in the wake of prenatal screening after World War II), nonfamilial adoption became a way to reconcile the ideal American nuclear patriarchal family with punishing and rehabilitating unmarried mothers and regulating their behavior and sexuality.[45] However, when motherhood, respectability, and health were taken into account during abortion debates, new opportunities for disagreement emerged.

To the Border 7

"Tijuana Abortions" and Legal Vagueness

> He went away across the corridor and into another room that we could not see, leaving us with the three people. They were not talking and it was strangely quiet all through the building. Everybody looked at everybody else in a nervous kind of way that comes when time and circumstance reduce us to seeking illegal operations in Mexico.
>
> —Richard Brautigan, 1970

By the 1950s and 1960s the border had become more visible to Americans through continued, and increased, regulation—specifically with Operation Wetback in 1954, the 1955 Senate committees on vice, and the Bracero program, which began during World War II and continued through 1964.[1] Along the border with Mexico concerns about illegal immigration added to the stereotype of the U.S.-Mexico border as a lawless place, while borders, smuggling, and crime "were hotly debated in the public arena."[2] Discussions about migration and deportation of Mexicans along the border also served to reinforce the idea that "countless illegal immigrants were pouring across the border on a daily basis."[3] With deportation programs tied to racial slurs and with legal immigration and illegal immigration often conflated in the case of Mexicans, newspapers, with their sensational coverage, helped to "explicitly linked the 'illegal Mexican aliens'" with criminal activity and other vices.[4]

The border also played an important role in the context of heightened Cold War fears about national security. In public opinion border cities and towns were thought to be "particularly susceptible to corruption and crime."[5] These concerns about borders emerged when unprecedented numbers of Americans were traveling across them and yet when fear "of subversion from the outside" was at its peak.⁶ As Mexican border towns became sites of American decadence, abortions made their way into this space as well. Although American women had traveled to other countries for abortions for years, in the 1950s and 1960s California women increasingly sought abortions across the border in light of therapeutic abortion committees' more judicious interpretations of legal abortion and the increasing ease with which white Americans could cross the border.

Southern California's landscape had transformed drastically in the first half of the twentieth century. As noted previously, during World War II California saw a massive population influx brought on by wartime industries—specifically ship production in Northern California and plane production in Southern California. Postwar prosperity, the Servicemen Readjustment Act, and the growth of the non-white population in the cities allowed for the expansion of suburbs as well. Defense spending after the war and the military-industrial complex fueled the region's growth. As more migrants came to California to find work in one of its many industries, the need for housing increased. The homeowners of the 1940s and 1950s built communities that centered around labor, self-reliance, patriotism, middle-class values, family, and racial separation.⁷ Places like San Diego and Long Beach—former outskirts of Los Angeles—grew increasingly connected to the sprawling metropolitan area. Automobile manufacturing necessitated the expansion of the existing WPA-funded roads and infrastructure. World War II facilitated increased highway construction, while individuals' ownership of automobiles allowed freedom from unwanted socio-spatial interactions in an increasingly non-white urban metropolis.⁸ Automobiles and freeways increased Americans' ability to travel, and California became the center of America's automobile culture early on. The birth of this new kind of freedom facilitated tourism among average middle-class Americans— whether that tourism was intrastate, interstate, or international.

Migration and mobility had become central to California, and one never had to look very far to find echoes of Mexico—whether metaphorically in the Spanish fantasy past or literally in the U.S.-

Mexico border. Mexico represented a sense of freedom to some, an exotic untamed land, or an easy last resort for escape in the event that criminal activity went bad. In fact in the late nineteenth century newspaper articles about escaped murderers and criminals crossing back and forth across the border were common, advancing the idea that Mexico and the border were wild and untamed.[9] Perhaps because of this perception, from the late nineteenth through the twentieth century the U.S.-Mexico border had become a place where "[American] tourists could fulfill their desire for exotic diversions."[10] In the 1910s, for example, progressive campaigns against vice in Los Angeles and San Diego accelerated the growth of vice industries on the Mexican side of the border. Tijuana represented a "den of vice" and a "shame and a disgrace" at America's southernmost gate.[11] Nevertheless, the gambling houses and pool halls at the border were just a short trip from San Diego, and they were even connected by rail.

Beginning in the late nineteenth century northern Mexico was increasingly exposed to American markets and quickly saw the potential benefits of economic trade and alliances with its northern neighbor. In addition, political instability—most notably the Mexican Revolution (1910–20)—transformed life in Mexico, forcing some to seek opportunities beyond the pale of reputable employment, whether in smuggling alcohol, drugs, ammunition, or flesh. The development of an illicit market is predicated on what Steven Bender describes as "the role of law as a motivation of the first order."[12] Others have said, more simply, "Mexicans have always been available to supply whatever Americans want but cannot obtain legally in their own country—just as Americans have always been ready to provide whatever Mexicans want and cannot acquire readily in Mexico."[13] When a national boundary marked one side as Mexican and the other as American, the structure of everyday transactions was permanently altered. The border became an "arbitrary restriction" as the people who lived there "sought to continue carrying goods freely across the Rio Grande."[14] As these people continued their interactions in a manner to avoid regulations and tariffs, their actions became criminal, and soon the perception of the border as criminal, lawless, or a haven for illicit behavior permeated American popular culture. Despite some Americans' best attempts to suppress vice at the border, gambling halls, racetracks, and saloons thrived. American tourists, disgruntled drinkers under the yoke of Prohibition, gamblers, and families alike crossed the border in order to experience the novelty of an exotic country and culture or to enjoy illicit drinking and gambling in relative peace.[15]

Marking a non-white space as a place wherein one could indulge in licentiousness or liberty was not a novel concept. The creation of "world" spaces in the 1893 Columbian Expositions opposite the "white city," for example, were similar instances wherein whites could partake and witness the foreign exoticness of non-white "primitivism" and "backwardness." "Slumming" in late nineteenth- and early twentieth-century cities provided reformers and middle-class consumers an opportunity to observe the poverty and "peculiarity" of ethnic enclaves. Similarly the Panama-California Exposition in San Diego (1915–17) juxtaposed sultry señoritas and lazy Hispanic performers with models of modern agriculture and California bungalows.[16] Southern Californians' ability to mobilize a non-white area and characterize it as a place where they could engage in behaviors unsuitable in *American* civilization was merely an extension of these earlier practices. To Americans the border towns of Mexico existed for their pleasure. While to reformers the border functioned as a way to contain vice in Mexico and keep it out of the United States, it meant little for Americans traveling to Mexico. They continued to travel across the border with relative ease at the same time that crossing the border for Mexicans became a regimented process. While there had been "lax immigration procedures" before the Johnson-Reed Act of 1924, afterward Americans saw the border between the United States and Mexico as not only a national boundary, but "a cultural and racial boundary" as well. As a result, "Mexicans coming to the United States encountered a new kind of border"—one that was concerned with regulating migration one way but not the other.[17]

As immigrants, criminals, and tourists made their ways back and forth across this shared border, U.S. law enforcement officials decried the bureaucratic processes necessary to extradite American fugitives who had found refuge in Mexico. One of the most notorious examples of such processes was when Jack Johnson fled to Mexico to escape charges of violating the Mann Act. Johnson, the first Black boxing heavyweight champion, inspired outrage after his victory. Not only had he dethroned the white heavyweight champ in an era when that was the epitome of the racial and masculine idea, but he had made open and flagrant displays of his relationships with white women. He immediately became a target of the White-Slave Traffic Act, or the Mann Act. The Mann Act made it a federal offense to transport women across state lines for immoral purposes. The mother of his white girlfriend, Lucille Cameron, accused Johnson of kidnapping her daughter. In the ensuing legal battle, Johnson was found guilty of transporting a white woman across state lines for immoral purposes and was sentenced to a year of prison. Instead Johnson fled to Canada, Spain, and Cuba before eventually settling down in Mexico. Mexican president Venustiano Carranza had befriended Johnson and ignored American pressure to extradite him for punishment.[18] Some accounts claimed that hundreds of American offenders lived in Mexico without "molestation in that country" since attempts at their return "proved futile." Furthermore, the extradition process was drawn out and burdensome. For example, when Dr. James Petrie fled to Mazatlán after he performed a fatal abortion, detectives in Los Angeles had to go to Sacramento for extradition papers. These papers had to be sent to Washington DC before they were forwarded to the president of Mexico in Mexico City.[19]

The Mexican government first addressed abortion in 1931. According to Mexican law, abortion was illegal except in cases of "negligence of the mother," if continuation of the pregnancy endangered the life of the mother, or if the pregnancy had resulted from rape.[20] Under this law abortion was punishable with one to three years or three to six years of prison for the provider, depending on whether the woman had consented to the abortion. There was no penalty for individuals who provided abortions for rape victims. The "negligence of the mother" portion, though vague, was designed to protect women who miscarried through no deliberate fault of their own. Although abortion on demand was not an option in Mexico, "the U.S. demand for abortions produced a surreptitious market. Particularly in the 1960s, Tijuana and nearby Ensenada served as an 'abortion emporium' for U.S. women who faced the alternative in the United States of back-alley abortions or safer but cost-prohibitive abortions by U.S. doctors acting illegally. Tijuana was a cheaper option.... It provided a whole coterie of movie stars with well-publicized 'miscarriages.' Mexican abortions entered the [American] cultural mainstream."[21]

The border became more visible in American abortion legislation after the case of the *People of the State of California v. Buffum* in 1953. The development of this "surreptitious" abortion market would not have been possible without it; the case accelerated the abortion-tourism industry at the border and allowed providers of illegal abortions to profit immensely. In the *Buffum* case Reginald Rankin and Roy L. Buffum were indicted for violating sections 182 and 274 of the California Penal Code.[22] Unlike Rankin's earlier legal battles, Rankin and Buffum won their appeal on what on the surface might appear to have been a technicality. Specifically the initial *Buffum* decision was reversed because the actual abortions did not take place in California; they took place across the border in Tijuana. The idea that abortionists could move around to perform a procedure was a product of the increased mobility and infrastructure in Southern California. Abortionists were quick to take advantage of the region's roads and freeways. Leaders in the PCAR, for example, regularly moved and rotated their abortionists, by car and plane, from clinic to clinic. In 1948 five people in Oakland were arrested for performing abortions in the back of a specially equipped trailer.[23] In 1958 and 1959 a six-month investigation led to the arrest of a half a dozen men and women who had operated a "floating" abortion ring in which the steerers took women to constantly changing clinic locations in Anaheim, Long Beach, or Los Angeles.[24] Coroner's reports beginning in 1954 even added new statistical categories or annotations: "found dead at scene" and "died under observation," perhaps further examples of the effects that mobility had on the abortion industry.[25] Using freeways, roads,

5. Body of teenage bride found, 1959. "Sgt. Ron Smith and Officer A. J. Rodriguez, holding shoe, examine area where body of Mrs. Brenda Lenore Emerson, 16, was found on strip of grass near St. Joseph Hospital Saturday night. Girl's body was fully clothed, and her shoes were found nearby. Preliminary autopsy has failed to show cause of girl's mysterious death." *Valley Times* Collection. Los Angeles Public Library.

and personal vehicles, Rankin and Buffum mobilized their new plan for the abortion industry.

Rankin had not pulled Buffum out from obscurity. Buffum was born in Lafayette, Illinois, on February 9, 1881. He received his bachelor's degree from Williams College in 1905. He went to Rush Medical School in Chicago and interned at the Presbyterian and Children's Hospitals of Chicago. He graduated from Rush in 1909. From 1910 to 1913 he maintained a practice in Toulon, Illinois. In 1915 he, his wife Bess, and their three children moved to Long Beach, California, where his older brothers, Charles Abel Buffum and Edwin E. Buffum, were already established. They had moved to Long Beach in 1904 and opened a successful chain of upscale department stores. Charles eventually became the mayor of Long Beach and likely benefited from a promising marriage between his daughter, Dorothy, and Norman Chandler, publisher of the *Los Angeles Times*.[26] Roy Buffum established an obstetrics and general practice in Long Beach.

In 1928 Buffum came to the California BME's attention while it was investigating an abortion case. A woman from San Pedro claimed that Buffum had performed an abortion on her.[27] Special Agent Albert Carter of the BME claimed he hadn't looked into the matter but complained of the inability to prosecute the physician without corroborative evidence. In 1929 Buffum allegedly peddled narcotics; he was accused of selling drugs outright without a prescription.[28] Though he was acquitted in criminal court, the BME found him guilty of prescribing narcotics to an addict and sentenced him to five years of probation. In 1931 Buffum's name came up in another abortion case investigation; however, the BME dismissed the case without prejudice.[29] In 1934 Special Agent Carter wrote to Charles Pinkham of the need to take action against "the more prominent abortionists in Los Angeles ... [as] they are the hardest ones to obtain evidence against."[30] He mentioned that Buffum had recently had a case against him dismissed but had his license revoked on another charge. In September 1935 a motion was made in a meeting of the Los Angeles County Medical Association to have Buffum's application for readmission referred back to the membership committee. With his application tabled, Buffum made a separate application in 1936 but also "failed of election to membership."[31]

Rankin and Buffum first met in the 1930s. During the first *Rankin* trial the prosecution called on Buffum as one of its witnesses. On the stand Buffum stated that Rankin had approached him in 1935, while he was on probation for violation of the state's Medical Practice Act. He claimed that Rankin wanted him to join PCAR and to be in charge of a new clinic he planned to open. He further claimed he had refused the offer, even when Rankin visited him a second time with Byrne.[32] It isn't clear how Rankin and Buffum became reacquainted after Rankin returned from Reno, but by 1950 Rankin had settled in Arcadia. Since abortions were lucrative and he was well known among abortionists' networks, he likely went back to the industry he knew. Rankin had rushed into his Oakland/Reno endeavor and probably did not want to make those same mistakes again. Though the landscape of Southern California had changed, this was Rankin's home.

According to the *Buffum* indictment, Buffum and Rankin operated an office in Long Beach, where they made arrangements with women seeking abortions. The arrangements would include taking the women's phone numbers, calling them, and arranging a designated meeting point. At the meeting point Buffum or Rankin would transport the women to an office in Tijuana, where another man would perform the procedure. After the procedure Buffum or Rankin would drive the women back. Once they returned to Long Beach, they all went their separate ways. In the abortions that brought about Buffum and Rankin's arrests, four women had been transported to Tijuana, and three had required hospitalization after their abortions. While they were hospitalized, it became clear that these women had had illegal abortions; this discovery led to an investigation. Buffum was taken into custody on Thursday, June 15, 1950. He was apprehended at Los Angeles International Airport while waiting to board a plane to Boston. Some believe that they won their appeal because Buffum was so well connected to the wealthy and powerful Chandler family.[33] While this connection may have been significant, it was more important that the court reversed its decision because it recognized the limits of its power; as noted, the abortions had taken place outside the reaches of California law.[34]

Although there was ample evidence to corroborate that Rankin and Buffum conspired in California, the fact that the crime had been performed in Mexico led to disagreements over whether Section 182 of the California Penal Code applied. Specifically the court stated that although the statute made "no reference to the place of performance of an abortion, [it] must assume that the Legislature did not intend to regulate conduct taking place outside the borders of the state."[35] Furthermore, during the initial trial prosecutors mentioned that the men had violated Mexico's laws against abortion—a statement that may have been prejudicial since the California jurors may have judged the men culpable of violating Mexican law. And California's conspiracy statute did not apply to conspiracies to violate Mexican law. Thus the judgment was reversed, the court recognizing that the state's existing statutes did not "provide a punishment for such conduct."[36] In reversing its decision, the court effectively stated it had no jurisdiction in the matter.

To be clear, this was not the first time women had crossed a national border to acquire abortions. Women of means had been doing so for some time, traveling as far as Mexico City, Japan, and even Sweden, where laws were more relaxed or where their money could go further.[37] In 1969 a couple described to a *Chicago Tribune* journalist their experience of flying to Mexico City in order to obtain an abortion, while other journalists wrote about clinics and lying-in homes like "la Casa de las Gringas," a title that translates roughly as "the American Girls' House" or "the White Girls' House." La Casa de las Gringas was one of the busiest abortion mills in Mexico City, and it generated up to $1,300 per abortion.[38] One couple spent over $1,100 for an abortion: $500 for the procedure itself, $400 for airfare, and over $200 for hotel and transportation fees. But this couple paid to get an abortion from a licensed physician in obstetrics and gynecology (OB/GYN) in Mexico City.[39] What was different was the postwar ease with which women and abortionists were able to navigate, acquire, and perform this procedure. After *Buffum* women did not have to get plane tickets or prepare for an extended stay. Southern California's proximity to Mexico meant that a woman could obtain an abortion across the border during a day trip. Foreign abortions were no longer a hassle or major inconvenience; rather they were relatively simple considering how easy it was for Californians to travel to Mexican border towns.

The *Buffum* decision opened the floodgates of American abortion tourism in nearby border cities. It essentially condoned the proliferation of an illegal abortion industry just across the border and contributed to the development of California's 1950s to 1960s Tijuana abortions phenomenon. In 1962 Joel M. Taylor, a special agent for the California Department of Justice, reported the following: "District attorney's investigators of San Diego and Orange counties and other law enforcement officials have pointed out that the Buffum decision prohibits prosecution for an offense committed in Mexico even though the arrangements for the act were made in this country by citizens of California."[40] Efforts to close the *Buffum* loophole were fruitless. Despite undercover assignments and surveillance in Tijuana by the Los Angeles BME, authorities were unable to put a stop to the surge of American women procuring abortions along the border. One report in 1967 estimated that there were about seventy-five abortionists operating regularly in Tijuana "and a few fly-by-nighters besides."[41] Border abortions were not limited to Tijuana, though, and this estimate did not include other border cities like Mexicali, Juarez, or Ensenada, which all had their own abortion businesses. The *Buffum* decision allowed women and steerers to make arrangements in California for illegal abortions that would be carried out in Mexico. Women in colleges up and down the state would charter buses and go across the border in order to secure abortions. One group of six young women from Berkeley paid a contact $600 each to transport them to Juarez. Instead of taking them to a clinic, though, the contact took them to the police, took their money, and fled to El Paso. The women were detained in Juarez and were unable to get their abortions.[42] Some would meet steerers in parking lots, and the steerers would transport them. Others would go to a local car rental agency and rent a car for a day.

According to Gene Allen, chief investigator for the San Diego district attorney, the process by which women and abortionists made contact seldom varied. In most cases once the woman had found an abortionist and made initial contact, she would be "instructed to get a motel room near the border or in Tijuana."[43] The woman would then make a call to the abortionist once she got to the motel or designated landmark. (For example, in Richard Brautigan's novel *The Abortion*, once he and his girlfriend, Vida, arrived in Tijuana, they were instructed to make a call from the pay phone outside of the local Woolworth's department store.) Once the woman made contact, she would often be instructed to go to a bar, restaurant, or some other public place where one of the abortionist's associates would transport her to the location where the procedure would take place. After the abortion the woman was often in charge of her own transportation. The abortionist would frequently tell the women to look happy when returning to the United States so as to not arouse suspicion from border patrol agents.

The preponderance of transborder abortions and the inability to successfully convict anyone for their practice prompted the state to revise its abortion law. According to the San Diego district attorney, Don Keller, law enforcement officials, "including members of the Department of Professional and Vocational Standards, agreed that the *Buffum* case virtually prohibits prosecution for abortions even in cases where the abortionist meets the victim in California, accepts a fee, transports the victim to Tijuana, and performs an operation. It appears that as long as the *Buffum* case stands, the wholesale abortion mills will continue to operate in Mexico."[44]

After the *Buffum* case legislators in California attempted to close the loophole that had freed Buffum and Rankin. In 1959 California's chief deputy attorney general expressed concern over the international abortion ring in Mexico and was assured that local and federal agencies were preoccupied with developing "new legislation to combat the problem."[45] These agencies were able to bring about legislation that made it illegal to conspire to commit an abortion outside of California, even if the abortion was legal in the jurisdiction in which it was performed. But these efforts did little to stymie the practice of transborder abortions. In 1962 the California Department of Justice still lamented the "considerable abortion activity in the Tijuana area" and pointed specifically to San Diego and Orange Counties as points of contact before transport.[46]

As the abortion industry on the border grew, unskilled abortionists had greater opportunities to offer their services. Desperate women— many of whom simply crossed the border and asked around—rarely looked for the most qualified abortionist and accepted the services of the first one they found. These unskilled abortionists did not necessarily kill, maim, or butcher their patients. Rather women who went to unskilled abortionists did not get hygienic treatment, pain relievers, or even complete abortions. When they returned to the United States, they often had to go to a hospital emergency room so that they could either get a complete abortion or have their lives saved.[47] In American emergency rooms the women were treated for infections or had D & Cs performed to complete the partial abortion begun in Mexico.

In 1966 Los Angeles County General Hospital experienced a brief surge in tetanus infections from women attempting to self-induce miscarriage. According to hospital officials, the cases were "typical of an alarming upswing in the number of women who are turning to 'old wives' remedies" and self-induced abortions.[48] Some people, like Pat Maginnis, realized that some women's *only* option was to do it themselves. Recognizing this, she and her partners orchestrated workshops where they told women how to perform abortions themselves and how to know when a trip to the hospital was absolutely necessary. These were the options for "women with less than two hundred dollars who hope they can get the county hospital to finish the abortion" once it got under way.[49] These do-it-yourself abortion methods utilized knitting needles, coat hangers, Lysol, bleach, turpentine, kerosene, rubber catheters, or even raw spaghetti.

Generally tetanus infections stemming from abortions were rare, but as a whole officials at Los Angeles County General claimed that the hospital saw about one hundred patients per month with complications from illegal abortions. One staff physician claimed that the hospital had "more experience treating women who had become infected due to an abortion than any other hospital in the state and perhaps in the country."[50] Some physicians, reflecting on their county hospital residencies from the 1940s to the 1960s, recalled "Monday morning abortion lineups." Women who received paychecks on Friday had abortions over the weekend, and by Monday morning many lined up outside the emergency room, hemorrhaging or septic and requiring treatment.⁵¹ Some residents would X-ray the women to see if there were knitting needles, catheters, or coat hangers inside them, while other residents would check for gas gangrene. Once the most severe emergency cases had been cleared, residents would perform D&Cs until Tuesday morning.⁵²

The staff physician at Los Angeles County General believed the hospital had such a workload because of its proximity to Tijuana. Pat Maginnis too recognized the potential dangers that existed when women crossed the border for abortions, and she often passed out leaflets with the names of physicians in Mexico whom she believed to be reputable and safe.⁵³ While Maginnis and her "Army of Three" (Maginnis, Lana Phelan, and Rowena Gurner) attempted to maintain a list of reliable providers, some "butchers" preyed on the countless American women who went across the border. In addition, the occasional crackdown from American and Mexican officials complicated efforts to keep the list up to date. In their leaflets Maginnis, Phelan, and Gurner provided tips to help identify reputable abortionists who would, for example, provide pain reliever before the procedure and an antibiotic afterward—like Dr. Alfonso Paris, an abortionist in Tijuana who was frequently under investigation by the California Department of Justice. One investigator stated, "Dr. Paris and a male assistant appeared to be highly trained professional people. The office was well equipped, smelled of disinfectant, and all instruments appeared to be sterile. Dr. Paris performed the abortion in a highly efficient manner [and] gave ... a sedative prior to the operation and an antibiotic [after]."⁵⁴ Maginnis encouraged women to look around once they arrived in Mexico by asking taxi drivers for abortionists or regular gynecologists. She and her colleagues also cautioned that if an abortion was less than $300, "you may not be too sure of getting a licensed physician. Ask to see a license if you are uncertain as to whether you are getting a bona fide physician."⁵⁵

Ultimately Mexico became both a beacon and a specter—a possibility for women to find relief, as well as a synonym for the potential dangers and perils of illegal operations in a "vice-ridden," "uncivilized" country. The husband of the couple who told the *Chicago Tribune* of their experience in Mexico City expressed anger and frustration at their predicament. While the woman was satisfied with the care and treatment she had received, her husband said he couldn't help but wonder what they were doing there. He said it made him "feel like a criminal . . . to have to go to a hot, dirty, foreign country." He continued, "I'm sure it was done as well as it could be done in Mexico. Still, why did it have to be done *there*?"[56] While this couple was privileged enough to pay for the services of a legitimate Mexican gynecologist, the $300 to ensure a bona fide physician may have been too great a price for some women traveling across the border. Unsure and unfamiliar with the foreign space of the border, some women took their chances with self-inducing, while others took their chances with cheaper abortionists. While some women self-induced and had complications, well-to-do women who had complications from Tijuana abortions also had to go to a hospital if they experienced complications or if they wanted to maintain a sense of anonymity and avoid their personal physicians (who may have refused to help them with their abortions in the first place).

Fears of Tijuana abortions added to the bleak reality that about one-third of Los Angeles County's maternal deaths each year were a result of abortions—"the majority [of which were] married women who have young children."[57] Since most of these women were victims of illicit abortions, these statistics added fuel to the burning fire of reform. In 1959 the American Law Institute (ALI), an independent organization comprised of various legal scholars, made a sweeping effort to standardize American abortion laws. In light of most states' amorphous abortion statutes, the ALI's goal of standardization was laudable. The ALI molded the law upon the bases "which most legislators have accepted" as justifiable for abortions.[58] These categories included the following: (1) when the life or health of the mother was in danger; (2) if sound medical judgment found it likely that the child would be born with a serious congenital abnormality; (3) if a pregnant girl was very young or if the pregnancy was the result of rape or incest. While this model law provided for an expansion of abortion rights for women in some states, the drafters of the model law actually believed that the problem with existing abortion laws was not that they were too restrictive but rather that they were too lax and open to interpretation. For example, in the case of the *People of the State of California v. Francis Edgar Ballard* (1959) the court seemed to double "over backwards to let a doctor go," even though the case had "all the earmarks of a criminal abortion."[59] Since the physician was well respected in his community, the court instead focused on the law's lack of clarity, stating at the outset that "a great deal of misunderstanding would be avoided in abortion matters if they were considered in the light of the fact that an abortion is not necessarily, in and of itself, an illegal procedure or act. In other words, not all abortions are illegal."[60] In California efforts to delineate the parameters of legal abortion were stifled by the differing opinions of those defining and defending the law.

In San Diego in 1962 the Assembly Interim Committee on Criminal Procedure gathered for a hearing on bill AB 2614. The bill held that abortions could be performed in hospitals if the hospitals' therapeutic abortion committees determined that "the continuance of pregnancy involves substantial risk that the mother of the child will suffer grave and irremediable impairment of physical or mental health of if the pregnancy resulted from rape or incest."[61] Recognizing the ambiguity in the existing law, this committee attempted to determine whether this bill, which was based on the ALI model law, would clear up the definition of legal abortion.

At the time of the San Diego hearing medical experts in the United States believed that the number of abortions performed in the country ranged between 375,000 and 2 million per year, with 1 million being a conservative figure. Although it is difficult to get precise figures for black market commodities and services, the medical experts estimated around 5,000 deaths per year as a result of poorly performed abortions. In Los Angeles County abortions continued to remain an insignificant portion of the coroner's caseload (see table 3).[62] In the fifteen fiscal years from 1954 to 1970 abortions represented an average of .09 percent of the total number of coroner cases, with a high of .188 percent and a low of .007 percent. The percentages of abortion deaths

Table 3. Los Angeles County Coroner's Office abortion cases, 1954–70

Fiscal year	Total number of coroner cases	Number of abortion cases
1954–55	8,634	14
1955–56	9,450	11
1956–57	9,584	18
1957–58	9,959	8
1958–59	9,950	11
1959–60	10,786	10
1960–61	10,825	17
1961–62	12,073	13
1962–63	12,516	15
1963–64	12,642	7
1964–65	12,670	7
1965–66	13,128	5
1966–67	12,387	3
1967–68	13,781	1
1968–69	—	—
1969–70	14,035	4 mothers and 1 fetus

Source: Los Angeles County Coroner's Office, annual reports.

represented in the Los Angeles County Coroner's Office had steadily and consistently declined since the 1920s and 1930s, yet abortion was becoming more visible in public discourse. One attorney at the time of the San Diego hearing explained that it was rare to find instances of the word "abortion" in newspapers since it was a taboo subject, "fit to be discussed only in medical journals."[63] However, with the continued coverage of "illegal operations" and "illegal surgeries" in daily newspapers, it became clear "that the abortion problem would never improve until it could be fully discussed."[64] According to Kristin Luker, efforts to standardize abortion law generated greater publicity and brought abortion into the public purview. As abortion became increasingly legislated and moved from the home to the hospital, "with the involvement of other people, widely varying interpretations of when an abortion is justified came into public view. The more public abortions became, the more opportunities for conflict arose."[65]

Though World War II had ruptured gender norms, the return of men from the war signaled a necessary return of women to the home. Abortion and maternal mortality thus became important figures in representing America as a modern nation. The potential lives of fetuses had gained new meaning. Babies born in the postwar era experienced a social, cultural, and medical world different from that of their parents. Postwar parents of the middle and upper classes spent more on their babies, "dressed their babies in new clothes, served them store-bought baby foods, spent more on their medical services, and purchased toys designed to promote . . . physical and mental development."[66] As babies became precious to postwar suburban families, motherhood gained new meaning and significance. Though maternal mortality had decreased over time, the shocking deaths of the women who did die threatened to ruin the reputation of the United States as a modern nation of technological advancement. As stated previously, advances in medical technology made it increasingly rare for a disease to preclude a woman from pregnancy or childbearing. Therefore, ideally speaking, women who wanted to abort their pregnancies were anomalies in the baby boom era unless their desire for an abortion fell within certain parameters: there was a problem with her, the baby, or the pregnancy. For example, San Diego lawmakers claimed that the thought of aborted fetuses was disgusting to society, but "the scale begins to tip" toward the mother if she was young, raped, a victim of incest, or "in a serious mental state."[67]

Despite legislators' best attempts to leave little room for interpretation, the thalidomide tragedy and rubella outbreaks, which resulted in the birth of infants with severe defects, complicated the abortion issue.[68] The use of thalidomide in Europe led to the death and deformation of thousands of babies. Thalidomide was a pharmaceutical drug that many pregnant women took to help them sleep or to fight nausea or morning sickness. In 1962 its effects became known worldwide.[69] European doctors began to notice higher rates of birth defects among women who took the drug. Most commonly thalidomide affected embryonic limb development and growth, which manifested in phocomelia, a rare disorder where the limbs and extremities were never fully formed or developed in utero.[70] While Americans did not experience an outbreak on the scale in Europe, it was enough to produce an "anxiety about pregnancy."[71]

The rubella, or German measles, epidemic of 1963–65 was particularly significant in changing public perceptions and laws regarding abortion in the United States.[72] While rubella caused only a minor rash and fever in women, it had particularly catastrophic effects if the women were pregnant. It could cause miscarriages, infant deaths, or defects such as intellectual disability, blindness, deafness, and heart malformations. According to the Centers for Disease Control and Prevention (CDC), during the 1960s rubella was responsible for some 11,000 miscarriages or abortions, 2,100 infant deaths, and the birth of about 20,000 babies with congenital rubella syndrome (CRS).[73] There was no cure for rubella (the first strains of the vaccine were licensed in 1963, and mass vaccination did not begin until the late 1960s), so pregnant women who had contracted the disease faced a difficult decision. Since rubella did not pose an imminent threat to the mother, it was up to doctors and committees to determine whether the possibility of fetal maladies was enough to justify a therapeutic abortion.

Physicians disagreed whether a rubella diagnosis in a pregnant woman justified abortion. As a result hospitals and therapeutic abortion committees were uneven in their application of California's abortion statute when it came to rubella patients. One investigation of several hospitals in the San Francisco Bay Area from August 1, 1964, to August 9, 1965, found that three had performed therapeutic abortions following rubella diagnoses in a woman's first trimester of pregnancy.[74] Another three had performed therapeutic abortions following rubella diagnoses for psychiatric reasons—particularly suicidal tendencies. Another would allow therapeutic abortions for rubella diagnoses within the first fourteen weeks of pregnancy *if* a physician saw the woman while she was infected. Most hospital representatives recognized that their therapeutic abortions did not follow a strict interpretation of the law. While the CDC urged pregnant women to stay away from the disease during the first trimester, they also claimed there was a relatively low risk of having deformed babies.[75] Since the victims of the German measles epidemic were predominately white, middle-class women with normative sexual practices, the outbreak opened the door for discussion about abortion as a public health measure and helped make abortion acceptable (at least in these instances).[76] After all, perfectly healthy white babies were valuable. Disabled babies, at this time, were not.[77]

In accordance with most hospitals' procedures, women who wanted a therapeutic abortion because of rubella exposure would enlist the help of their physicians to petition a hospital's therapeutic abortion committee. One doctor who performed rubella-related abortions for two of his patients at St. Luke's Hospital in San Francisco stated that the hospital did not have "an established policy regarding the handling of therapeutic abortions for rubella cases" and instead considered "each case individually."[78] When law enforcement and the BME discovered this physician's actions, they investigated one of his abortion patients. The patient, whose husband was a physician, stated that she had three children—aged nine, six, and fifteen months. She had her physician perform a house call, and she discovered that she and her nine-year-old son had rubella. She was pregnant at the time, "and neither she nor her husband want[ed] a malformed child."[79] As white, middle-class, heterosexual families weighed scientific risks, abortion "came to be associated with respectable mothers and families in the midst of this epidemic."[80] It became a means through which husbands and wives negotiated and discussed their families' possibilities for the future. It is important to reiterate that in order for abortion to be a respectable, therapeutic procedure, it had to include husband and wife discussions in addition to consultations with a physician. One petition for a rubella-related therapeutic abortion read: "This patient is being submitted for your consideration because of the following information: Her last menstrual period was 7 weeks ago. She had rubella when she was 10 days overdue. She was seen and diagnosed during this illness by her private physician. It is my understanding

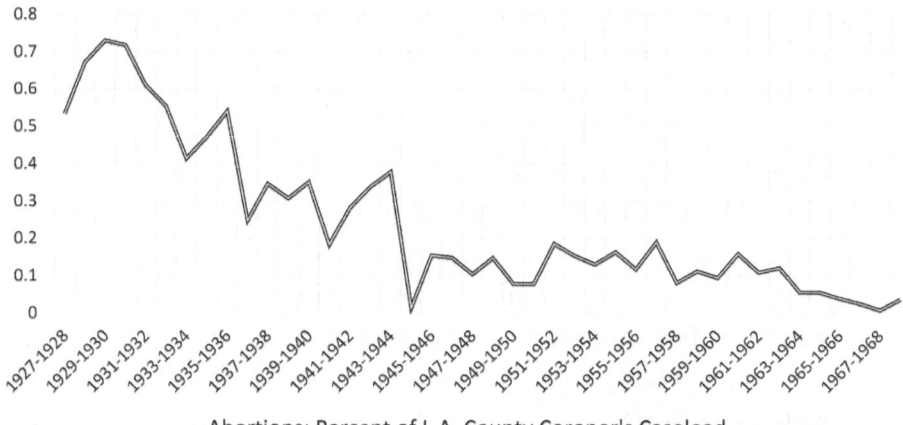

─ Abortions: Percent of L.A. County Coroner's Caseload

6. Abortions as a percentage of Los Angeles County Coroner's Office caseload. Source: Los Angeles County Coroner's Office, annual reports.

that there is a 50% chance of malformation of the embryo in this early stage of the pregnancy. The patient has requested this procedure *and her husband is in accord with it.*"[81]

These were not careless, unwed women. Together with their husbands, they were respectable parents whose concerns about their children's livelihoods fit within the parameters of the postwar period's focus on "the family, sexuality, and reproduction" in addition to "recrafted aspects of better breeding."[82] Together these families utilized a new vocabulary of family planning and genetics to argue for their need for legal abortions when the woman's life was not at risk. These women, who felt justified enough to petition for legal abortions, represented only a portion of the women wanting abortions in the postwar period, and they were typically the subjects ignored when officials attempted to characterize—or mischaracterize—abortion recipients.

According to Zad Leavy, a Beverly Hills attorney and a witness for the San Diego abortion hearing discussed previously, it was impossible to disregard the stereotype of married women who ended up in hospitals as a result of falling down the stairs and spontaneously aborting. Leavy claimed that women suffered only because they went "outside the medical profession" due to their utter "disregard of the law."[83] In many cases, however, it wasn't "disregard of the law" that compelled women to pursue potentially dangerous illegal abortions. Some women used abortions as a means of navigating complex relationships in which they had limited agency. When Barbara Jackson, a college student, discovered she was pregnant again, she was unsure of what to do. She already had a child with her ex-husband, from whom she received $150 per month. She and her boyfriend discussed their options. At first they considered getting married quickly but worried that having a child out of wedlock or shortly after their wedding "would give the father of her 3-year-old child some power to find her an unfit mother and take the child away." Sometimes women chose to have abortions because they were in unhappy marriages and did not want to bring another child into the mix. One nineteen-year-old woman sought an abortion because she and her husband were having marital trouble, had already separated on many occasions, and already had a fourteen-month-old child.[84] In other cases, estranged husbands reported their wives' abortions, or intentions to abort, to authorities as a means of control, in an attempt to shame them, or to exact revenge for their having left.

In 1967 Republican governor Ronald Reagan signed the Therapeutic Abortion Act (TAA), which was based on ALI's model law. The act was an attempt to liberalize the existing abortion law and clarify the criteria for legal abortions. While the basic tenets of this new law provided a measure of uniformity, the law still did not address the issue of choice. It still prohibited abortions but provided exceptions within the first twenty weeks of pregnancy when necessary to preserve the life of the mother, when pregnancy would impair the physical or mental health of the mother, or if a girl under the age of fifteen had become pregnant through rape or incest. Because the model law specifically outlined the reasons for which abortion was allowable—physical and mental health of the mother, disease or abnormality of the fetus, or pregnancy resulting from "felonious intercourse"—it was more rigid and restrictive, leaving little room for interpretation. Furthermore, the model law stated that the abortions had to be performed by licensed physicians in hospitals accredited "by the Joint Commission on Accreditation of Hospitals."[85] Under the watch of zealous hospital committees on therapeutic abortions, women were no longer able to navigate the previously imprecise terrain of abortion through negotiation with their physicians.

It didn't take long for women and physicians to grow tired of the TAA. It made abortions a tiresome bureaucratic process, and it stripped physicians of their autonomy. Unbridled and unburdened by a law they were ignoring, providers of illegal abortions were ultimately the only persons responding to the wants and needs of women. Whether working for moral or ethical reasons or for fee and profit, abortionists—driven by their own ingenuity or connivance—made California's abortion statute untenable. When Dr. Leon Belous referred a woman to an illegal abortionist because he feared she would turn to "butchery" in Tijuana, his case was the final straw before Section 274 of the California Penal Code was successfully overturned.

In the midst of the civil rights struggles of the 1960s second-wave feminists linked the lack of reproductive freedom to social and political inequalities. The ability to control one's own reproduction was a hallmark of individual freedom and also was a step toward larger goals of social and political equality. As reported in the *Los Angeles Times*, one Colorado state legislator noted that women en masse were "realizing that they don't have to be brood animals."[86] The feminist movement of the 1960s and 1970s was centered on debates about personal choice and privacy. Women increasingly linked reproductive control to the burgeoning civil rights movement and claimed that women would never achieve full equality if they lacked control of their own bodies.[87] One abortionist—who described himself as the unofficial abortionist of college women in the Northeast and Midwest—claimed to have performed over thirty thousand abortions during his career. He went to prison six times and described his efforts to provide abortions as a form of "civil disobedience."[88] The challenges to California's abortion statute came at a time when politically underrepresented groups were challenging their inequality in the broader political arena, and it meant that reproductive rights, and a woman's right to control her own body, were a part of the movement for civil rights.

The calls for reproductive control challenged the notion of idealized motherhood. It is not surprising that these calls resulted in backlash. Individuals who opposed abortion and birth control for moral and religious reasons argued that women wanted birth control in order to engage in casual sex and be promiscuous. Evangelicals referenced tradition, family values, and the Bible to bolster their arguments against contraception. Others even claimed that contraception was antifeminist, that women didn't know what they wanted, or that abortion was "a symptom of men's failures"—specifically their failures to take responsibility as the heads of household.[89] Despite this backlash, a loose coalition of women, birth control advocates, and medical professionals united under the banner of birth control, a spectrum of contraceptive rights that also included abortion.[90]

Physicians' perspectives on abortion waxed and waned in response to their own professional concerns. In the second half of the twentieth century physicians feared a large medical-industrial complex would replace their professional autonomy with mega-corporations, insurance companies, and federal oversight, setting fixed costs and removing physicians from economic control of their own labor. Many physicians believed that this was the beginning of an era of "deprofessionalization" or socialized medicine, where federal regulations were stripping them of their autonomy and intervening in their professional lives.[91] When Belous referred a patient to an abortionist without her having a justifiable reason to need an abortion, he may have been responding to a series of regulations that limited his ability to function as an autonomous medical care provider. Regardless of whether that was Belous's intent, he applied pressure to the existing abortion laws and followed in the footsteps of a series of physicians and abortionists who had challenged California's abortion statute before him.

Belous was a Russian-born obstetrician and gynecologist. In 1931 he was licensed to practice medicine in California and was on the attending staff at Cedars of Lebanon Hospital in Los Angeles. For all intents and purposes he was a respected member of the medical community in the city. He was a fellow of the Los Angeles Obstetrical and Gynecological Society, the Abdominal Surgery Society, the Geriatric Society, and the American College of Obstetrics and Gynecology. He was also on the board of directors of the California Committee on Therapeutic Abortion. Outspoken, he "had become a leading crusader against California's anti-abortion laws."[92] Belous was following a long line of medical professionals and abortionists who had responded to women's desires for a medical procedure legally out of reach.

In 1966 Belous referred Cheryl Bryant to an unlicensed physician for an illegal abortion. Belous was found guilty, and in 1969 he appealed his conviction, defending his actions.[93] He believed nineteen-year-old Bryant and her fiancé were determined to terminate the pregnancy one way or another. But Belous told the couple he wanted to *liberalize* the law, not break it. He urged the couple to marry and deal with the pregnancy. Though the couple planned to marry, they worried that having a child would disrupt their professional goals. Belous refused to perform the procedure himself, but he decided to refer Bryant to a physician-friend, Dr. Karl Lairtus. Though Lairtus did not have a license to practice medicine in the United States, he was a licensed physician in Mexico, where he and Belous had met. Belous had witnessed Lairtus's work and found him to be a skilled practitioner. Belous ultimately referred Bryant for the illegal procedure with his colleague because he worried that the couple's desperation would push them to do anything to get an abortion, including "butchery in Tijuana or self-mutilation."[94] Having witnessed the results of several Tijuana abortions, Belous knew of their dangers.[95] He even went so far as to tell the couple that when women went to Tijuana for abortions, they "were taking their lives in their hands."[96] Rather than adhere to the strict interpretation of the abortion statute, Belous believed that Cheryl Bryant's life was in danger, so he referred her to Lairtus.

On May 10, 1966, Lairtus performed an abortion on Cheryl Bryant in a Chula Vista apartment office for $500. The police received a tip from an unknown woman, and when they arrived, they found Cheryl recovering from her procedure. The police arrested Lairtus; while searching the office, they found notebooks that suggested Belous had referred thirteen other women before. Belous was arrested, indicted, and ultimately found guilty of abortion and conspiring to commit abortion. The court of appeals affirmed the lower court's decision, so Belous took his case to the California Supreme Court, where he challenged the constitutionality of California's abortion statute.[97]

When *People of the State of California v. Belous* made its way to the California Supreme Court, the case drew national attention. The press immediately recognized its potential as a landmark for abortion legislation. The professional medical community overwhelmingly respected Belous. The public even felt sympathy for Bryant. In a letter to the *Los Angeles Times* Mrs. Franklin P. Marder of Sherman Oaks expressed that most women were caught in the crosshairs of an increasingly tense battle over abortion legislation. She posed several questions to *Times* readers, asking which was better: for a doctor to perform the procedure safely or to send women off to abortion clinics in Tijuana? Marder argued that countless young girls would be saved by not having to resort to the "thousands of disgusting leeches" who profited from botched abortions. She asked whether it was right to allow men to "force a woman to carry a child" she did not want. Finally, she noted the hypocrisy "of our lawmakers when they send our boys (those who are born and [have] grown to learn the beauties of life) overseas to kill and be killed."[98] To close her letter Marder posed one final question to *Times* readers: "Which is better? Legalizing abortion or allowing countless numbers of senseless deaths to be caused by our *present antiquated laws*?"[99]

Belous believed that the potential "butchery," whether imagined or imminent, was sufficient for him to state that Bryant's life was in danger. His fears were not simply based on some idea about racial, ethnic, or nationalistic superiority. In fact just weeks after Cheryl Bryant's abortion, twenty-four-year-old Elyse Khedari, the wife of a Woodland Hills dentist, was found dead in a physician's office in Tijuana after an illegal abortion. Khedari had made arrangements for the abortion in Chula Vista, California. On Wednesday, June 8, 1966, a man picked her up from a motel at approximately seven thirty in the morning. Her parents were told to meet her at a local bar three hours later to take her back home. Khedari never showed up. Her body was found the following morning. The physician who leased the office where her body was discovered—Dr. Miguel Sanchez Punzo—fled the city with his family.[100] That a physician had performed Khedari's abortion meant little. What set the two abortions apart was geography—Bryant's abortion in the United States, and Khedari's in Mexico—and the fact that the latter died and the former didn't.

When Belous appeared before the California Supreme Court, he and his attorneys argued that California's abortion statute was vague and unconstitutional. Specifically Belous's argument challenged the validity of the "necessary to preserve life" clause in the abortion statute. According to their argument, the requisite phrase had no "clear meaning."[101] Was potential danger an acceptable justification for legal abortion? Or did the danger need to be imminent? Since there was no clear meaning, a physician had to speculate whether, or when, an abortion was medically necessary. However, if arrested and convicted because a jury found the procedure to be *unnecessary*, the physician was "denied his liberty without due process of law."[102]

The California Supreme Court justices debated tirelessly over this case. At the center were two innocuous words: "necessary" and "preserve." The justices found no definition of either word that allowed them to sustain the existing law. Furthermore, the courts had already rejected the interpretation that the statute required certainty or immediacy of death in *People of the State of California v. Abraham R. Abarbanel* (1965) and *People v. Ballard* because the requirement would abridge a woman's constitutional rights—specifically her right to privacy and her right to life (since childbirth involved a risk of death, albeit small). Furthermore, the U.S. Supreme Court's decision in *Griswold v. Connecticut* (1965) held that couples had a right to marital privacy that protected their use of contraceptives to control family size. Since approximately 90 percent of abortions were performed on married women, it might appear that abortions fell within *Griswold*'s purview.[103]

As the arguments continued, there emerged a recognition that abortion laws did not reduce the number of abortions; rather they simply reduced the number of safe abortions. According to contemporary evidence, hygienic abortions performed early in pregnancy resulted in minimal risks to women, while illegal abortions were the greatest cause of maternal death in California.[104] While not all illegal abortions resulted in death, the rate of infection from criminal abortions was also significantly greater than from legal abortions. In an amicus brief submitted to the court, 178 deans of medical schools from California and the rest of the country stated that the unfortunate reality was that the "statute designed in 1850 to protect women from serious risks to life and health has in modern times become a scourge."[105]

After determining that the state's abortion law did not protect women, the court discussed whether the state had an interest in protecting the fetus. In examining legal precedents, the court found that there were differences in how the legal system punished the killing of a born child versus that of an unborn child. In another amicus brief filed on behalf of Belous, a group of lawyers and law professors argued against fetal personhood by stating that "unless an embryo develops to live birth as a child, it achieves no right to inherit, sue, or even receive a birth certificate."[106] The court concluded that fetal rights did not exist. In addition, if fetuses did have rights, then the court could not allow the therapeutic abortions of embryos resulting from incest or rape while forbidding the abortions that resulted from consensual sex. Doing so would mean the court recognized the rights of only *some* embryos and discriminated against others. The court pressed further by saying that even if fetuses did have rights, "fetal rights were insufficient to justify the state in limiting the woman's constitutional rights."[107] Also, the pregnant woman's rights should take precedence over those of the unborn. While the justices debated whether the state's interest in the fetus could ever take precedence over the mother, they decided that they could not forbid any abortion where the result of childbirth could be death.

This case about women's legal access to abortions generated a meaningful discussion about physicians' rights as well. The court recognized that physicians were the responsible parties who had to determine whether women needed abortions. While physicians did not face criminal charges if their refusal to grant an abortion resulted in a woman's death, they could face charges for performing an abortion if they were accused of being too lenient in their application of the statute. If a physician decided a woman was entitled to an abortion and a court decided the physician was wrong, the physician was punished, even if the physician had been exercising an abundance of caution in relation to the woman's life or health. The phrase "necessary to preserve" hinted to a degree of certainty that could not be measured or confirmed by the operating physician. Yet in having the punishments skewed to one side, a physician's rights to due process and his or her right to practice medicine were denied; furthermore, the structure of the law might compel some physicians to refuse all abortions—a position that would then be detrimental to their female patients.

The California Supreme Court ruled in Belous's favor. The basis for his challenge had been an assumption about what border abortions meant for American women. Specifically Belous feared that Cheryl Bryant would "seek an illegal abortion in Tijuana under substandard medical conditions."[108] This assumption rested on several premises, including the following: that illegal abortions were dangerous; that Mexican border towns offered American women an abortion emporium; and, most important, that illegal abortions in Mexico were inferior to abortions in the United States. That the judges took on Belous's case—and California's antiquated law—suggests that the California Supreme Court accepted this fear of border abortions as a reasonable premise. While Mexico offered real relief for countless women, the problem with Mexican abortions was the American law that drove women to them and made them so profitable. While legislators in California grappled with their fears of Tijuana abortions, they failed to recognize that it was actually California's law that made women unsafe. In the end the California Supreme Court found the abortion statute "void for vagueness." The vagueness doctrine posited that law-abiding citizens would not have a clear sense of what was criminal or not. In this case doctors have no clear sense of what

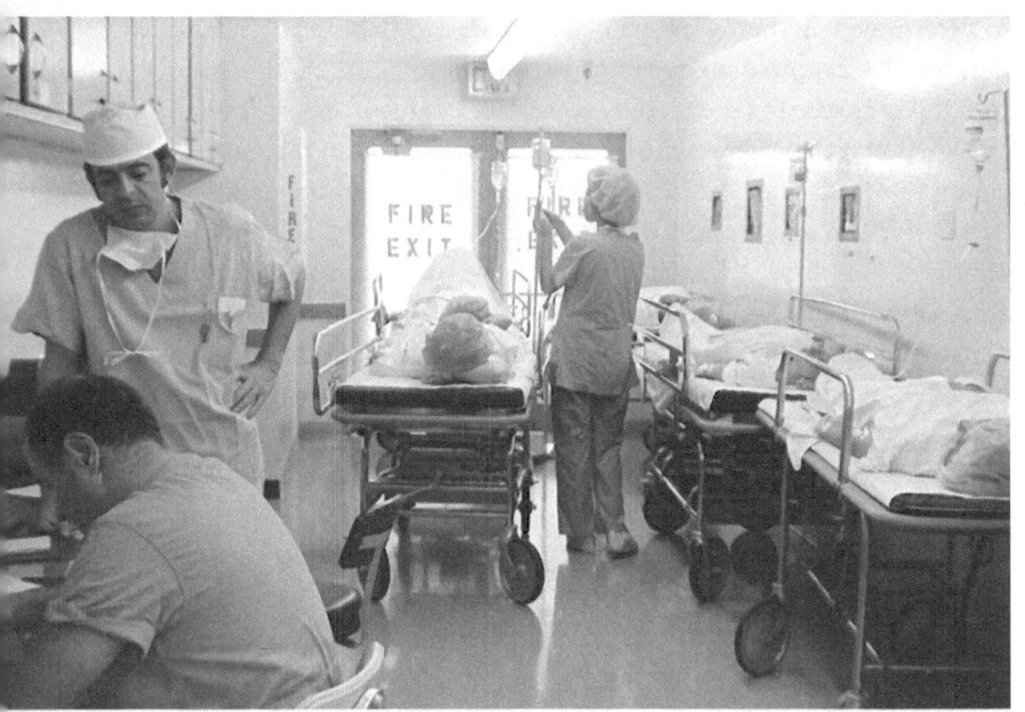

7. Patients on gurneys in corridor as they are prepped for abortion operations at Montclair Hospital, California, 1971. Photo by Harry Chase. *Los Angeles Times* Photographic Archive. Department of Special Collections, Charles E. Young Research Library, UCLA.

conditions would render an abortion criminal or legal, rendering the existing statute vague and void. Thought the court did discuss other wording options to make the law clearer, it didn't know how to fix the language and ultimately gave up.

The *Belous* case promoted the "ultimate goal" of "abortion on request by a licensed physician."[109] Without a legal recognition of fetal rights or personhood, any laws that attempted to prevent women from getting an abortion—at least at the beginning of their pregnancy—denied them bodily autonomy. With that recognition brought to the fore, the "probable fate of all current abortion legislation" was abortion on demand by a licensed medical practitioner.[110] Since physicians had largely been responsible for the criminalization of abortion in the nineteenth century, the *Belous* case—with a recognized and respectable OB/GYN—provided a logical bookend for California's abortion statute.

Since more than half of the country had abortion laws with language similar to California's, other states began to challenge their abortion statutes as well. Shortly after *Belous* was decided, four physicians in New York filed a suit in federal court against their state's abortion statute, and a deluge of others followed. California decriminalized abortion shortly before other states explicitly legalized it. While other states would have followed even if California had not been first, California's ruling in *Belous* represents a shift toward legalization. In the context of the civil rights movement and shifting public sentiments, the California Supreme Court abandoned its efforts to continue criminalizing abortion, perhaps recognizing the sea change that was about to occur.

Conclusion

> The end goal of the anti-abortion movement in America has never been a series of incremental, piecemeal abortion restrictions in red states. Their objective is nothing less than a U.S. Supreme Court decision overturning *Roe v. Wade* and, preferably, federal legislation making abortion illegal even in states . . . like New York or California.
>
> —Robin Marty, 2018

The story of women who have sought abortions despite the legal ramifications is not unique to California. It is a quintessential example of women who have sought to exercise an iota of reproductive control when the law did not allow it. This story is shared by many women in the United States in the pre-*Roe* era. However, the cat-and-mouse game between law enforcement and providers of illegal abortions has not been explored in depth before. Providers of illegal abortions were instrumental to abortion legalization. Providers of illegal abortions were not simply "criminal abortionists"—static, unchanging, forever nefarious; rather they were nuanced, changed over time, and were real people. They were not all simply clichéd back alley butchers (though some were). While it might be convenient to rely on that trope, the reality is that such providers were specialists, physicians, and surgeons, some highly trained, some lacking any skills, and many somewhere in between. Their work shaped and shifted investigative practices and even the law. California led the nation in the history of abortion decriminalization, but this feat was largely due to the work of the illegal abortion providers, who changed and adapted their business practices to continue serving the women who needed them. This book has focused primarily on the role that providers of illegal played in shaping California's legal landscape so as to highlight the *Rankin* decision's significance as a turning point in the prosecution and conviction of such providers and to show how "Tijuana abortions" contributed to abortion decriminalization in the state.

This book disagrees with earlier works that suggest that the period between 1880 and 1960 was characterized by "silence" or a lack of public discourse about abortion. My research shows that women were not silent, and it also shows that they didn't just speak in secret within female networks. Instead women often found themselves speaking openly in trials and for investigators. There were limitations to the agency that these women had, no doubt. Most, if not all, were coerced to testify for the prosecution. However, once they were on the stand, these women spoke their own words and thoughts. Though they had the "ability" to speak openly about their own experiences, these women resented it. They did not seek to speak, and they protested incursions into the intimate details of their lives before the *Buffum* decision paved the way. While women had a chance to speak in the 1940s and 1950s, it was only in the context of the civil rights movement that they realized they could use their voices for change instead of letting the prosecution monopolize their voices for shame, punishment, or humiliation.[1]

While advances in medicine had all but eradicated "justifiable" reasons for therapeutic abortions, the perceived threat of Tijuana abortions revived earlier discussions about physicians' ability to act in the face of assumed, or probable, threats to women's lives or health. In arguments like those of earlier physicians, doctors in the middle of the twentieth century asked whether they were expected to turn away women whose desperation would drive them—quite literally—to the abortionists of Mexico. Citing fears of potential butchery, doctors claimed that *not* being able to provide these women safe abortions was the danger. The malleability and flux that characterized abortion made it difficult to establish "a fixed standard of guilt" to determine whether a physician had acted inappropriately.[2] As a result, after nearly 120 years on the books, the California Supreme Court found its abortion statute void for vagueness, and by 1970 a number of states had pushed for repeals of their existing abortion laws, while several others legalized abortion on demand—including Hawaii, Alaska, New York, and Washington. Nevertheless, the issue had not yet been decided at the federal level, and it would not be until *Roe v. Wade* (1973).

A generation of women would grow up taking the *Roe* decision for granted, even in the wake of a series of legal efforts to chip away at its foundation. As the pendulum began to swing toward abortion liberalization in the 1960s, anti-abortion groups mobilized and became increasingly organized after *Roe*.[3] The passage of the Hyde Amendment in 1976 prohibited federal dollars from being used for abortion. This ruling specifically affected Medicaid users and prohibited poor women (and predominately women of color) from acquiring legal abortions affordably. Though abortions were legal in 1977 when Rosie Jiménez needed an abortion, the $400 fee for a legal abortion was cost-prohibitive for Jiménez; she was a student, single mother, and relied on welfare. Her desire to seek a cheaper, unlicensed abortionist so that she could save her money ended up costing her her life. The U.S. Supreme Court would later decide that states were not required to pay for, or refund, abortions for Medicaid recipients and that the Hyde Amendment did not violate women's constitutional rights.[4] Abortions were legal yet out of reach. But is that different from abortions being illegal? Is legal-but-out-of-reach actually better than just plain illegal? Both situations can result in desperation and extreme circumstances. When Pennsylvania decided to stop allocating Medicaid funds for abortions in 1985, one women's center volunteer noted that the center began to receive phone calls from desperate women asking whether ingesting full bottles of aspirin or falls down the stairs would be enough to induce a miscarriage.[5]

In 1989 Pennsylvania governor Bob Casey signed the Abortion Control Act. This ruling was one of the first attempts by an individual state to restrict abortion rights after *Roe*. The act had several provisions that were designed to limit abortions: informed consent, spousal notification, parental notification, and a twenty-four-hour waiting period. In addition, clinics would be required to report demographic data of women acquiring abortions to the state. Under the "informed consent" provision physicians who were going to provide an abortion had to inform the prospective recipient of abortion alternatives (including adoption, child support, and state assistance); risks associated with abortion; and the estimated gestational age of the fetus so that the woman could make an informed decision. The "spousal notification" provision required women seeking abortions to notify their husbands before the procedure, much as the "parental notification" required unemancipated minors to get consent from their parents or guardians. When Casey signed the act, it was immediately challenged by a number of abortion providers, counselors, and doctors and turned into a class action lawsuit: *Planned Parenthood of Southeastern Pennsylvania v. Casey*.

It was 1992 by the time *Casey* made its way to the U.S. Supreme Court. The attorneys for the appellants argued that Pennsylvania's Abortion Control Act effectively overturned *Roe* since it imposed so many regulations on the women seeking abortions and the doctors providing them. On the other hand, the attorneys for the defendants argued they were not overturning *Roe*; they were simply regulating abortion. It was then a matter of determining whether the provisions of Pennsylvania's Abortion Control Act constituted an "undue burden."[6] In prior challenges to *Roe* the U.S. Supreme Court had already decided two things: (1) the existence of a fundamental right (like abortion) and the enjoyment of a fundamental right were mutually exclusive; and (2) since the state had an interest in potential life, it could favor or encourage pregnancy and childbirth so long as it did not *prevent* women from getting abortions.[7] The majority held on to the three fundamental tenets of the *Roe* decision: women had the right to an abortion before fetal viability, the state had the right to restrict abortions after viability, and the state has an interest in protecting the life of the woman and the potential child. Nevertheless, in their opinion for this case the majority opted for an "undue burden" standard over the existing trimester system since it was more flexible and reflected the state's interest in potential life.[8] Furthermore, the majority felt that Pennsylvania's abortion regulations (with the exception of spousal notification) did not violate the Constitution and did not constitute "undue" burdens.[9]

In moving from the trimester system to a system based in determining whether abortion regulations were "undue burdens," abortion decisions effectively went away from the doctor-patient relationship and back into the courts, where they were subject to legal interpretation. In their biting dissent to *Casey*, the minority wrote the following:

> [The "undue burden" standard has] no basis in constitutional law, and will not result in the sort of simple limitation, easily applied.... To evaluate abortion regulations under that standard, judges will have to make the subjective, unguided determination whether the regulations place "substantial obstacles" in the path of a woman seeking an abortion, undoubtedly engendering a variety of conflicting views. The standard presents nothing more workable than the trimester framework the joint opinion discards, and will allow the Court, under the guise of the Constitution, to continue to impart its own preferences on the States in the form of a complex abortion code.[10]

Casey was a compromise—to an extent. Those who identified as anti-abortion saw *Casey* as a victory. Although abortion remained legal in the United States, the ruling allowed for the creation of new regulations that severely limited abortions or at least made them incredibly inconvenient. Those who identified as pro-choice were at least pleased that the basic tenets of the 1973 decision remained intact; however, the U.S. Supreme Court's protections for abortion are hollow and meaningless if states can make it as inconvenient as possible to obtain an abortion. Since the *Casey* decision a number of states began to follow Pennsylvania's example by implementing their own abortion restrictions (which are put in effect until petitioners are able to prove in court that the restrictions are unduly burdensome).

Now some would argue that an American woman's access to abortion is more defined by *Casey* than it is by *Roe v. Wade*. In an episode of *Last Week Tonight with John Oliver*, the pundit discussed a recent barrage of anti-abortion measures. In Oliver's recorded interview with Andrea Ferrigno, the corporate vice president of Whole Woman's Health, Ferrigno said, "I told her [the reference is to a client] you can come to San Antonio and we can help you here, and she said, 'I can't; I don't have the means—there's no way I can get to San Antonio. So what if I tell you what I have in my kitchen cabinet and you tell me what I can do?'" Oliver noted that the surge of these new restrictions was forcing women to partake in "the most depressing quickfire challenge in *Top Chef* history."[11] It would hardly seem, then, that abortions were accessible—even if they were legal.

Despite their legality, abortions, and the people who provide them, remain stigmatized. According to the Guttmacher Institute, from 2011 to 2013 more states enacted abortion restrictions than in any other previous decade. In 2013 alone twenty-two states passed seventy anti-abortion measures. Today most women of reproductive age in the United States live in areas that are considered hostile to abortion.[12] It is difficult to imagine the previous sentence with the word "abortion" replaced with any other medical procedure. "Majority of American Women Now Live in Areas Considered Hostile to Breast Augmentations" sounds like a piece in *The Onion*, and if physicians and lawmakers suddenly grew averse to vasectomies, appendectomies, or even breast augmentations, they'd be swiftly dismissed by mainline medicine and society.

The midterm elections of 2014—which shifted both houses of Congress to Republican majorities—ensured a continuing assault on women's reproductive rights. In 2015 lawmakers across the nation deliberated over 514 abortion provisions, 396 of which "sought to restrict access to abortion services."[13] The recent barrage of anti-abortion measures overwhelmingly call for mandatory waiting times, parental notification, ultrasounds, and the prevention of the dispensation of the abortion drugs Mifepristone and Misoprostol in clinics without an operating room. Some more radical states have even proposed eliminating legal access to abortion at six to eight weeks' gestation—measures Iowa and Ohio passed among the 308 other abortion restrictions that were introduced in thirty-seven states in the first quarter of 2018.[14] In 2019 more than a dozen states introduced legislation to ban abortion as early as six weeks into a pregnancy—that is, two weeks after a late period. Anti-abortion activists and legislators have been emboldened. While such proposed laws have been subject to legal challenges, they represent part of an aggressive pattern to shorten the window of time a woman has to legally access a safe abortion—or, put another way, they shorten the window of time a woman has to access a safe and legal abortion.

Many, if not all, of these regulations disproportionately affect young women, women of color, low-income women, and women who live in rural areas. Conservatives argue these bills are inconsequential, that they are about preventing fetal pain and protecting women's health and safety. Critics of these restrictions argue that they are efforts to shame and demean women out of getting the procedure or to impose so many regulations that it's infeasible for women to get procedures at all. What has become clear, however, is that conservatives are digging through the wastebasket of abortion legislation's past. Instead of accepting the mountain of evidence that shows that abortion restrictions cause more harm than good, conservatives simply want to make abortion gory again. The *Roe* decision declared that all women had the right to safe, legal abortions in their first trimester; however, depending on where a woman lives, the reality of that decision may not extend to her. As reproductive justice activists and scholars have noted extensively, there is no "choice" and there are no rights where there is no *access*.

Despite the abortion restrictions that are playing out at the national level, abortion is currently "strongly protected" in the state of California.[15] Nationwide 39 percent of American women of reproductive age live in the 90 percent of American counties without abortion clinics, but only about 43 percent of California counties lack an abortion clinic, and these counties account for only about 5 percent of California women.[16] In addition, California does not have any major regulations that restrict either access or state funds to abortion. Nevertheless, a recent U.S. Supreme Court decision in a California case related to abortion will likely have major national implications.

In 2015 California passed the Reproductive FACT Act.[17] The act, which was an amendment to the Health and Safety Code, required that licensed reproductive health facilities provide comprehensive information to patients regarding California programs and services, including access to abortion. Unlicensed health facilities—that is, fake abortion clinics or "crisis pregnancy centers"—would be required to state that they are not licensed medical facilities.[18] Any facility that failed to comply with the bill, which included rules for signs, postings, and fonts, would be subject to a civil penalty. The act was challenged immediately by "a licensed pregnancy center, an unlicensed pregnancy center, and an organization composed of crisis pregnancy centers."[19] Since the act required anti-abortion pregnancy centers to provide information about abortion, the appellants argued that they were being forced to speak against their consciences, and the majority of the Supreme Court justices agreed that the "content-based regulation" sufficiently altered the petitioners' speech and violated their First Amendment rights.[20] While proponents of the law argued that women entering the facilities had the right to truthful information, the victory in this case belongs to fake clinics.[21]

At this point it would appear that overturning *Roe* would be more symbolic than anything. *Roe* has been weakened to the point that its overturning would simply open the door for those states hostile to abortion to recriminalize the procedure—a step that would be a continuation of the processes and patterns that have been ongoing since the 1970s. Yet in the face of such anti-abortion fervor, the rates of abortion in the United States have steadily declined.[22] Some argue that the decline in abortion rates is a result of increased access to effective birth-control methods like condoms, the pill, the morning after pill, and IUDs. Others attribute the decline to increased societal acceptance of single motherhood, coupled with the decreasing importance of marriage. Consequently conservatives have resigned themselves, perhaps even embraced, single parenthood as an alternative to abortion.[23] Though fewer people are having abortions, abortions have not lost their significance. Abortion restrictions prevent women from exercising the right to make decisions of their own.[24] Historically laws that restrict abortion have done little more than make the procedure more dangerous for the women seeking them.[25] Abortion laws have not discouraged desperate women from submitting themselves to unknown practitioners—as, I hope, this book has illustrated. Rather abortion restrictions do nothing but advance the notion that women cannot be trusted with their own bodies.

AFTERWORD

To the Back Alley and Border again? Abortion Post-*Dobbs*

On May 2, 2022, an unprecedented, leaked U.S. Supreme Court opinion draft signaled that abortion rights were at risk. The ninety-eight-page document indicated that the court majority believed "*Roe* and *Casey* must be overruled," and that abortion laws should be left to state legislators to decide. When the official decision was handed down on June 24, 2022, outrage was plentiful, but few were truly shocked. *Dobbs v. Jackson* was a Mississippi case whose central issue was to determine whether the state's Gestational Age Act was constitutional. The Act prohibited abortions past fifteen weeks gestation except in cases of medical emergency, "or in the case of a severe fetal abnormality."[1] With this decision, the U.S. Supreme Court essentially upheld legal vagueness and demonstrated how a general ignorance about women's health permeates U.S. political decision-making.

Calculating gestational age is not the same as measuring height, weight, or even age. In fact, an OB-GYN 101 course module in the Johns Hopkins School of Medicine states, "If everyone had normal, regular periods, every 28 days, and could remember exactly when their last period was, and ovulation always occurred on day #14 of the menstrual cycle, then gestational age determination would be easy."[2] The sheer number of ways to calculate gestational age suggests it cannot be determined without some margin of error. Would a physician who judged a pregnancy to be at fourteen weeks gestational age, who performed an abortion, be denied due process because another physician estimated the gestational age to be sixteen weeks? Or fifteen weeks?

As many of the examples in this book have shown, medical emergencies and abnormalities were not easy to define in the 1950s and 1960s, and they are even less distinguishable today. Our pronatalist society often fails to recognize that pregnancy is not health neutral. Some women experience pregnancy with few complications; others lose the ability to perform routine tasks.

For all women, the maternal mortality rate in the United States was higher in 2020 than it was in 2019. It's even worse for Black women, who had a maternal mortality rate of 55.3 deaths per 100,000 live births—a significant increase from 2019 when the maternal mortality rate for Black women was 44 deaths per 100,000 live births. According to the *American Journal for Managed Care*, the United States ranks lowest among other developed nations in maternal care and mortality.[3] Based on those statistics alone, it might appear that being pregnant in America, and especially Black and pregnant in America, already constitutes a medical emergency.

Given the risks associated with pregnancy and delivery in the United States, taking away federal protections to terminate pregnancies is tone deaf and will also have disastrous consequences. In the few months since *Dobbs* was decided, several states have already implemented abortion restrictions with similar wording to Mississippi's Gestational Age Act. As one can imagine, this has created problems for pregnant persons and medical professionals who now fear arrest for providing medical treatment (abortions) to women experiencing ectopic pregnancies, who are pregnant with fetuses with fatal abnormalities, or who have experienced spontaneous abortions (miscarriages). In several of these cases, women were denied prompt medical treatment or were urged to return to the hospitals when their lives and health were *clearly* at risk. For a court claiming its ruling is consistent with protecting life, its cavalier attitude toward women's health and safety is decidedly telling.

Aside from vagueness in calculating gestational age and medical emergencies, there is also vagueness in determining exceptions like a "fetal abnormality." In the 1960s during the Thalidomide tragedy and the Rubella outbreak, concerns over the possibility of fetal abnormalities in the era before disability rights prompted some medical professionals and members of the public to demand access to abortion and more liberal abortion laws. Now, however, as Katie O'Connell so eloquently argued, the anti-abortion movement "has successfully seized control" over the conversation about disability and abortion. Within the anti-abortion movement, "fetal disability narratives are central to pro-life rhetoric, where they decry abortions of fetuses with disabilities as a form of eugenics," thus making the anti-abortion movement's co-opting of disability rights difficult to address.[4] No one wants to sound like they are espousing eugenic ideologies.

Nevertheless, a reproductive *justice* framework stresses personal autonomy and the ability for individuals to make decisions for themselves. Often people's decisions to terminate pregnancies stem from the options that they have. Given the state of our health care system and the lack of adequate programs and funding to support parents in general—and especially parents of children with disabilities—the anti-abortion movement's seeming embrace of individuals with disabilities is hollow at best.

Furthermore, as we saw in the past and will continue to witness, safe and legal abortions will ultimately become luxuries that are only accessible to some. In his analysis of California's 1967 Therapeutic Abortion Act (TAA), one legal scholar was able to recognize one of the main problems that plagued hospital therapeutic abortions and their committees: inequity.[5]

Legal, therapeutic abortions were often easiest for white women of means to acquire. Even after the TAA, poor women and women of color still relied heavily on illegal abortions. In a 1970 report to the California State Legislature, the Bureau of Maternal and Child Health found that nonwhite women underwent illegal abortions at a rate of 313 per 1,000 conceptions, while white women underwent illegal abortions at a rate of 103 per 1,000. 98 percent of the abortions performed on nonwhite women were illegal.[6] When we look at data for those who acquired therapeutic abortions from 1967 through

1969, between 85.8 and 91 percent of all therapeutic abortion recipients were white women, most of these patients used insurance or private payment, and less than 15 percent of these abortions were performed in county hospitals—meaning most were performed at private hospitals.[7]

As some states begin to ban abortion or implement restrictions that make them more difficult to access, women with resources will be able to skirt around their own state laws by traveling to other destinations where abortion is still legal, paying out of pocket for services by sympathetic medical professionals, or purchasing abortion drugs through the mail. However, this, too, may be at risk given the current lawsuit pending in Texas that may result in a nationwide ban on mifepristone (based on completely unfounded arguments about its safety and efficacy).

In the 1969 case *People v. Belous*, the California Supreme Court examined the state's abortion statute. The court stated:

> The problem caused by the vagueness of the statute is accentuated because ... the doctor is ... delegated the duty to determine whether a pregnant woman has the right to an abortion and the physician acts at his peril if he determines that the woman is entitled to an abortion. He is subject to prosecution for a felony and to deprivation of his right to practice medicine if his decision is wrong. Rather than being impartial, the physician has a "direct, personal, substantial, pecuniary interest in reaching a conclusion" that the woman should not have an abortion. . . . The inevitable effect of such delegation may be to deprive a woman of an abortion when ... she would be entitled to such an operation, because the state ... has skewed the penalties in one direction: *no* criminal penalties are imposed where the doctor refused to perform a necessary operation, even if the woman should in fact die because the operation was not performed. . . . A woman whose life is at stake may be as effectively condemned to death as if the law flatly prohibited all abortions.[8]

This also holds true for the Mississippi Gestational Age Act and many of the other post-*Dobbs* abortion restrictions. In crafting an abortion law that limits legal abortion to only certain criteria, physicians will be tasked with determining whether their patients fit these narrow categories. However, physicians will also be the ones at risk of penalties if their judgement is challenged. In the 1950s and 1960s, California attempted to change their abortion laws. Instead they bureaucratized a medical decision best left to patients and their own medical providers.

The U.S. Supreme Court's decision in *Dobbs v. Jackson* will have negative consequences for women of childbearing age throughout the country. The reality is that many of those who are anti-abortion believe abortion is a black-and-white issue when in reality it is mostly gray. If those who were anti-abortion listened to the voices of those who had abortions instead of pontificating to them, they might be able to see that. In bureaucratizing health care, we're delaying and making inaccessible treatment many women will need. In compelling birth without increasing access to health care or welfare, we're showing we care more about an uncomplicated, abstract, potential life than a real child or an adult pregnant person. You can't have it both ways. You cannot force birth or life without some guarantee about quality of life.

Ultimately all the anti-abortion movement has shown us so far is that they lack the ability to learn from the past. As anti-choice legislators continue to deny science and recycle bad law, pregnant people will suffer.

NOTES

Introduction

Epigraph: Laws of the State of California, *Statutes and Amendments to the Codes*, 1935, Section 274.

1. The name has been changed.
2. Joel M. Taylor, Special Agent, Bureau of Criminal Identification and Investigation Report, California Department of Justice, March 14, 1962, BME, F3760:821.
3. Quoted in Joel M. Taylor, Special Agent, Bureau of Criminal Identification and Investigation Report, California Department of Justice, March 14, 1962, BME, F3760:821.
4. Luker, *Abortion and the Politics of Motherhood*, 40.
5. Reagan, *When Abortion Was a Crime*, 21.
6. *People of the State of California v. Reginald L. Rankin, et al.* (1937). I will use "PCAR," "Watts-Rankin Outfit," and "*Rankin* case" interchangeably. All refer to the PCAR and the trial *People of the State of California v. Reginald L. Rankin et al.*
7. *People of the State of California v. Reginald L. Rankin, et al.* (1937).
8. *People of the State of California v. Buffum*, 256P.2d 317 (1953).
9. Luker, *Abortion and the Politics of Motherhood*; and Reagan, *When Abortion Was a Crime*.
10. Alexander Fleming discovered penicillin, the first antibiotic, in 1928. His findings were first published in 1929. Though research began in the 1930s, penicillin was not widely used until the 1940s.
11. Luker, *Abortion and the Politics of Motherhood*, 100.
12. Gootenberg, "Talking about the Flow," 13–46.
13. Gootenberg, "Talking about the Flow," 25.
14. Gootenberg, "Talking about the Flow," 33.
15. Gootenberg, "Talking about the Flow," 38.

1. From Back Alley

Epigraph: Philip M. Lovell, "Care of the Body—After the Abortion?" *Los Angeles Times*, December 20, 1931.

1. John J. Donovan, "Find Parts of Woman's Body in Suit Case in Merrimac," *Boston Daily Globe*, September 2, 1923, 1.
2. Donovan, "Find Parts of Woman's Body," 1, 8.
3. Donovan, "Find Parts of Woman's Body," 1, 8.
4. See Brodie, *Contraception and Abortion in Nineteenth-Century America*, 253–88; L. Gordon, *Woman's Body, Woman's Right*, 36–38; Dayton, "Taking the Trade," 20; and Acevedo, "Abortion in Early America," 163.
5. Reagan, *When Abortion Was a Crime*, 8–9.
6. Gibson, "The Termination of the Quickening Doctrine."
7. Mohr, *Abortion in America*, 3; and Brind'Amour, "Quickening."
8. Reagan, *When Abortion Was a Crime*, 9.
9. Dayton, "Taking the Trade."
10. Acevedo, "Abortion in Early America," 163 (my emphasis).
11. See Dayton, "Taking the Trade," 20; and Brodie, *Contraception and Abortion in Nineteenth-Century America*, 253–88.
12. Luker, *Abortion and the Politics of Motherhood*, 58.
13. Mohr, *Abortion in America*, 7.
14. Mohr, *Abortion in America*, 20–45.
15. Mohr, *Abortion in America*, 32–33.
16. Engelman, *A History of the Birth Control Movement in America*, 10.
17. Mohr, *Abortion in America*, 22.
18. California Grand Jury (Nevada County), "Indictment of Julia Moore," September 19, 1859, Huntington Library.
19. For an analysis of abortion in mid-nineteenth-century California, see Hurtado, *Intimate Frontiers*.
20. Crimes and Punishment Act § 45 (Stats 1850 ch 99 § 45).
21. California's abortion statute underwent a series of revisions. The original abortion statute was introduced in 1850 and was revised in 1861, 1872, and 1935, but the basic tenets remained the same.
22. A curette was a gynecological tool that was shaped like a spoon or scoop and was used to remove material from the uterus.
23. Tone, *Devices and Desires*, 14.
24. Comstock himself probably did not distinguish between contraception and abortion; however, to use precise language, I have separated the two.
25. Tone, *Devices and Desires*, 8.

26. For more on Anthony Comstock, see A. L. Bates, *Weeder in the Garden of the Lord*; Beisel, *Imperiled Innocents*; and Comstock, *Traps for the Young*.
27. Albanesi and Olivetti, *Maternal Health and the Baby Boom*; Sheppard-Towner Maternity and Infancy Act, 42 Stat. 224 (1921); "Achievements in Public Health, 1900–1999."
28. Unfortunately because of the nature of my sources, I am arguably supporting a generalization that suggests that abortion is dangerous or deadly. However, as mentioned, because of the social stigma associated with premarital sex, sex outside of procreation, and abortion, most women who successfully had abortions did not leave evidence of them in the public record. Because I focus on documented abortions, I must refer to the records that made abortion visible.
29. Reagan, *When Abortion Was a Crime*, 125.
30. D'Emilio and Freedman, *Intimate Matters*.
31. Horatio Storer, "Contributions to Obstetric Jurisprudence," *North American Medico-Chirurgical Review*. Reprinted in Storer, *On Criminal Abortion in America*, 5.
32. Storer, "Contributions to Obstetric Jurisprudence." Reprinted in Storer, *On Criminal Abortion in America*, 10.
33. Drake, *What a Young Wife Ought to Know*, 124.
34. Reagan, *When Abortion Was a Crime*, 116.
35. Beisel and Kay, "Abortion, Race, and Gender in Nineteenth-Century America"; Brodie, *Contraception and Abortion in Nineteenth-Century America*, 266–75; Higham, *Strangers in the Land*; and Schrag, *Not Fit for Our Society*.
36. Storer, *Criminal Abortion*, 4.
37. My own data from the Los Angeles County Coroner's Office will show such a personification in subsequent chapters. In addition, Leslie Reagan has also referred to this personification in *When Abortion Was a Crime*, 39.
38. Lears, *Rebirth of a Nation*; McGerr, *A Fierce Discontent*; and Wiebe, *The Search for Order*.
39. "Shame and a Shroud," *National Police Gazette*, October 22, 1881, 3.
40. "Ruin and Death," *Los Angeles Herald*, February 12, 1882, 3.
41. "Ruin and Death," 3.
42. "Ruin and Death," 3.
43. Lears, *Rebirth of a Nation*; McGerr, *A Fierce Discontent*; and Wiebe, *The Search for Order*.
44. Davis, *Living Up to the Ads*; Dumenil, *The Modern Temper*; and Lemons, *The Woman Citizen*.
45. Bailey, *From Front Porch to Back Seat*, 13.
46. Margaret Sanger et al., *Birth Control Review* 1, no. 1 (February 1917): 3.

47. Baker, *Margaret Sanger*; Chesler, *Woman of Valor*; Coates, *Margaret Sanger and the Origin of the Birth Control Movement*; "Biographical Sketch."
48. Engelman, *A History of the Birth Control Movement in America*.
49. Letter from Albert Carter, BME Special Agent, to Dr. O. D. Young, June 30, 1926, BME, F3760:819.
50. California Penal Code §1108 (my emphasis).
51. California Penal Code §1108 and §1111.
52. Federal Rules of Evidence, Legal Information Institute, Cornell Law School, https://www.law.cornell.edu/rules/fre.
53. "Dying Declaration," Wex Legal Dictionary, Legal Information Institute, Cornell Law School, https://www.law.cornell.edu/wex/dying_declaration.
54. Orenstein, "Her Last Words," 1412.
55. This idea obviously existed well before the time period under discussion here. See, for example, Shakespeare's play *King John*: "Have I not hideous death within my view / Retaining but a quantity of life / Which bleeds away, even as a form of wax / Resolveth from this figure 'gainst the fire? / What in the world should make me now deceive / Since I must lose the use of all deceit? Why should I then be false, since it is true / That I must die here and live hence by truth?" William Shakespeare, *King John*, act V, scene IV (1596), OpenSourceShakespeare, George Mason University, https://www.opensourceshakespeare.org/views/plays/playmenu.php?WorkID=kingjohn.
56. LACC, vol. 312, pp. 142, 198, 233.
57. Draper, "Criminal Abortion with a 'Dying Declaration,'" 461.
58. Draper, "Criminal Abortion with a 'Dying Declaration,'" 461.
59. Orenstein, "Her Last Words," 1418.
60. This stance also speaks to a general attitude toward dying declarations. They were only recognized, or accepted, in homicide cases due to the exigent circumstances.
61. "Criminal Abortion," 36.
62. "Woman Freed on Charge of Murder," *San Francisco Call*, March 8, 1910, 8.
63. "Woman Freed on Charge of Murder," 8.
64. Reagan, *When Abortion Was a Crime*, 126.
65. Reagan *When Abortion Was a Crime*, 126–27, 131.
66. MacGibbon, "The Abortion Narrative in American Film," 10.
67. MacGibbon, "The Abortion Narrative in American Film," 36.
68. MacGibbon, "The Abortion Narrative in American Film," 38.
69. Reagan, *When Abortion Was a Crime*, 167.
70. "Historical Sketch of Galen R. Hickok," 397.
71. "Historical Sketch of Galen R. Hickok," 397; and Grant Historical Society and Museum, *The First 100 Years*.

72. Grant Historical Society and Museum, *The First 100 Years*.
73. "Historical Sketch of Galen R. Hickok," 397.
74. Zangwell's family included his wife, Julia; Julia's daughter from an earlier marriage, Madeline; and Zangwell and Julia's son, Max.
75. "Historical Sketch of Galen R. Hickok," 397.
76. Communication from California BME Attorney H. T. Morrow to BME, May 15, 1911. Cited in "Historical Sketch of Galen R. Hickok," 398.
77. An article in the *California State Journal of Medicine* claimed that "Dr. Hickok" lived in Los Angeles until 1914.
78. "Historical Sketch of Galen R. Hickok," 397–98; *Pacific Medical Journal* 54, no. 6 (June 1, 1911): 335; "Says Doctor Performed a Criminal Operation," *San Francisco Chronicle*, September 22, 1912, 64.
79. Some sources list Dr. Reinhart's name as Dr. Allen Reinhart and others as Dr. Reinhart Allen (or variations thereof).
80. "Physicians Convicted"; "Mystery Castle Raided," *Daily Oregonian*, September 4, 1920; and "Bones Dug Up at 'Castle,'" *San Francisco Chronicle*, September 2, 1920, 1.
81. "Girls' Tales Shake Calm of Dr. Hickok," *San Francisco Chronicle*, December 4, 1920, 4; *Sausalito News* 35, no. 50 (December 11, 1920); *People v. Hickok*, 204 P. 555 (Cal. Ct. App. 1921); "Convicted Physician Loses on Appeal," *San Francisco Chronicle*, December 31, 1921.
82. "Dr. Hickok Slated to Lose License," *Berkeley Daily Gazette*, May 11, 1921; and "Proprietor of 'Castle' Once Here," *Los Angeles Times*, September 8, 1920, III 4.
83. "Sleuths Look for Bodies of Missing Girls," *Oakland Tribune*, August 31, 1920, 1.
84. "Mottard's Patient Maimed after Death, Grand Jury Is Told," *New York Herald, New York Tribune*, April 24, 1925, 6.
85. "'Dr. Green' Held on Homicide Count," *New York Times*, April 10, 1925, 3.
86. "Autopsy of Mrs. Allison Indicates an Operation," *New York Herald, New York Tribune*, April 17, 1925, 11.
87. "Autopsy of Mrs. Allison Indicates an Operation," 11; "Mottard's Patient Maimed after Death, Grand Jury Is Told," *New York Herald, New York Tribune*, April 24, 1925, 6.
88. "Seek Missing Infants on Long Island Farm," *Bridgeport Telegram*, April 10, 1925, 1.
89. "Crime Bared in Probe of Kidnaping," *Ogden Standard Examiner*, April 9, 1935, 1.
90. "'Dr. Green' Held on Homicide Count," *New York Times*, April 10, 1925, 3.
91. "Mottard Is Arrested as Baby Slayer," *Appleton Post Crescent*, April 24, 1925, 7; "Chiropractor Held in Jail," *Ogden Standard Examiner*, April 10, 1925, 3; "Baby Farm Suspect in Cops' Nets," *Helena Independent*, April 9, 1925, 1.

92. "Parents Waver on Girl's Identity," *Fitchburg Sentinel*, April 9, 1925, 4.
93. "Parents Waver on Girl's Identity," 4; and "Search for Bodies of Missing Babies on Doctor's Farm," *Hartford Courant*, April 10, 1925, 1.
94. "Mottard Is Out on Bail," *New York Times*, May 5, 1925, 11.
95. Luker, *Abortion and the Politics of Motherhood*, 75.

2. Regular Physicians

Epigraph: John Campbell, "The Position of the Medical Practitioner Called in to Attend a Case of Procured Abortion," *British Medical Journal*, December 10, 1921.

1. McWilliams, *Southern California*, 98.
2. "Good Thing for Glendale," *Los Angeles Times*, August 14, 1904, A1.
3. "Eat California Fruit," 5.
4. For more on California as a health destination, see Baur, *The Health Seekers of Southern California*; Molina, *Fit to Be Citizens?*; Rothman, *Living in the Shadow of Death*; A. M. Stern, *Eugenic Nation*.
5. LACMA, vol. 1.
6. California medical societies allowed female physicians to join their membership from the beginning. There was at least one woman present at LACMA's first meeting in 1871. In April 1876 the California Medical Association voted to admit women on the same basis as men. In June of that same year the AMA admitted the first female physician to its ranks.
7. Wilson, "Medical College of the Pacific."
8. P. Mitchell, *Coyote Nation*.
9. I refer to "modernity" here in the sense that medicine, as a *profession*, had become increasingly specialized—and separate—from other trades. Though there were many religious physicians, the majority overwhelmingly believed the field was rational, scientific, and progressive. Medical associations and societies also operated a form of surveillance to ensure that their constituents adhered to the tenets of the profession. See Foucault, *Discipline and Punish*, esp. 170–94.
10. P. Mitchell, *Coyote Nation*, 125–26.
11. Crimes and Punishment Act § 45 (Stats 1850 ch 99 § 45), as amended Stats 1861 ch 521 § 1.
12. McWilliams, *Southern California*, 114.
13. Ulin, *Literary Los Angeles*, 51.
14. "In 1890, 24 percent of all American homes had running water. And not until the 1930s would the entire urban population have running water, while most of the rural population would not until after 1945." Hoy, *Chasing Dirt*, 15.

15. Molina, *How Race Is Made in America*, 27; A. Kaplan, *The Anarchy of Empire in the Making of U.S. Culture*.
16. McWilliams, *Southern California*, 339.
17. Wagner, *Film Folk*, 257.
18. Jou, "Calorie Counting."
19. Peters, *Diet and Health with Key to the Calories*.
20. Quoted in Lulu Hunt Peters, "Diet and Health: Wasn't It?" *Los Angeles Times*, October 6, 1926, A7.
21. Richard Henry Little, "Barkless Airedales of Hollywood," *Chicago Daily Tribune*, October 28, 1923, E1.
22. Wagner, *Film Folk*, 250, 252.
23. Antoinette Donnelly, "Reducing with the Stars," *Chicago Daily Tribune*, October 18, 1925, B4.
24. Donnelly, "Reducing with the Stars," B4.
25. Klumph and Klumph, *Screen Acting*, 215–16.
26. Marcie Bianco and Merryn Johns, "Classic Hollywood's Secret: Studios Wanted Their Stars to Have Abortions," *Vanity Fair*, July 15, 2016, www.vanityfair.com/hollywood2016/07/classic-hollywood-abortion. The article also provides suggestions for other readings on Hollywood scandals.
27. Willis Kent Productions, *Road to Ruin*.
28. McWilliams, *Southern California*.
29. A letter from Los Angeles mayor Frank Shaw to members of the Los Angeles City Council, dated July 23, 1937, reads as follows: "I wish to state that during the time I was a member of the Los Angeles County Board of Supervisors many hundreds of thousands of dollars of public funds were saved annually through repatriation of migratory indigents who came to us from other parts of the United States and from Mexico. Under the State Welfare Act as amended in 1933 which requires residence in the County for one year and in the State for three years before an individual is eligible to public aid, our practice was to give indigent transients such emergency assistance as might be necessary to prevent suffering from want of food and clothing, and then to return them promptly to their communities of legal residence where the responsibility for their care properly belonged. By so doing, and adhering to the provisions of the Social Welfare Act, we protected the interests of our own citizens, of whom there are approximately 88,000 employable now dependant [sic] upon relief in this County. Indigent transients are annually willing to accept jobs at a much lower rate of pay and lower standard of working conditions that our own residents expect, which makes enforcement of the Welfare Act necessary for the defense of jobs and employment for our own citizens, as

well as [for] saving millions of dollars in taxes." Los Angeles City Council Files, 1937-3014.
30. Natalia Molina has shown the correlation between the onset of the Depression and the racial scapegoating and racism that became prevalent in the 1920s and 1930s. Alexandra Stern and Miroslava Chávez-García have also made connections between the sterilization of ethnic Mexicans and concerns about eugenics and criminal heredity respectively. See Sánchez, *Becoming Mexican American*, 210.
31. Chávez-García, *States of Delinquency*, 69–70 (my emphasis).
32. Chávez-García, *States of Delinquency*, 83.
33. *Buck v. Bell*, 274 U.S. 200 (1927). In this case the U.S. Supreme Court upheld the constitutionality of Virginia's sterilization law. Virginia's law—which had been modeled on that of the ERO—paved the way for states to begin sterilizing en masse.
34. Stern, *Eugenic Nation*, 110, 112.
35. Stern, *Eugenic Nation*, 113.
36. Stern, *Eugenic Nation*, 111.
37. Stern, *Eugenic Nation*, 24.
38. In *The History of Sexuality* Michel Foucault describes sexuality as a "dense transfer point for relations of power." He goes on to outline four strategies that became essential to power and knowledge production in the domain of sexuality, one of those being "a hysteriziation of women's bodies." Under this strategy women's bodies were analyzed "as being thoroughly saturated with sexuality; whereby it was integrated into the sphere of medical practices, by reason of a pathology intrinsic to it; whereby, finally it was placed in organic communication with the social body (whose regulated fecundity it was supposed to ensure), the family space (of which it had to be a substantial and functional element), and the life of children (which it produced . . .)." Foucault, *The History of Sexuality*, 104.
39. Molina, *Fit to be Citizens?*, 117.
40. The highest number of major mine disasters in the United States up to that point was recorded in 1910, with nineteen coal mining disasters and six metal/nonmetal mining disasters. It was also the first year that the Pullman Company made mine-rescue railroad cars. In the first five years of their use there were "300 mine accidents, including explosions, fires, and cave-ins." See Sherard, "Arizona Fatal Mining Accidents."
41. L. Gordon, *The Great Arizona Orphan Abduction*, 57.
42. "Tragedy Halts Delphine Walsh's Rise from Obscurity," *Los Angeles Times*, May 11, 1929, A3; and various playbill listings and announcements in newspapers.

43. There are some conflicting dates in the sources. Some claim Delphine saw Drs. Traxler and Lantern on April 27, 1929, and died April 29, 1929, while the majority of the sources say she died on May 2 or 3, 1929 (late night or early morning).
44. Banner, *American Beauty*, 183.
45. A. Fine, "Scandal, Social Conditions, and the Creation of Public Attention," 300; and Johnson, "Fatty Arbuckle Trials (1921–1922)," 242–43.
46. "Murder Charge Placed against Fatty Arbuckle," *Indianapolis Star*, September 12, 1921, 1.
47. Quoted in "Murder Charge Placed against Fatty Arbuckle," 2.
48. Quoted in M. Russell, "Drive Out the Rotters," 104.
49. M. Russell, "Drive Out the Rotters," 104.
50. M. Russell, "Drive Out the Rotters," 104.
51. "Movie Morals under Fire," *New York Times*, February 12, 1922, 80.
52. "Movie Morals under Fire," 80.
53. G. A. Fine, "Scandal, Social Conditions, and the Creation of Public Attention," 298.
54. G. A. Fine, "Scandal, Social Conditions, and the Creation of Public Attention," 304.
55. Banner, *American Beauty*, 183–84.
56. "Dancer's Death Quiz Continues," *Los Angeles Times*, May 8, 1929, A12; "Dancer Clews Lead Nowhere," *Los Angeles Times*, May 10, 1929, A5; and "Dancer Death Trial Upset," *Los Angeles Times*, September 3, 1929, A2.
57. "Coroner Attacks Woman and Is Jailed," *Los Angeles Times*, December 18, 1907.
58. "Dr. Lanterman under Arrest," *Los Angeles Times*, July 20, 1916, 111; "Physician's Hearing Set in September," *Los Angeles Times*, July 21, 1916, 116; and "Dr. Lanterman Loses License," *Los Angeles Times*, October 7, 1916, 113.
59. "Dr. Lanterman under Arrest," *Los Angeles Times*, July 20, 1916, 111.
60. "Coroner Attacks Woman and Is Jailed," *Los Angeles Times*, December 18, 1907; Larry Harnisch, "What's in That Embalming Fluid?" *Daily Mirror*, December 18, 2006; "Dr. Lanterman Loses License," *Los Angeles Times*, October 7, 1916, 113.
61. "Physicians Face Death Complaint," *Los Angeles Times*, May 5, 1929, D8.
62. Reagan, *When Abortion Was a Crime*, 131.
63. Reagan, *When Abortion Was a Crime*, 131.
64. "Dancer Clews Lead Nowhere," *Los Angeles Times*, May 10, 1929, A5.
65. "Dancer's Death Quiz Continues," *Los Angeles Times*, May 8, 1929, A12.
66. "Dancer Clews Lead Nowhere," *Los Angeles Times*, May 10, 1929, A5; "Dead Dancer's Letter Sought," *Los Angeles Times*, May 9, 1929, A5; "Dancer's Death Quiz Continues," *Los Angeles Times*, May 8, 1929, A12.

67. "Dancer's Death Quiz Continues," *Los Angeles Times*, May 8, 1929, A12; "Tragedy Halts Delphine Walsh's Rise from Obscurity," *Los Angeles Times*, May 11, 1929, A3; "Dancer Clews Lead Nowhere," *Los Angeles Times*, May 10, 1929, A5.
68. "Legal Debate Delays Trial," *Los Angeles Times*, August 29, 1929, A2.
69. "Twelve Doctors Accused," *Los Angeles Times*, October 3, 1929, 8.
70. "Medical Board Dismisses Case," *Los Angeles Times*, October 23, 1929, 8.
71. "Doctor Asks Court to Lift License Ban," *Los Angeles Times*, April 15, 1931, 19; "Medical License Plea Up Today," *Los Angeles Times*, April 24, 1933, A5.
72. Traxler and Lanterman are possibly in earlier editions of the BME directory as well, but I was unable to locate earlier editions where their names might be listed.
73. Hadley Meares, "Lanterman House: The Enduring Legacy and Forgotten Scandals of La Cañada's First Family," KCET, August 6, 2015, https://www.kcet.org/history-society/lanterman-house-the-enduring-legacy-and-forgotten-scandals-of-la-canadas-first.
74. "Youths Named in Dead Girl's Diary Sought in Murder Inquiry," *Los Angeles Times*, September 23, 1930, A12.
75. "Youths Named in Dead Girl's Diary," A12.
76. "Evidence Ready in Girl's Death," *Los Angeles Times*, September 24, 1930, A5.
77. "Doctor Blamed in Girl's Death," *Los Angeles Times*, September 27, 1930, A2.
78. "Doctor Tells of Girl's Death," *Los Angeles Times*, December 10, 1930, A19; "Dr. W. C. Fiske Goes to Trial," *Los Angeles Times*, December 9, 1930, A8.
79. "Girl Hunted in Death Case," *Los Angeles Times*, December 11, 1930, A8; "Dr. Fiske Case Jury Locked Up," *Los Angeles Times*, December 13, 1930, A2.
80. Harry Carr, "The Lancer," *Los Angeles Times*, May 14, 1929, A1.
81. See, for example, L. Gordon, *Woman's Body, Woman's Right*, xii, 3; and MacKinnon, "Feminism, Marxism, Method, and the State," 515.
82. The earliest year for which the Los Angeles County Coroner's Office had an annual report was 1927.
83. I made no distinction among surgeons, chiropractors, or other types of medical professionals who performed the procedures. However, I cannot attest to the categories the coroner used to identify these professionals.
84. LACC, book 312, 233. The probable cause for the abortion was listed separately from the cause of death, which in Sullivan's case was listed as "endometritis from abortion of foetis with septicemia," meaning inflammation or irritation of the endometrium (lining of the uterus) caused by an infection—in this case, septicemia, a life-threatening blood infection that was quite common in abortion deaths.
85. Reagan, *When Abortion Was a Crime*, 43.

3. Inconceivable Blackness

Epigraph: Kletzing and Crogman, *Progress of a Race*, 281–82.

1. Morgan, *Laboring Women*.
2. Schwartz, *Birthing a Slave*, 98.
3. Schwartz, *Birthing a Slave*, 93.
4. See McGuire, *At the Dark End of the Street*.
5. McGuire, *At the Dark End of the Street*, 91.
6. "Negro Mortality at the South," *Nation*, August 15, 1872, 105–6 (emphasis in original).
7. "Negro Mortality at the South," 106.
8. Hoffman, *Race Traits and Tendencies of the American Negro*, 37.
9. Hoffman, *Race Traits and Tendencies of the American Negro*, 236.
10. See Downs, *Sick from Freedom*; and M. Mitchell, *Righteous Propagation*.
11. Hoffman, *Race Traits and Tendencies of the American Negro*, viii.
12. Hoffman, *Race Traits and Tendencies of the American Negro*, 217.
13. Gillette, "Modernism's Scarlet Letter," 124.
14. "Popular Education in Sexual Matters," 46.
15. Frazier, "The Negro and Birth Control," 68.
16. Reagan, *When Abortion Was a Crime*, 137.
17. M. Mitchell, *Righteous Propagation*, 78–79.
18. Engelman, *A History of the Birth Control Movement in America*, 160.
19. Rhetta, "A Plea for the Lives of the Unborn," 202. Ironically Dr. Rhetta and his son, Dr. Barnett M. Rhetta Jr., would be arrested on charges of abortion some forty years later. "Jail 2 Baltimore Medics on Abortion Charges," *Jet*, April 14, 1955, 25.
20. Burwell, "The Fertility of Woman," 227.
21. Burwell, "The Fertility of Woman," 229.
22. Schoen, *Choice and Coercion*; and Nelson, *Women of Color and the Reproductive Rights Movement*.
23. "Birth Control or Race Control?"
24. Garvin, "The Negro Doctor's Task," 269.
25. Garvin, "The Negro Doctor's Task," 270.
26. Reagan, *When Abortion Was a Crime*, 156–58.
27. Fisher and Buckley, *Black Doctors of World War I*, 73–74.
28. *People v. DeVaughan*, 105 Cal. App. 516 (1930). The spelling is different for Oscar Wilson DeVaughn in this case and the one that follows (where it appears as "DeVaughn"). After searching the 1920 and 1930 censuses and looking at DeVaughn's military records, I feel comfortable asserting that the two men are one and the same and that the spelling was simply erroneous in

this case. "United States World War I Draft Registration Cards, 1917–1918," Oscar W. Devaughn, 1917–1918, NARA microfilm M1509 (Washington DC), FHL microfilm 1,558,448; "United States, Veterans Administration Master Index, 1917–1940," Oscar Wilson De Vaughn, June 27, 1918, Military Service, NARA microfilm publication 76193916 (St. Louis); "United States World War II Draft Registration Cards, 1942," NARA microfilm publications; and "United States Census, 1930," Enumeration District 208, Sheet 6A, Line 9, Family 89, NARA microfilm publication T626 (Washington DC), Roll 110, FHL microfilm 2,339,845.

29. *People v. DeVaughan*, 105 Cal. App. 516 (1930).
30. *People v. DeVaughan*, 105 Cal. App. 516 (1930).
31. Fisher and Buckley, *Black Doctors of World War I*, 73–74.
32. *People v. DeVaughn*, 2 Cal. App. 2d 447 (1934).
33. "Communication from Secretary of State Board of Medical Examiners to Association Secretary," 70; and Fisher and Buckley, *Black Doctors of World War I*, 74.
34. *People v. DeVaughn*, 2 Cal. App. 2d 447 (1934).
35. *People v. DeVaughn*, 2 Cal. App. 2d 447 (1934).
36. *People v. DeVaughn*, 2 Cal. App. 2d 447 (1934) (my emphasis).
37. "Communication from Secretary of State Board of Medical Examiners to Association Secretary."
38. "Communication from Secretary of State Board of Medical Examiners to Association Secretary."
39. Rhodes, *A History of Flint Medical College, 1889–1911*.
40. Flamming, *Bound for Freedom*, 2.
41. Flamming, *Bound for Freedom*, 192–225.
42. Marques Vestal, "Mathew J. Marmillion Bio," draft of document used in research for Dr. Marmillion's entry in UCLA's Black Prisoners Project online database. Available at blackprisonersproject.omeka.net. According to the 1932 Los Angeles city directory, Marmillion's address was 3315 S. Central Avenue, about seven blocks north of where the Somerville Hotel (later the Dunbar Hotel) would become the "vibrant center of black life" in Los Angeles. Flamming, *Bound for Freedom*, 262.
43. Flamming, *Bound for Freedom*, 296.
44. Flamming, *Bound for Freedom*, 296.
45. This campaign was referred to as "Don't Spend Your Money Where You Cannot Work"; Flamming, *Bound for Freedom*, 300.
46. There are a few spelling variations for Archie's last name, including Hairston, Harrison, and Harriston.

47. Despite repeated attempts, I was unable to gain access to Hairston's student records.
48. "Free Dr. Marmillion!" *Los Angeles Sentinel*, September 20, 1934, 1.
49. "Marmillion Trial Opens," *California Eagle*, June 16, 1933, 1.
50. Beito and Beito, *Black Maverick*, 24.
51. "Young Woman's Death," *Los Angeles Herald*, November 28, 1903, 8 (my emphasis).
52. For one of the more recent studies on the intersections of race and gender in media coverage, see Neely, *You're Dead, So What?*
53. *People v. Marmillion*, Crim. No. 2435, Court of Appeal of California, Second Appellate District, Division One, 135 Cal. App. 560; 27 P.2d 649; 1933 Cal. App., December 4, 1933, Decided.
54. "Free Dr. Marmillion!" *Los Angeles Sentinel*, September 20, 1934, 1.
55. Beito and Beito, *Black Maverick*, 24.
56. Ward, *Black Physicians in the Jim Crow South*, 150–51.
57. I found no examples of Black female physicians accused of performing abortions.
58. "Bail for Negro Physician," *Washington Post*, July 4, 1905, 4.
59. "Thousands of Babies Slain in Year, Is Charge," *Chicago Daily Tribune*, December 7, 1918, 5.

4. "The Mid-Wife Type"

Epigraph: Testimony from Assembly Interim Committee on Criminal Procedure, Abortion Hearing, AB 2614, San Diego, California, December 17–18, 1962, John A. O'Connell, chairman.

1. Drake, *What a Young Wife Ought to Know*, 133.
2. V. Russell and Malleson, "The Problem of Abortion," 101–6.
3. "Thousands of Babies Slain in Year, Is Charge," *Chicago Daily Tribune*, December 7, 1918, 5.
4. Bederman, *Manliness and Civilization*.
5. Beisel and Kay, "Abortion, Race, and Gender in Nineteenth-Century America," 507.
6. *Digest of American Medical Association Official Actions*, 50, 60 (my emphasis).
7. Drake, *What a Young Wife Ought to Know*, 123–34.
8. Beisel and Kay, "Abortion, Race, and Gender in Nineteenth-Century America," 507.
9. Drake, *What a Young Wife Ought to Know*, 126.
10. D'Emilio and Freedman, *Intimate Matters*, 146.
11. Michelet, *L'Amour*, 1.
12. Bederman, *Manliness and Civilization*, 14.
13. Tone, *Devices and Desires*, 18.

14. Tone, *Devices and Desires*, 18.
15. Bederman, *Manliness and Civilization*; and L. Gordon, *The Moral Property of Women*.
16. L. Gordon, *Woman's Body, Woman's Right*, 102–15.
17. Stanton and Anthony also spoke out openly against marital rape. They argued that women were not in a position to deny their husbands' advances. Marital rape was not considered a crime in the United States until well into the twentieth century. Under the doctrine of coverture (or "marital privilege") it was considered impossible for a husband to rape his wife since she became his property once they were married. Efforts to make marital rape a criminal act on par with non-marital rape began in the late nineteenth century but did not have tangible results. Many still view marital rape as somehow different from non-marital rape. For example, the 1962 Model Penal Code—a joint scholarly effort to standardize American law—provided its interpretation of the felony of rape in the first, second, and third degrees. All three descriptions included the clause "not his wife"—specifically, rape is recognized as a forced sexual encounter between a man and a woman who is *not his wife*. A handful of states still make exceptions for rape cases involving married couples, and several more treat marital rape as a lesser crime than non-marital rape. For more on marital rape, see Hasday, "Contest and Consent."
18. Storer, *On Criminal Abortion in America*, 55.
19. Storer, *On Criminal Abortion in America*, 56.
20. Whiteley, "Monstrous, Demonic and Evil," 91–94.
21. Whiteley, "Monstrous, Demonic and Evil," 95.
22. Whiteley, "Monstrous, Demonic and Evil," 97.
23. "72 Women Die in 1921, Death Toll of Abortionists," *Chicago Daily Tribune*, January 13, 1922, 17.
24. "'Hush' Officials Permit Abortion Ring to Grow," *Chicago Daily Tribune*, June 1, 1915, 6.
25. "Restell the Female Abortionist," *National Police Gazette*, March 13, 1847, 212; and "Ann Trow Lohmann."
26. "Restell the Female Abortionist," 212; and "Ann Trow Lohmann."
27. "Restell the Female Abortionist," 212; and "Ann Trow Lohmann."
28. "Margaret Browning Is Held for Murder, Death Farm Probed," *Madera Daily Tribune*, November 25, 1932, 1.
29. "Mrs. Browning Is Taken on Murder Charge," *Santa Cruz Sentinel*, November 24, 1932, 1.
30. The amount of $15,000 in November 1932 had the same buying power as approximately $340,000 in 2023.
31. "Selection of Jury in Trial of Mrs. Browning Progressing Rapidly," *Madera Daily Tribune*, January 9, 1933, 4.

32. Browning's defense attorney attempted to get a new judge for the new trial but was unable to do so.
33. "Guilty Verdict in Browning Case," *Healdsburg Tribune*, March 3, 1933, 5.
34. "Margaret Browning Will Seek Release Writ Habeas Corpus," *Madera Daily Tribune*, March 4, 1933, 4.
35. "Rapid Progress Browning Trial," *Madera Daily Tribune*, April 6, 1933, 4.
36. "Abortion Farm Verdict Upheld Appeals Court," *Madera Daily Tribune*, May 20, 1933, 1.
37. "Mrs. Browning Loses Again in Rehearing Move," *Santa Cruz Sentinel*, June 21, 1933, 1.
38. "Deny Scandal Parole Given Mrs. Browning," *Madera Daily Tribune*, December 29, 1934, 1.
39. "Mrs. Browning Paroled," *Madera Daily Tribune*, December 19, 1934, 4.
40. "Prison Board Asked Explain," *Madera Daily Tribune*, January 2, 1935, 2.
41. "Surprise Party Given on Birthday," *Madera Daily Tribune*, April 16, 1964, 6.
42. "Girl's Death Leads to Arrest of Bay Woman Physician," *Detroit Free Press*, February 21, 1915, 1.
43. "Criminal Operation on Healdsburg Wife Charged to Woman," *Press Democrat*, October 28, 1921, 5.
44. "Takes Poison as Police Wait," *Sun*, May 27, 1915, 14.
45. "Woman Accused in Girl's Death Tries Suicide," *Chicago Daily Tribune*, February 18, 1929, 13.
46. "Woman Is Arrested in Court as Slayer Suspect," *Los Angeles Herald*, night edition, June 12, 1920, 1.
47. Letter from Albert Carter to Dr. Charles B. Pinkham, June 29, 1928, BME, F3760:817.
48. Paul Drexler, "Inez Burns: A Necessary Evil," *San Francisco Examiner*, March 13, 2016; Powell, *The Browns of California*, 60; Riggin, *San Francisco's Queen of Vice*.
49. Interrogation of Marjorie Krebs, April 12, 1937, BME, F3760:817.
50. "Court Denies Divorce to Woman Aborter," *Chicago Daily Tribune*, June 1, 1915, 6.
51. Notes from Tehachapi, in Laura Miner's Private Collection and Correspondence.
52. Notes from Tehachapi.
53. Notes from Tehachapi.
54. Notes from Tehachapi.
55. Tone, "Making Room for Rubbers," 65.
56. Notes from Tehachapi.

5. The Pacific Coast Abortion Ring

Epigraph: Sullivan, "Smashing California's $100,000,000 Abortion Ring."

1. Tolnai, "The Abortion Racket," 176.
2. Reagan, *When Abortion Was a Crime*, 135; and Tolnai, "The Abortion Racket," 176.
3. Kenney, *Organized Crime in America*.
4. Kaplan, "Abortion as a Vice Crime," 153.
5. Luker, *Abortion and the Politics of Motherhood*, 75.
6. Bates, "The Abortion Mill," 157.
7. *People of the State of California v. Rankin, et al.* Court transcript, 7.
8. As discussed in chapter 4, "steerers" solicited business for the clinics. They would approach pharmacists and doctors and encourage them to "steer" potential clients to their clinics. In exchange, steerers promised the pharmacists and doctors a referral bonus.
9. Sullivan, "Smashing California's $100,000,000 Abortion Ring," 72; Beers, "Laura Miner."
10. All the abortionists, with the exception of Laura Miner, were male.
11. Pinkham, "The Pacific Coast Abortion Ring," 350.
12. With inflation, $35–$50 in 1936 would have had the same buying power as approximately $760–$1,100 in 2023.
13. *People of the State of California v. Rankin, et al.*, 258.
14. Exhibit 24 in *People of the State of California v. Rankin, et al.*, 254–55.
15. *People of the State of California v. Rankin, et al.*, 707.
16. The statement read: "This is to certify that the two gentlemen with Mr. Cunningham [the police investigator] are not the men who performed the operation on me." *People of the State of California v. Rankin, et al.*, 904.
17. Letter from Dr. Pinkham to [Los Angeles district attorney] Buron Fitts and V. L. Ferguson, September 22, 1934, BME, F3760:820.
18. Letter from Dr. Pinkham to Buron Fitts and V. L. Ferguson, September 22, 1934, BME, F3760:820.
19. *People of the State of California v. Rankin, et al.*, 772–75.
20. Letter from Dr. Pinkham to Buron Fitts and V. L. Ferguson, September 22, 1934, BME, F3760:820.
21. Letter from Dr. Pinkham to Buron Fitts and V. L. Ferguson, September 22, 1934, BME, F3760:820.
22. Sullivan, "Smashing California's $100,000,000 Abortion Ring," 15.
23. A D&C involves dilating the cervix, accessing the uterus, and performing a curettement—that is, scraping and removing material or tissue from the uterus with a curette, or spoonlike medical instrument.

24. *People of the State of California v. Rankin, et al.*, 760.
25. *People of the State of California v. Rankin, et al.*, 333–34.
26. Solinger, *The Abortionist*, 83.
27. Letter from Special Agent Albert Carter to Dr. Pinkham, December 11, 1934, BME, F3760:819.
28. An interesting side note: during World War II De Gaston was interned as a German sympathizer in an American concentration camp. Later he would eventually emerge as one of the primary suspects questioned in the Black Dahlia case.
29. Sullivan, "Smashing California's $100,000,000 Abortion Ring," 12.
30. Sullivan, "Smashing California's $100,000,000 Abortion Ring," 12.
31. Sources vary on whether Eilert was twenty-two or twenty-five years old.
32. "Death Inquiry Has New Turn," *Los Angeles Times*, August 14, 1934, A8; "Chemists Offer Testimony in Operation Case," *Los Angeles Times*, December 18, 1934, A1.
33. *People of the State of California v. Rankin, et al.*, 102.
34. *People of the State of California v. Rankin, et al.*, 235.
35. *People of the State of California v. Rankin, et al.*, 240.
36. *People of the State of California v. Rankin, et al.*, 245.
37. Letter from Special Agent Albert Carter to Dr. Pinkham, June 23, 1935, BME, F3760:820.
38. Ruth Attaway died of a septic infection following her abortion with Heddens. Heddens gave the police a full confession and claimed his wife wasn't involved. He later recanted and argued that his confession was obtained under duress. The police did not believe in Rose Marie's innocence and tried her as well. The pair ultimately pled guilty to manslaughter and were both incarcerated. By 1940 Rose Marie had been released, took custody of their daughter, and moved in with her parents. Harley was paroled, but in 1940 he was accused of murdering Bertha Hewitt following an illegal abortion. He fled San Francisco, began working as a manager for an electrical company, and eventually became a vaudeville mind reader. He was captured in Indiana in 1941, extradited to California in 1941, and died while on parole in 1952.
39. Sollinger, *The Abortionist*.
40. Sullivan, "Smashing California's $100,000,000 Abortion Ring," 12.
41. Sullivan, "Smashing California's $100,000,000 Abortion Ring," 12.
42. Sullivan, "Smashing California's $100,000,000 Abortion Ring," 13.
43. Sullivan, "Smashing California's $100,000,000 Abortion Ring," 72.
44. In 1936, $5,000 had the same buying power as almost $90,000 in 2018.
45. Sullivan, "Smashing California's $100,000,000 Abortion Ring," 73.

46. Ferguson, "Illegal Operations, INC."; and Ledbetter, "Smashing the West Coast's Worst Racket."
47. Dr. Eric Wilson, *What a Racket!*, BME, F3760:823.
48. Sullivan, "Smashing California's $100,000,000 Abortion Ring," 74. The full list of those indicted is as follows: Reginald Rankin, Dr. George E. Watts, John A Creeth, Joseph Shinn, Marvin Raithel, Dr. William Norman Powers, Dr. Valentine St. John, Dr. Harry L. Houston, Dr. James Beggs, Paul De Gaston, William Byrne, Dr. Lawrence Guibinni (also known as Victor Angelo), Dr. F. B. Smith, J. C. Perry, E. T. Patee, Violet Rankin, Violet Pellegrini, Leola Habel, Dr. Jesse Ross, Ruth Hanson, Viola Warner, Laura Miner, Josephine Follet, Nedra Arden (also known as Nedra Cordon), Grace Moore, Mary Wilson, Lillian Wilson, Gladys Korf, Bessie McCarthy, Beatrice Bole, and Zora McEwen. Of these, Nedra Arden, Paul De Gaston, Josephine Follet, Zora McEwen, Laura Miner, William Powers, and Marvin Raithel turned state's evidence in exchange for immunity or lighter sentences. Powers pled guilty to the charges in order to avoid facing trial.
49. Ferguson, "Illegal Operations, INC.," 35.
50. "Criminal Syndicate Witness Is Guarded," *Reading Eagle*, October 21, 1936, 2.
51. Kaley, "This Business of Abortion," 34.
52. Kaley, "This Business of Abortion," 34.
53. Ferguson, "Illegal Operations, INC.," 34.
54. Ledbetter, "Smashing the West Coast's Worst Racket," 14.
55. Kaley, "This Business of Abortion," 35.
56. Kaley, "This Business of Abortion," 35.
57. Kaley, "This Business of Abortion," 36.
58. Kaley, "This Business of Abortion," 36.
59. C. A. Gordon, "Abortion and Contraception," 678.
60. V. Russell and Malleson, "The Problem of Abortion," 102.
61. Joan Malleson was actually the initial doctor whom the pregnant rape victim in the Bourne case asked for help. Malleson wrote to Bourne while simultaneously contacting others in the medical community to support the abortion.
62. V. Russell and Malleson, "The Problem of Abortion," 105.

6. After PCAR

Epigraph: Notes from Tehachapi, in Laura Miner's Private Collection and Correspondence.

1. Inez Brown changed her name to Burns when she married in 1932.
2. The first two trials, in 1945 and 1946, resulted in deadlocked juries. The third trial resulted in a guilty verdict for all five defendants. The defendants were

sentenced to two to five years in prison. After exhausting their appeals, the defendants were told to serve out their sentences.
3. Report #154 from W. N. Anderson, Acting Assistant Special Agent to the San Diego County Board of Medical Examiners of the State of California, June 22, 1937, BME, F3760:817.
4. Stern, "Abortion," 87.
5. Reports conflict on whether the victim was feebleminded. One report claimed she was healthy. It isn't clear if the diagnosis of feeblemindedness was related to her rape and subsequent abortion (as a marker of social deviance) or if it was deliberately employed to bolster the idea that her abortion was medically necessary to preserve her fragile mental state.
6. "Noted Surgeon Challenges Law," *Los Angeles Times*, July 2, 1938, 7.
7. "Criminal Law," 109.
8. "Doctors Back Obstetrician," *Los Angeles Times*, July 19, 1938, 1.
9. Aleck Bourne, "Correspondence: *Rex v. Bourne*, to the Editor of *The Lancet*," *Lancet*, July 30, 1938, 280.
10. "Criminal Law," 111.
11. Reagan, *When Abortion Was a Crime*, 63.
12. Reagan, *When Abortion Was a Crime*, 68–69 and 200–201.
13. Laws of the State of California, *Statutes and Amendments to the Codes*, 1935, Section 274.
14. D'Emilio and Freedman, *Intimate Matters*, 253.
15. Joffe, *Doctors of Conscience*, 64.
16. C. A. Gordon, "Abortion and Contraception," 675.
17. C. A. Gordon, "Abortion and Contraception," 676.
18. C. A. Gordon, "Abortion and Contraception," 676.
19. Ruth Barnett was an Oregon abortionist and was introduced to the business after she received an abortion from none other than Dr. George E. Watts.
20. St. John was sentenced to four to ten years after the *People v. Rankin* ruling. However, his sentence was later reversed on a technicality. With many of his co-conspirators out of the way, he reportedly went back to the abortion business on his own. The fact that St. John already had his own abortion business may have been why Rankin latched onto him.
21. Report, Re: Rankin, February 26, 1945, BME, F3760:825a.
22. Hunter, "Harvesters of the Unborn."
23. The charge against the defendants was that they "willfully, unlawfully and feloniously" used an unknown instrument "in and about and upon and within the body of one B. Price" to induce a miscarriage that was "not at all necessary to preserve the life of the said B. Price, or that of the child whereof she was pregnant." *State of Nevada v. Paul Cushing and R. L. Rankin*, No. 3343,

Respondent's Answering Brief, August 22, 1941, Supreme Court of the State of Nevada.
24. St. John jumped bail and was a wanted fugitive at the time of the trial.
25. Report, Re: Rankin, February 26, 1945, BME, F3760:825a.
26. Before Miner and her children moved to Los Angeles, she was in the spotlight following an operation upon Mrs. Lauretta Hazel Reese. Miner was held on $1,000 bail for the procedure, and Reese was not expected to survive. According to Reese's dying declaration, the procedure occurred on April 16, 1937, in Miner's home. It is unclear what happened after the procedure, but Reese wound up in the county hospital, where she received multiple blood transfusions. A week after her procedure it appeared Reese's condition was improving; however, on April 29 she died. Before Reese died, the police escorted Miner to Reese's deathbed, where Reese made a positive identification. Though the police in San Diego were aware of Miner's previous involvement in PCAR and despite pressure to charge Miner with murder, it does not appear that she served any time for Reese's death, and Miner makes no mention of the incident in any of her own documents that I was able to view.
27. Johns, *Perilous Times*, 8–9.
28. Chadwick, a San Diego native, would become famous for being the first woman to swim the English Channel in both directions.
29. *People of the State of California v. Laura K. Miner, Josephine M. Page, and Nedra Cordon*, No. 149586, Reporter's Transcript, filed November 10, 1948, 67. In Miner, Laura Miner's Private Collection and Correspondence.
30. *People of the State of California v. Laura K. Miner, Josephine M. Page, and Nedra Cordon*, No. 149586, Reporter's Transcript, filed November 10, 1948, 67. In Laura Miner's Private Collection and Correspondence.
31. Letter from George E. Jordan (Assistant Special Agent) to Dr. C. B. Pinkham, October 23, 1937, BME, F3760:819.
32. Confidential Report, Re: Miner Case, Operative J-9. In Laura Miner's Private Collection and Correspondence.
33. Gillette, "Modernism's Scarlet Letter," 137.
34. Gillette, "Modernism's Scarlet Letter," 137. In addition, according to Alexandra Minna Stern, the postwar "revision of eugenics" opened the door for "various psychogenic and psychoanalytic explanations of human development and deviance." Stern, *Eugenic Nation*, 152.
35. Dating patterns, the end of World War II, and the GI Bill had also dramatically lowered the average age of marriage in the postwar period. Fessler, *The Girls Who Went Away*, 29.
36. Fessler, *The Girls Who Went Away*, 103.

37. Names have been changed. Letter from Special Agent W. N. Anderson to C. B. Pinkham, May 24, 1940, BME, F3760:817a.
38. Letter from Special Agent W. N. Anderson to C. B. Pinkham, May 24, 1940, BME, F3760:817a.
39. Names have been changed. Joel M. Taylor, Special Agent, Bureau of Criminal Identification and Investigation Report, California Department of Justice, March 14, 1962, BME, F3760:821.
40. Names have been changed. Joel M. Taylor, Special Agent, Bureau of Criminal Identification and Investigation Report, California Department of Justice, March 14, 1962, BME, F3760:821.
41. Fessler, *The Girls Who Went Away*.
42. Fessler, *The Girls Who Went Away*; and Solinger, *Wake Up Little Susie*.
43. Wilson-Buterbaugh, *The Baby Scoop Era*.
44. Stern, *Eugenic Nation*, 166.
45. Wilson-Buterbaugh, *The Baby Scoop Era*.

7. To the Border

Epigraph: Brautigan, *The Abortion*.

1. See Hernández, *Migra!*; Luibhéid, *Entry Denied*; and Ngai, *Impossible Subjects*.
2. Karibo, "Swashbuckling Criminals and Border Bandits," 706.
3. Karibo, "Swashbuckling Criminals and Border Bandits," 711.
4. Karibo, "Swashbuckling Criminals and Border Bandits," 711.
5. Karibo, "Swashbuckling Criminals and Border Bandits," 727.
6. Karibo, "Swashbuckling Criminals and Border Bandits," 727.
7. Nicolaides, *My Blue Heaven*.
8. Avila, *Popular Culture in the Age of White Flight*.
9. Some examples of the border as wild and untamed: "Chinese Coming by Way of Mexico," *San Francisco Chronicle*, April 7, 1890, 3; "A Queer Case: Arrest of an American Citizen in Lower California," *Los Angeles Times*, September 20, 1893, 2; and "Murderer Morales Near San Diego," *Los Angeles Times*, November 11, 1901, 11.
10. Medrano, "Sexuality, Migration, and Tourism," 236; and Schantz, "From the *Mexicali Rose* to the Tijuana Brass."
11. "Vice at Tia Juana," *Los Angeles Times*, January 21, 1916, I14.
12. Bender, *Run for the Border*, 53.
13. Reuter and Ronfeldt, *Quest for Integrity*, 10.
14. Díaz, *Border Contraband*, 13.
15. St. John, "Selling the Border," 114.
16. Kropp, *California Vieja*.
17. Ngai, *Impossible Subjects*, 67.

18. Runstedtler, *Jack Johnson*, 223–30.
19. "Extradition Fight for Doctor Launched," *Los Angeles Times*, November 25, 1941, A2.
20. Faithful, "Mexico's Choice." See also Cardona, "Politics, Religion and Morality"; and Jelen and Bradley, "Abortion Opinion in Emerging Democracies."
21. Bender, *Run for the Border*, 81.
22. Section 182 of the California Penal Code states, "If two or more persons conspire: 1. To commit any crime ... they are punishable as follows: When they conspire to commit any felony, they shall be punishable in the same manner and to the same extent as is provided for the punishment of the said felony."
23. "Illegal Operation: 'Travelling Abortion Mill' in California," *South China Morning Post and the Hong Kong Telegraph*, August 26, 1948, 7.
24. From the documents I saw my understanding of "floating" is that the headquarters and operation locations changed and circulated. Initially I was hoping it meant that a ring was conducting its surgeries offshore. It does not appear that was the case, but if it were, it would not have surprised me.
25. These categories lasted only a couple fiscal years because by the report of July 1, 1956–June 30, 1957, the coroner's office and reports had been reorganized.
26. Howe, *Decennial Record of the Class of 1905*, 44.
27. Letter from Albert Carter to Dr. Charles B. Pinkham, June 29, 1928, BME, F3760:817.
28. "Operator Describes Drug Deal," *Los Angeles Times*, July 17, 1929, 2.
29. Letter from Albert Carter to Dr. Charles B. Pinkham, December 11, 1934, BME, F3760:819.
30. Letter from Albert Carter to Dr. Charles B. Pinkham, December 11, 1934, BME, F3760:819.
31. LACMA, vol. 18.
32. "Clinic Tales Link Byrne," *Los Angeles Times*, October 16, 1936, A12.
33. Assembly Interim Committee on Criminal Procedure, Abortion Hearing, AB 2614, San Diego, California, December 17–18, 1962, John A. O'Connell, chairman.
34. *People of the State of California v. Buffum*, 40 Cal.2d 709, Crim. No. 5293 (1953).
35. *People of the State of California v. Buffum*, 40 Cal.2d 709, Crim. No. 5293 (1953).
36. *People of the State of California v. Buffum*, 40 Cal.2d 709, Crim. No. 5293 (1953).
37. Abortions were legal in Japan and Sweden at the time.
38. Ruth Moss, "Not to the Jurist, Nor to the Respectable Surgeon," *Chicago Tribune*, October 19, 1969, J34; and Jacquin Sanders "The Shadow World of the Abortionist," *Austin Statesman*, June 7, 1970, B4.
39. In 1969, $1,100 would have had the same buying power as over $9,200 in 2023.

40. Joel M. Taylor, Special Agent, Bureau of Criminal Identification and Investigation Report, California Department of Justice, March 14, 1962, BME, F3760:821.
41. Marine and Goldberg, "Abortion Reform," 46.
42. "Women Seeking Abortion Stranded in Juarez," *Sun Reporter*, December 7, 1958, 17.
43. Joel M. Taylor, Special Agent, Bureau of Criminal Identification and Investigation Report, California Department of Justice, March 14, 1962, BME, F3760:821.
44. Joel M. Taylor, Special Agent, Bureau of Criminal Identification and Investigation Report, California Department of Justice, March 14, 1962, BME, F3760:821.
45. Letter from Archie D. Ross, Assistant Secretary, to Richard R. Rogan, Chief Deputy Attorney General, July 28, 1959, BME, F3760:818.
46. Joel M. Taylor, Special Agent, Bureau of Criminal Identification and Investigation Report, California Department of Justice, March 14, 1962, BME, F3760:821.
47. In some instances abortionists simply packed women with gauze in order to induce premature labor. The abortion would be complete once another physician removed the gauze.
48. Wayne Clark, "Orange County: Abortion Deaths Trigger Investigation of 'Murder,'" *Los Angeles Times*, November 6, 1963, F8.
49. Phelan and Maginnis, *The Abortion Handbook for Responsible Women*, 135.
50. Harry Nelson, "Illegal Abortions Bring on Tetanus, Many Other Infections," *Los Angeles Times*, June 21, 1966, A1.
51. Joffe, *Doctors of Conscience*, 60.
52. Joffe, *Doctors of Conscience*, 60–61.
53. Reagan, "Crossing the Border for Abortions," 323.
54. Joel M. Taylor, Special Agent, Bureau of Criminal Identification and Investigation Report, California Department of Justice, March 14, 1962, BME, F3760:821.
55. "Letters to the Army of Three," Walker Art Center.
56. Quoted in Ruth Moss, "Not to the Jurist, Nor to the Respectable Surgeon," *Chicago Tribune*, October 19, 1969, J76 (my emphasis).
57. Harry Nelson, "Illegal Abortions Bring on Tetanus, Many Other Infections," *Los Angeles Times*, June 21, 1966, A3.
58. K. P. Russell and Jackson, "Therapeutic Abortions in California," 758.
59. Assembly Interim Committee on Criminal Procedure, Abortion Hearing, AB 2614.

60. *People of the State of California v. Francis Edgar Ballard*, 167 Cal.App.2d 803 (1959), Crim. No. 6222, California Court of Appeals, Second Dist., Div. On., February 13, 1959.
61. Assembly Interim Committee on Criminal Procedure, Abortion Hearing, AB 2614.
62. In the July 1, 1956–June 30, 1957, fiscal year the coroner's office reorganized and altered its reports. Instead of detailed accounts and numbers, the reports became biennial and provided only selected statistics. Though they continued to provide the number of abortions, they ceased to list abortionist categories or marital statuses and ages of women obtaining abortions. The office continued to use this limited approach until the report of July 1, 1969–June 30, 1970, which for the first time specifically listed racial and ethnic data and fetal deaths. There is an issue with dates in the July 1, 1967–June 30, 1969, biennial report, so in table 3 I did not include the figures for 1968–69 because they appeared to be an accidental identical reprint.
63. Sands, "The Therapeutic Abortion Act," 285.
64. Sands, "The Therapeutic Abortion Act," 285.
65. Luker, *Abortion and the Politics of Motherhood*, 58.
66. Golden, *Babies Made Us Modern*, 185.
67. Assembly Interim Committee on Criminal Procedure, Abortion Hearing, AB 2614.
68. K. P. Russell and Jackson, "Therapeutic Abortions in California," 758.
69. Approximately seven thousand infants in about forty-eight countries were affected by thalidomide. Cooper-Roth, "The Effects of Thalidomide on Embryonic Development."
70. Vargesson, "Thalidomide-Induced Teratogenesis."
71. Reagan, *Dangerous Pregnancies*, 56.
72. Reagan, *Dangerous Pregnancies*, 1.
73. "Rubella in the U.S."
74. "Interdepartmental Communication from Department of Professional and Vocational Standards, Division of Investigation, to Wallace W. Thompson, Executive Secretary, BME," August 19, 1965, BME, F3760:822.
75. Reagan, *Dangerous Pregnancies*, 55.
76. Reagan, *Dangerous Pregnancies*, 6.
77. Golden, *Babies Made Us Modern*, 186.
78. Report on rubella, BME, F3760:822.
79. Report on rubella, BME, F3760:822.
80. Reagan, *Dangerous Pregnancies*, 142.
81. Medical Records, Report to Therapeutic Abortion Committee, May 18, 1965, BME, F3760:822 (my emphasis).

82. Stern, *Eugenic Nation*, 180.
83. Assembly Interim Committee on Criminal Procedure, Abortion Hearing, AB 2614.
84. Names have been changed. County of Santa Clara District Attorney Investigator's Report, December 21, 1960, BME, F3760:821.
85. K. P. Russell and Jackson, "Therapeutic Abortions in California," 757.
86. Lynn Lilliston, "Abortion Reform Bills 'Fall Short,'" *Los Angeles Times*, May 13, 1969, C1.
87. D'Emilio and Freedman, *Intimate Matters*, 314.
88. Jacquin Sanders, "The Shadow World of the Abortionist," *Austin Statesman*, June 7, 1970, B4.
89. Haugeberg, *Women against Abortion*, 26.
90. L. Gordon, *The Moral Property of Women*, 297.
91. Reed and Evans, "The Deprofessionalism of Medicine." It is interesting that some physicians also argued that performing abortions on demand relegated them to the status of "technicians," another form of deprofessionalization wherein physicians merely performed the patient's bidding.
92. Gene Blake, "Abortion: Court Ruling Could Be Landmark," *Los Angeles Times*, March 10, 1969, 1.
93. Jane Lang McGrew, "To Be or Not to Be," 643.
94. McGrew, "To Be or Not to Be," 643.
95. Gene Blake, "Abortion: Court Ruling Could Be Landmark," *Los Angeles Times*, March 10, 1969, 1.
96. *People of the State of California v. Belous*, Crim. 71 Ca1.2d 954 (1969), Crim. 12739.
97. The Therapeutic Abortion Act came up during the *Belous* case due to the fact that it still retained some of the original statute's wording—specifically "necessary to preserve." Therefore it also fell apart and became void upon the final *Belous* decision.
98. Mrs. Franklin P. Marder, "Letters to the Times: Woman Reader Probes Issue of Legal Abortion vs. Antiquated Law," *Los Angeles Times*, March 25, 1969, C8.
99. Marder, "Letters to the Times," C8.
100. "Authorities Free Parents of Dead Girl," *Los Angeles Times*, June 14, 1966.
101. "Abortion Statutes," 446.
102. "Abortion Statutes."
103. "Abortion Statutes."
104. CCTA, Amici Curiae Brief on Behalf of Medical School Deans and Others in Support of Appellant, p. 12, *People of the State of California v. Belous* (1969).
105. CCTA, Amici Curiae Brief on Behalf of Medical School Deans and Others in Support of Appellant, p. 12, *People of the State of California v. Belous* (1969).

106. CCTA, Application for Leave to File Brief Amici Curiae in Support of the Position of Appellant, p. 16, *People of the State of California v. Belous* (1969).
107. "Abortion Statutes."
108. Husse, "Abortion Law," 772.
109. Vogel, "Constitutional Law," 339.
110. Vogel, "Constitutional Law."

Conclusion

Epigraph: Robin Marty, "The Goal of Mississippi's 15-Week Abortion Ban Is to Overturn *Roe v. Wade*," NBC News, March 12, 2018, nbcnews.com.

1. As a side note, the sources also change as women speak more. In a sense there is a "silence" in the 1920s and early 1930s. There are more fatalities, and the voices that direct the narrative in this period are not the women's. They are those of police officers, coroners, friends, families, spouses, and members of the BME. After *Rankin* and through the 1950s the sources begin to allow women's voices to be heard. The women are subject to questioning and are put on trial. Many are defiant—unhappy to be on the stand, angry about being questioned, or emotionally or mentally spent. As we get to the 1960s, there is more power behind women's voices. Leslie Regan has documented some of the activists in the 1960s who share their abortion stories and speak out against law. Now they are unapologetic.
2. Harriman, "The Void for Vagueness Rule in California," 524.
3. Haugeberg, *Women against Abortion*.
4. *Harris v. McRae*, 448 U.S. 297 (1980); and "*Harris v. McRae*."
5. Rochelle Sharpe, "Abortion Funding Cuts Pose Dilemmas for Poor," *Desert Sun*, December 3, 1988, A9.
6. The standard of "undue burden" was introduced, or at least discussed, in the decisions for a series of cases after *Roe* (*Akron v. Akron Center for Reproductive Health* [1983], *Beal v. Doe* [1977], *Maher v. Roe* [1977], *Thorburgh v. American College of Obstetricians and Gynecologists* [1986], and *Webster v. Reproductive Health Services* [1989]). In their opinions several justices stated that regulations could not be unduly burdensome. Thus "the obverse of unduly burdensome was due burdens ... [and] the courts would have to decide what was ... 'due' or undue." Hull and Hoffer, *Roe v. Wade*, 226.
7. In his opinion in *Beal v. Doe*, which concerned the use of Medicaid funds for abortions in Pennsylvania, Justice Blackmun dissented and argued that the majority's decision "concedes the existence of a constitutional right, but denies the realization and enjoyment of that right on the ground that existence and realization are separate and distinct. For the individual woman concerned, indigent and financially helpless, as the Court's opinions in the three cases

concede her to be, the result is punitive and tragic." *Beal v. Doe*, 432 U.S. 438 (1977). In *Maher v. Roe* the state of Connecticut's policy of using Medicaid funds *only* for "medically necessary" abortions (and not non-therapeutic abortions) came under scrutiny since the state pays for childbirth. In the majority opinion the justices wrote: "The Connecticut regulation before us is different in kind from the laws invalidated in our previous abortion decisions. The Connecticut regulation places no obstacles—absolute or otherwise—in the pregnant woman's path to an abortion. An indigent woman who desires an abortion suffers no disadvantage as a consequence of Connecticut's decision to fund childbirth; she continues as before to be dependent on private sources for the services she desires. The State may have made childbirth a more attractive alternative . . . but it has imposed no restriction on access to abortions that was not already there. . . . There is a basic difference between direct state interference with a protected activity and state encouragement of an alternative activity consonant with legislative policy." *Maher v. Roe*, 432 U.S. 464 (1977).

8. In this case the court argued that "an undue burden exists . . . [and invalidates a provision of law] if its purpose or effect is to place substantial obstacles in the path of a woman seeking an abortion before the fetus attains viability." *Planned Parenthood of Southeastern Pennsylvania v. Casey*, 505 U.S. 833 (1992).
9. "Section 3209's husband notification provision constitutes an undue burden, and is therefore invalid. A significant number of women will likely be prevented from obtaining an abortion just as surely as if Pennsylvania had outlawed the procedure entirely. . . . Furthermore, it cannot be claimed that the father's interest in the fetus' welfare is equal to the mother's protected liberty, since it is an inescapable biological fact that state regulation with respect to the fetus will have a far greater impact on the pregnant woman's bodily integrity than it will on the husband." *Planned Parenthood of Southeastern Pennsylvania v. Casey*, 505 U.S. 833 (1992).
10. *Planned Parenthood of Southeastern Pennsylvania v. Casey*, 505 U.S. 833 (1992).
11. *Last Week Tonight with John Oliver*, Season 3, Episode 2, HBO, February 21, 2016.
12. "More State Abortion Restrictions Enacted in 2011–2013 Than in the Entire Previous Decade"; and Boonstra and Nash, "A Surge of State Abortion Restrictions," 9.
13. Nash et al., "Laws Affecting Reproductive Health and Rights."
14. Paige Winfield Cunningham, "The Coming Wave of Anti-Abortion Laws," *Politico*, November 28, 2014, http://www.politico.com/story/2014/11/the-coming-wave-of-anti-abortion-laws-113196.html; Laura Myers, "Abortion Issue Returning to Nevada Legislature in 2015," *Las Vegas Review-Journal*,

November 30, 2014, http://www.reviewjournal.com/politics/abortion-issue-returning-nevada-legislature-2015; David Boucher, "Bill Would Require Ultrasound before Abortion," *Tennessean*, November 14, 2014, http://www.tennessean.com/story/news/politics/2014/11/14/bill-require-ultrasound/abortion/19026477/; "Iowa's Republican Governor to Sign Law Banning Abortions at Six Weeks," *Guardian*, May 4, 2018, https://www.theguardian.com/world/2018/may/04/abortion-iowa-republican-governor-to-sign-law-six-weeks-ban; and Nash et al., "Policy Trends in the United States."

15. Under NARAL Pro-Choice America's rating system, reproductive rights access in California is rated as "strongly protected access." https://prochoiceamerica.org/state/California.

16. "State Facts about Abortion: California."

17. Reproductive FACT (Freedom, Accountability, Comprehensive Care, and Transparency) Act, AB-775.

18. "Crisis pregnancy centers," or fake abortion clinics, are designed to *look* like clinics that offer reproductive health services, but they are usually backed by religious or special-interest groups. Typically they do not employ trained medical professionals, and they use trickery and deceit to basically shame and mislead women or otherwise manipulate them out of getting an abortion. Since they are unlicensed, they do not fall under medical community guidelines or regulations, and many are considered religious outreach missions and are thus protected by the First Amendment. The HBO documentary *12th and Delaware* (2010) explores fake clinics by focusing on an intersection of Fort Pierce, Florida, where an abortion clinic and a crisis pregnancy center exist side by side.

19. *National Institute of Family and Life Advocates, et al. v. Becerra, et al.*, 585 U.S. 16-1140 (2018).

20. *National Institute of Family and Life Advocates, et al. v. Becerra, et al.*, 585 U.S. 16-1140 (2018). The Supreme Court also found the regulated speech unduly burdensome to the clinics.

21. Some legal scholars and journalists remain optimistic. Since First Amendment rights also protect the right to not speak, the upholding of First Amendment rights in this case may have implications in other states where doctors and abortion providers are required to tell women that fetuses can feel pain (most doctors have argued that this is simply not true) and that personhood begins at conception, or they can make any other statement that has not been thoroughly proven by reputable studies (like the link between abortion and increased risk of breast cancer). Only time will tell if that is true, though.

22. Pazol et al., "Abortion Surveillance."

23. Also known as "the Bristol Palin Effect." David Frum, "Why Is the Abortion Rate Falling?" *Atlantic*, December 1, 2014, http://www.theatlantic.com/politics/archive/2014/12/why-is-the-abortion-rate-falling/383300/?single_page=true.
24. Watt, *The Ethics of Pregnancy, Abortion and Childbirth*, 2.
25. Abortion critics are often quick to cite the recent example of Dr. Kermit Gosnell, the notorious abortion doctor in Philadelphia who drew nationwide attention for his "house of horrors" in 2011. His unsanitary clinic became fodder for pro-lifers, who saw this situation as an opportunity to increase restrictions. However, at the time Pennsylvania had among the strictest abortion laws in the nation, and Gosnell's clinic had not been investigated in years. I would suggest the issue was not that there was a lack of laws but that the laws were not enforced and that the state's hostility to abortion created an opportunity for someone like Gosnell to take advantage of the situation.

Afterword

1. Miss. Code Ann. § 41-41-191 (2018), § 4 (b).
2. Estimating Gestational Age. OB-GYN 101: Introductory Obstetrics & Gynecology, 2005, https://oacapps.med.jhmi.edu/OBGYN-101/Text/Pregnancy/estimating_gestational_age.htm.
3. Steven Ross Johnson, "The U.S. Maternal Mortality Rate Surged by Nearly 20% in 2020," *U.S. News & World Report*, February 23, 2022, https://www.usnews.com/news/health-news/articles/2022-02-23/u-s-maternal-mortality-rate-surged-in-2020 and Gianna Melillo, "US Ranks Worst in Maternal Care, Mortality Compared with 10 Other Developed Nations," *American Journal for Managed Care*, December 3, 2020, https://www.ajmc.com/view/us-ranks-worst-in-maternal-care-mortality-compared-with-10-other-developed-nations.
4. Katie O'Connell, "We Need to Talk About Disability as a Reproductive Justice Issue," ReproAction Blog, August 24, 2016, https://reproaction.org/we-need-to-talk-about-disability-as-a-reproductive-justice-issue/.
5. Brian Pendleton, "The California Therapeutic Abortion Act: An Analysis," *Hastings Law Journal*, vol. 19, no. 1 (1967): 242–255, p. 248–249.
6. Bureau of Maternal and Child Health, *A Report to the 1970 Legislature Third Annual Report on the Implementation of the California Therapeutic Abortion Act, Pursuant to Chapter No. 177 (ACR 113) 1967*, table 4. Department of Public Health, January 1970, Box 1, David S. Hall Papers (Collection 1193). Department of Special Collections, Charles E. Young Research Library, UCLA.
7. Bureau of Maternal and Child Health, *A Report to the 1970 Legislature*, table 3.
8. *People v. Belous*, 71 Cal.2d 954, September 5, 1969.

BIBLIOGRAPHY

Archives and Manuscript Materials

ACLU. American Civil Liberties Union of Southern California Records (Collection 900). UCLA Library Special Collections, Charles E. Young Research Library.

BME. Department of Consumer Affairs–Board of Medical Examiners Records, Abortion Investigation Files. California State Archives, Office of the Secretary of State, Sacramento.

California Digital Newspaper Collection. Center for Bibliographic Studies and Research, University of California, Riverside. http://cdnc.ucr.edu.

California Grand Jury. "Indictment of Julia Moore." September 19, 1859, Nevada County, California. Huntington Library, San Marino, California, HM 68279.

CCTA. California Committee on Therapeutic Abortion Records (Collection 1195). UCLA Library Special Collections, Charles E. Young Research Library.

LACC. Los Angeles County Coroner's Register Books. County of Los Angeles Medical Examiner–Coroner.

LACMA. Los Angeles County Medical Association Minute Books, 1871–1970. Huntington Library, San Marino, California.

Laura Miner's Private Collection and Correspondence. Courtesy of Linda Heisig and Robin Beers.

"Letters to the Army of Three." Walker Art Center. http://www.walkerart.org/magazine/2012/andrea-bowers-patricia-maginnis-abortion#.

Los Angeles City Council Files. City Archives and Records, Los Angeles, California.

Los Angeles County Coroner's Office Annual Reports. County of Los Angeles Medical Examiner–Coroner.

NAACP (National Association for the Advancement of Colored People), Region I Records, BANC MSS 78/180 c. Bancroft Library, University of California, Berkeley.

NARA. National Archives and Records Administration, St. Louis MO and Washington DC.

Pasadena Heritage Oral History Project. Pasadena Heritage. https://pasadenaheritage.org/oral-histories/.

Spingarn. Ephemera from the Arthur B. Spingarn Collection of Negro Literature (Collection 923). UCLA Library Special Collections, Charles E. Young Research Library.

Published Works

"Abortion Statutes: Are They Unconstitutional Per Se? *People v. Belous*, 458 P.2d 194 (1969)." *Washington University Law Review*, no. 4 (1969).

Acevedo, Zoila. "Abortion in Early America." *Women and Health* 4, no. 2 (Summer 1979): 159–67.

"Achievements in Public Health, 1900–1999: Healthier Mothers and Babies." *Morbidity and Mortality Weekly Report* 48, no. 38 (October 1, 1999): 849–58.

Albanesi, Stefania, and Claudia Olivetti. "Maternal Health and the Baby Boom." National Bureau of Economic Research (NBER) Working Paper No. 16146, July 2010.

"Ann Trow Lohmann." Assumption College, U.S. Women's History Workshop. http://www1.assumption.edu/WHW/done/webquest/lohman.html.

Archer, David F., et al. "A Statement on Abortion by 100 Professors of Obstetrics: 40 Years Later." *American Journal of Obstetrics and Gynecology* 209, no. 3 (September 2013): 193–99.

Avila, Eric. *Popular Culture in the Age of White Flight: Fear and Fantasy in Suburban Los Angeles*. Berkeley: University of California Press, 2004.

Bailey, Beth L. *From Front Porch to Back Seat: Courtship in Twentieth-Century America*. Baltimore: Johns Hopkins University Press, 1989.

Baker, Jean H. *Margaret Sanger: A Life of Passion*. New York: Hill and Wang, 2011.

Banner, Lois W. *American Beauty: A Social History . . . through Two Centuries of the American Idea, Ideal, and Image of the Beautiful Woman*. Los Angeles: Figueroa Press, 2003.

Bates, Anna Louise. *Weeder in the Garden of the Lord: Anthony Comstock's Life and Career*. Lanham MD: University Press of America, 1995.

Bates, Jerome E. "The Abortion Mill: An Institutional Study." *Journal of Criminal Law and Criminology* 45, no. 2 (1954): 157–69.

Baur, John E. *The Health Seekers of Southern California, 1870–1900*. San Marino: Henry E. Huntington Library and Art Gallery, 1959.

Bederman, Gail. *Manliness and Civilization: A Cultural History of Gender and Race in the United States, 1880–1917*. Chicago: University of Chicago Press, 1995.

Beers, Robin. "Laura Miner." Hillquest Urban Guide. http://www.hillquest.com/history/joyce-beers-mother-laura-miner/.

Beisel, Nicola Kay. *Imperiled Innocents: Anthony Comstock and Family Reproduction in Victorian America*. Princeton NJ: Princeton University Press, 1997.

Beisel, Nicola, and Tamara Kay. "Abortion, Race, and Gender in Nineteenth-Century America." *American Sociological Review* 69 (August 2004): 498–518.

Beito, David T., and Linda Royster Beito. *Black Maverick: T. R. M. Howard's Fight for Civil Rights and Economic Power*. Champaign: University of Illinois Press, 2009.

Bender, Steven W. *Run for the Border: Vice and Virtue in U.S.-Mexico Border Crossings*. New York: NYU Press, 2013.

"Biographical Sketch." Margaret Sanger Papers Project, New York University. https://www.nyu.edu/projects/sanger/aboutms/msbio.php.

"Birth Control or Race Control? Sanger and the Negro Project." Margaret Sanger Papers Project, New York University. https:www.nyu.edu/projects/sanger/articles/bc_or_race_control.php.

Boonstra, Heather D., and Elizabeth Nash. "A Surge of State Abortion Restrictions Puts Providers—and the Women They Serve—in the Crosshairs." *Guttmacher Policy Review* 17, no. 1 (Winter 2014): 9–15.

Branson, Helen K. *Let There Be Life: The Contemporary Account of Edna L. Griffin, M.D.* Kessinger Publishing Reprint Edition. Pasadena: M. S. Sen, 1947.

Brautigan, Richard. *The Abortion: An Historical Romance, 1966*. New York: Simon and Schuster, 1970.

Brind'Amour, Katherine. "Quickening." *The Embryo Project Encyclopedia*, October 30, 2007. https://embryo.asu.edu/pages/quickening.

Brodie, Janet Farrell. *Contraception and Abortion in Nineteenth-Century America*. Ithaca NY: Cornell University Press, 1994.

Burwell, L. L. "The Fertility of Woman: Its Effect Physically and Morally upon the Nation." *Journal of the National Medical Association* 5, no. 4 (October–December 1913).

Cardona, Rudy J. "Politics, Religion and Morality: An Obstacle to Women's Right to Legal Abortion in Mexico." *In-Verso Online Literary Journal*, California State University, Northridge. csun.edu.

Chávez-García, Miroslava. *States of Delinquency: Race and Science in the Making of California's Juvenile Justice System*. Berkeley: University of California Press, 2012.

Chesler, Ellen. *Woman of Valor: Margaret Sanger and the Birth Control Movement in America*. New York: Simon and Schuster, 2007.

Coates, Patricia Walsh. *Margaret Sanger and the Origin of the Birth Control Movement, 1910–1930: The Concept of Women's Sexual Autonomy*. Lewiston: Edwin Mellen Press, 2008.

"Communication from Secretary of State Board of Medical Examiners to Association Secretary." *California and Western Medicine* 42, no. 1 (1935).

Comstock, Anthony. *Traps for the Young*. New York: Funk and Wagnalls, 1883.

Cooper-Roth, Tristan. "The Effects of Thalidomide on Embryonic Development."

The Embryo Project Encyclopedia, September 12, 2010. https://embryo.asu.edu/pages/effects-thalidomide-embryonic-development.

"Criminal Abortion." *California State Journal of Medicine* 20, no. 1 (1922).

"Criminal Law: Abortion, Preservation of Health as a Justification." *University of Chicago Law Review* 6, no. 1 (December 1938).

Dana, Richard Henry, Jr. *Two Years before the Mast.* 1840. Available at https://www.gutenberg.org/files/2055/2055-h/2055-h.htm.

Davis, Simone Weil. *Living Up to the Ads: Gender Fictions of the 1920s.* Durham NC: Duke University Press, 2000.

Dayton, Cornelia Hughes. "Taking the Trade: Abortion and Gender Relations in an Eighteenth- Century New England Village." *William and Mary Quarterly* 48, no. 1 (January 1991): 19–49.

D'Emilio, John, and Estelle B. Freedman, eds. *Intimate Matters: A History of Sexuality in America.* New York: Harper and Row, 1988.

Díaz, George T. *Border Contraband: A History of Smuggling across the Rio Grande.* Austin: University of Texas Press, 2015.

Digest of American Medical Association Official Actions. Official Proceedings of the House of Delegates. Chicago: American Medical Association, June 1864.

Downs, Jim. *Sick from Freedom: African-American Illness and Suffering during the Civil War and Reconstruction.* Oxford: Oxford University Press, 2012.

Drake, Emma F. A. *What a Young Wife Ought to Know.* Philadelphia: The Vir Publishing Company, 1908.

Draper, F. W. "Criminal Abortion with a 'Dying Declaration.'" *Boston Medical and Surgical Journal* 112, no. 19 (November 9, 1899).

Du Bois, W. E. B., ed. *The Health and Physique of the Negro American.* Atlanta: Atlanta University Press, 1906.

Dumenil, Lynn. *The Modern Temper: American Culture and Society in the 1920s.* New York: Hill and Wang, 1995.

"Eat California Fruit: By One of the Eaters." San Francisco: Southern Pacific Company, 1904.

Engelman, Peter C. *A History of the Birth Control Movement in America.* Santa Barbara CA: Praeger, 2011.

Faithful, Sarah. "Mexico's Choice: Abortion Laws and Their Effects throughout Latin America." Council on Hemispheric Affairs, September 28, 2016. www.coha.org.

Ferguson, Vernon. "Illegal Operations, INC." *Official Detective Stories* 3, no. 6 (February 1, 1937).

Fessler, Ann. *The Girls Who Went Away: The Hidden History of Women Who Surrendered Children for Adoption in the Decades before* Roe v. Wade. New York: Penguin Press, 2006.

Fine, David. *Imagining Los Angeles: A City in Fiction*. Reno: University of Nevada Press, 2000.

Fine, Gary Alan. "Scandal, Social Conditions, and the Creation of Public Attention: Fatty Arbuckle and the 'Problem of Hollywood.'" *Social Problems* 44, no. 3 (August 1997): 297–323.

Fisher, W. Douglas, and Joann H. Buckley. *Black Doctors of World War I: The Lives of 104 Volunteers*. Jefferson: McFarland, 2016.

Flamming, Douglas. *Bound for Freedom: Black Los Angeles in Jim Crow America*. Berkeley: University of California Press, 2006.

Foucault, Michel. *Discipline and Punish: The Birth of the Prison*. Translated by Alan Sheridan. New York: Vintage Books, 1995.

———. *The History of Sexuality*. Vol. 1, *An Introduction*. Translated by Robert Hurley. New York: Vintage Books, 1990.

Frazier, Franklin. "The Negro and Birth Control." *Birth Control Review* 17, no. 8 (March 1933).

Garvin, Charles H. "The Negro Doctor's Task." *Birth Control Review* 16, no. 9 (November 1932).

Gibson, Beth. "The Termination of the Quickening Doctrine: American Law, Society, and the Advent of Professional Medicine in the Nineteenth Century." Master's thesis, Western Kentucky University, 1995.

Gillette, Meg. "Modernism's Scarlet Letter: Plotting Abortion in American Fiction, 1900–1945." PhD dissertation, University of Illinois at Urbana-Champaign, 2007.

Golden, Janet. *Babies Made Us Modern: How Infants Brought America into the Twentieth Century*. Cambridge: Cambridge University Press, 2018.

Gootenberg, Paul. "Talking about the Flow: Drugs, Borders, and the Discourse of Drug Control." *Cultural Critique* 71 (Winter 2009): 13–46.

Gordon, Charles A. "Abortion and Contraception for Indications Other Than Purely Medical." *American Journal of Surgery* 8, no. 3 (March 1930).

Gordon, Linda. *The Great Arizona Orphan Abduction*. Cambridge MA: Harvard University Press, 1999.

———. *The Moral Property of Women: A History of Birth Control Politics in America*. Urbana: University of Illinois Press, 1974.

———. *Woman's Body, Woman's Right: A Social History of Birth Control in America*. New York: Grossman Publishers, 1976.

Grant County Historical Society and Museum. *The First 100 Years: A Pictorial History of Grant County*. N.p.: Jostens Printing, 1990. http://www.grantcoks.org/DocumentCenter/.

Harriman, David Bruce. "The Void for Vagueness Rule in California." *California Law Review* 41, no. 3 (October 1953).

"Harris v. McRae." Center for Constitutional Rights, Historic Case. https://ccrjustice.org/home/what-we-do/our-cases/harris-v-mcrae.

Hasday, Jill Elaine. "Contest and Consent: A Legal History of Marital Rape." *California Law Review* 88, no. 5 (October 2000): 1373–505.

Haugeberg, Karissa. *Women against Abortion: Inside the Largest Moral Reform Movement of the Twentieth Century*. Urbana: University of Illinois Press, 2017.

Hayden, Tiana Bakić. "Private Bleeding: Self-Induced Abortion in the Twenty-First Century United States." *Gender Issues* 28 (2011): 209–25.

Hegar, et al. Texas Legislature Senate Bill 5. http://www.capitol.state.tx.us/tlodocs/831/billtext/html/SB00005H.htm.

Hernández, Kelly Lytle. *Migra! A History of the U.S. Border Patrol*. Berkeley: University of California Press, 2010.

Higham, John. *Strangers in the Land: Patterns of American Nativism, 1860–1925*. New Brunswick NJ: Rutgers University Press, 1983.

Hise, Greg. *Magnetic Los Angeles: Planning the Twentieth-Century Metropolis*. Baltimore: Johns Hopkins University Press, 1997.

"Historical Sketch of Galen R. Hickok." *California State Journal of Medicine* 18, no. 11 (November 1920).

Hoffman, Frederick L. *Race Traits and Tendencies of the American Negro*. New York: Macmillan, 1896.

Howe, Herbert Barber, ed. *Decennial Record of the Class of 1905: Williams College*. Watertown: Williams College, 1915.

Hoy, Suellen. *Chasing Dirt: The American Pursuit of Cleanliness*. Oxford: Oxford University Press, 1995.

Hull, N. E. H., and Peter Charles Hoffer. Roe v. Wade: *The Abortion Rights Controversy in American History*. 2nd ed. Lawrence: University Press of Kansas, 2010.

Hunter, T. P. "Harvesters of the Unborn: Crushing California's Abortion Syndicate." *Real Detective*, August 1941.

Hurtado, Albert L. *Intimate Frontiers: Sex, Gender, and Culture in Old California*. Albuquerque: University of New Mexico Press, 1999.

Husse, Edward. "Abortion Law—California Abortion Law Voided." *Dickinson Law Review*, 1969–70.

Jelen, Ted G., and Jonathan Doc Bradley. "Abortion Opinion in Emerging Democracies: Latin America and Central Europe." Western Political Science Association Annual Meeting, Portland, Oregon, March 2012.

Joffe, Carole E. *Dispatches from the Abortion Wars: The Costs of Fanaticism to Doctors, Patients, and the Rest of Us*. Boston: Beacon Press, 2009.

———. *Doctors of Conscience: The Struggle to Provide Abortion before and after Roe v. Wade*. Boston: Beacon Press, 1995.

Johns, Fran Moreland. *Perilous Times: An Inside Look at Abortion before—and after—Roe vs. Wade*. New York: YBK Publishers, 2013.

Johnson, Scott P. "Fatty Arbuckle Trials (1921–1922)." In *Trials of the Century: An Encyclopedia of Popular Culture and the Law*. Santa Barbara CA: ABC-CLIO, 2011.

Jou, Chin. "Calorie Counting." *Chemical Heritage Magazine* 29, no. 1 (Spring 2011). http://www.chemheritage.org/discover/magazine/articles/29-1-coubting-calories.aspx.

Kaley, Louis Blanchard. "This Business of Abortion." *Forum and Century* 100, no. 1 (July 1938).

Kaplan, Amy. *The Anarchy of Empire in the Making of U.S. Culture*. Cambridge MA: Harvard University Press, 2005.

Kaplan, John. "Abortion as a Vice Crime: A 'What If' Story." *Law and Contemporary Problems* 51, no. 1 (Winter 1988): 151–79.

Karibo, Holly M. "Swashbuckling Criminals and Border Bandits: Fighting Vice in North America's Borderlands, 1945–1960." *Social History* 47, no. 95 (November 2014).

Keene, Jennifer D., et al. *Visions of America: A History of the United States*. Boston: Pearson, 2013.

Kenney, Dennis. *Organized Crime in America*. Belmont: Wadsworth, Cengage, 1995.

Kletzing, H. F., and W. H. Crogman. *Progress of a Race . . . or . . . the Remarkable Advancement of the Afro-American Negro from the Bondage of Slavery, Ignorance and Poverty to the Freedom of Citizenship, Intelligence, Affluence, Honor and Trust*. Atlanta: J. L. Nichols, 1898.

Klumph, Inez, and Helen Klumph. *Screen Acting: Its Requirements and Rewards*. New York: Falk Publishing, 1922.

Koslow, Jennifer Lisa. *Cultivating Health: Los Angeles Women and Public Health Reform*. New Brunswick NJ: Rutgers University Press, 2009.

Kropp, Phoebe. *California Vieja: Culture and Memory in a Modern American Place*. Berkeley: University of California Press, 2006.

Kurashige, Scott. *The Shifting Grounds of Race: Black and Japanese Americans in the Making of Multiethnic Los Angeles*. Princeton NJ: Princeton University Press, 2008.

Langum, David J. *Crossing over the Line: Legislating Morality and the Mann Act*. Chicago: University of Chicago Press, 1994.

Lears, Jackson. *Rebirth of a Nation: The Making of Modern America*. New York: Harper Perennial, 2009.

Ledbetter, M. H. "Smashing the West Coast's Worst Racket." *Master Detective*, July 1937.

Lemons, J. Stanley. *The Woman Citizen: Social Feminism in the 1920s*. Charlottesville: University Press of Virginia, 1990.

Luibhéid, Eithne. *Entry Denied: Controlling Sexuality at the Border*. Minneapolis: University of Minnesota Press, 2002.

Luker, Kristin. *Abortion and the Politics of Motherhood*. Berkeley: University of California Press, 1985.

MacGibbon, Heather. "The Abortion Narrative in American Film: 1900–2000." PhD dissertation, New York University, 2007.

MacKinnon, Catharine A. "Feminism, Marxism, Method, and the State: An Agenda for Theory." *Signs: Journal of Women in Culture and Society* 7, no. 3 (1982): 515–44.

Marine, Gene, and Art Goldberg. "Abortion Reform: A Big Step Forward? No." *Ramparts*, July 1967.

McGerr, Michael. *A Fierce Discontent: The Rise and Fall of the Progressive Movement in America*. Oxford: Oxford University Press, 2003.

McGrew, Jane Lang. "To Be or Not to Be: The Constitutional Question of the California Abortion Law." *University of Pennsylvania Law Review* 118, no. 643 (1970).

McGuire, Danielle L. *At the Dark End of the Street: Black Women, Rape, and Resistance—A New History of the Civil Rights Movement from Rosa Parks to the Rise of Black Power*. New York: Alfred A. Knopf, 2010.

McWilliams, Carey. *Southern California: An Island on the Land*. Layton UT: Gibbs Smith, 2010.

Medrano, Marlene. "Sexuality, Migration, and Tourism in the 20th Century U.S.-Mexico Borderlands." *History Compass* 11, no. 3 (2013): 235–46.

Michelet, Jules. *L'Amour*. Translated by J. W. Palmer. New York: Carleton, 1868.

Mitchell, Michele. *Righteous Propagation: African Americans and the Politics of Racial Destiny after Reconstruction*. Chapel Hill: University of North Carolina Press, 2004.

Mitchell, Pablo. *Coyote Nation: Sexuality, Race, and Conquest in Modernizing New Mexico, 1880–1920*. Chicago: University of Chicago Press, 2005.

Mohr, James C. *Abortion in America: The Origins and Evolution of National Policy*. Oxford: Oxford University Press, 1979.

Molina, Natalia. *Fit to Be Citizens? Public Health and Race in Los Angeles, 1879–1939*. Berkeley: University of California Press, 2006.

———. *How Race Is Made in America: Immigration, Citizenship, and the Historical Power of Racial Scripts*. Berkeley: University of California Press, 2013.

Morais, Herbert M. *The History of the Negro in Medicine*. Association for the Study of Negro Life and History. New York: Publishers Company, 1967.

"More State Abortion Restrictions Enacted in 2011–2013 Than in the Entire Previous Decade." New York: Guttmacher Institute, January 2, 2014. https://guttmacher.org/media/inthenews/2014/01/02/index.html.

Morgan, Jennifer L. *Laboring Women: Reproduction and Gender in New World Slavery*. Philadelphia: University of Pennsylvania Press, 2004.

Nash, Elizabeth, et al. "Laws Affecting Reproductive Health and Rights: 2015 State Policy Review." New York: Guttmacher Institute, 2016.

———. "Policy Trends in the United States: First Quarter 2018." Guttmacher Institute, April 2018. https://guttmacher.org/article/2018/04/policy-trends-states-first-quarter-2018.

Neely, Cheryl L. *You're Dead, So What? Media, Police, and the Invisibility of Black Women as Victims of Homicide.* East Lansing: Michigan State University Press, 2015.

Nelson, Jennifer. *Women of Color and the Reproductive Rights Movement.* New York: New York University Press, 2003.

Ngai, Mae M. *Impossible Subjects: Illegal Aliens and the Making of Modern America.* Princeton NJ: Princeton University Press, 2004.

Nicks, Denver. "Wendy Davis on the Filibuster That Mattered to Her Most." *Time,* September 10, 2014. http://time.com/3318582/wendy-davis-filibuster-memoir.

Nicolaides, Becky M. *My Blue Heaven: Life and Politics in the Working-Class Suburbs of Los Angeles, 1920–1965.* Chicago: University of Chicago Press, 2002.

Odem, Mary E. *Delinquent Daughters: Protecting and Policing Adolescent Female Sexuality in the United States 1885–1920.* Chapel Hill: University of North Carolina Press, 1995.

Olasky, Marvin. *Abortion Rites: A Social History of Abortion in America.* Washington DC: Regnery Publishing, 1992.

———. *The Press and Abortion, 1838–1988.* Hillsdale NJ: Lawrence Erlbaum Associates, 1988.

Orenstein, Aviva. "Her Last Words: Dying Declarations and Modern Confrontation Jurisprudence." *University of Illinois Law Review,* Paper 6 (January 2010): 1411–60.

Pazol, Karen, et al. "Abortion Surveillance—United States, 2011." *Surveillance Summaries,* Centers for Disease Control and Prevention, 63, SS11 (November 28, 2014): 1–41.

Peters, Lulu Hunt. *Diet and Health with Key to the Calories.* Chicago: Reilly and Lee, 1918. Available at http://www.gutenberg.org/files/15069/15069-h/15069-h.htm.

Peyton, Thomas Roy. *Quest for Dignity: An Autobiography of a Negro Doctor.* Los Angeles: W. F. Lewis, 1950.

Phelan, Lana Clark, and Patricia Therese Maginnis. *The Abortion Handbook for Responsible Women.* North Hollywood: Contact Books, 1969.

"Physicians Convicted." *Journal of the American Medical Association* 76, no. 15 (April 2, 1921).

Pinkham, Charles B. "The Pacific Coast Abortion Ring." *California and Western Medicine* 46, no. 5 (May 1937).

"Popular Education in Sexual Matters." *Journal of the National Medical Association* 4, no. 1 (January–March 1912).

Powell, Miriam. *The Browns of California: The Family Dynasty That Transformed a State and Shaped a Nation*. New York: Bloomsbury, 2018.

Reagan, Leslie. "Crossing the Border for Abortions: California Activists, Mexican Clinics, and the Creation of a Feminist Health Agency in the 1960s." *Feminist Studies* 26, no. 2 (Summer 2000): 323–48.

———. *Dangerous Pregnancies: Mothers, Disabilities, and Abortion in Modern America*. Berkeley: University of California Press, 2010.

———. *When Abortion Was a Crime: Women, Medicine, and Law in the United States, 1867–1973*. Berkeley: University of California Press, 1998.

Reed, Ralph R., and Daryl Evans. "The Deprofessionalism of Medicine: Causes, Effects, and Responses." *Journal of the American Medical Association* 258, no. 22 (December 11, 1987): 3279–82.

Reuter, Peter, and David Ronfeldt. *Quest for Integrity: The Mexican-U.S. Drug Issue in the 1980s*. Santa Monica CA: RAND Corporation, 1991.

Rhetta, Barnett M. "A Plea for the Lives of the Unborn." *Journal of the National Medical Association* 7, no. 3 (July–September 1915).

Rhodes, Desha P. *A History of Flint Medical College, 1889–1911*. New York: iUniverse, 2007.

Riggin, Lisa. *San Francisco's Queen of Vice: The Strange Career of Abortionist Inez Brown Burns*. Lincoln: University of Nebraska Press, 2017.

Rothman, Sheila M. *Living in the Shadow of Death: Tuberculosis and the Social Experience of Illness in American History*. Baltimore: Johns Hopkins University Press, 1994.

"Rubella in the U.S." Centers for Disease Control and Prevention, March 31, 2016. https://cdc.gov/rubella/about/in-the-us.html.

Runstedtler, Theresa. *Jack Johnson, Rebel Sojourner: Boxing in the Shadow of the Global Color Line*. Berkeley: University of California Press, 2012.

Russell, Keith P., and Edwin W. Jackson. "Therapeutic Abortions in California." *American Journal of Obstetrics and Gynecology* 105, no. 5 (1969).

Russell, Marion, ed. "Drive Out the Rotters from the Film Industry." *Billboard* 33, no. 39 (September 24, 1921).

Russell, Violet, and Joan Malleson. "The Problem of Abortion." *Public Health*, January 1938.

Sánchez, George J. *Becoming Mexican American: Ethnicity, Culture, and Identity in Chicano Los Angeles, 1900–1945*. Oxford: Oxford University Press, 1993.

Sands, Michael S. "The Therapeutic Abortion Act: An Answer to the Opposition." *UCLA Law Review* 13 (1966).

Schantz, Eric Michael. "From the *Mexicali Rose* to the Tijuana Brass: Vice Tours of the United States–Mexico Border, 1910–1965." PhD dissertation, University of California, Los Angeles, 2001.

Schoen, Johanna. *Choice and Coercion: Birth Control, Sterilization, and Abortion in Public Health and Welfare*. Chapel Hill: University of North Carolina Press, 2005.

Schrag, Peter. *Not Fit for Our Society: Immigration and Nativism in America*. Berkeley: University of California Press, 2010.

Schwartz, Marie Jenkins. *Birthing a Slave: Motherhood and Medicine in the Antebellum South*. Cambridge MA: Harvard University Press, 2006.

Sherard, Gerald E. "Arizona Fatal Mining Accidents, 1912–1929." 2007. http://digital.denverlibrary.org/cdm/ref/collection/p16079coll16/id/449.

Sides, Josh. *L.A. City Limits: African American Los Angeles from the Great Depression to the Present*. Berkeley: University of California Press, 2004.

Solinger, Rickee. *The Abortionist: A Woman against the Law*. New York: Free Press, 1994.

———. *Wake Up Little Susie: Single Pregnancy and Race before Roe v. Wade*. New York: Routledge, 2000.

"State Facts about Abortion: California." Guttmacher Institute, May 2018. https://www.guttmacher.org/fact-sheet/state-facts-about-abortion-california.

Stern, Alexandra Minna. *Eugenic Nation: Faults and Frontiers of Better Breeding in Modern America*. Berkeley: University of California Press, 2005.

Stern, Loren G. "Abortion: Reform and the Law." *Journal of Criminal Law and Criminology* 59, no. 1 (1968): 87.

St. John, Rachel. "Selling the Border: Trading Land, Attracting Tourists, and Marketing American Consumption on the Baja California Border, 1900–1934." In *Land of Necessity: Consumer Culture in the United States–Mexico Borderlands*, edited by Alexis McCrossen. Durham NC: Duke University Press, 2009.

Storer, Horatio. *Criminal Abortion: Its Nature, Its Evidence, and Its Law*. Boston: Little, Brown, 1868.

———. *On Criminal Abortion in America*. Philadelphia: J. B. Lippincott, 1860.

Sullivan, Edward S. "Smashing California's $100,000,000 Abortion Ring." *Real Detective*, February 1937. In BME, F3760:823.

Tolnai, B. B. "The Abortion Racket." *Forum and Century* 94, no. 3 (September 1935).

Tone, Andrea. *Devices and Desires: A History of Contraception in America*. New York: Hill and Wang, 2001.

———. "Making Room for Rubbers: Gender, Technology, and Birth Control before the Pill." *History and Technology* 18, no. 1 (2002): 51–76.

Ulin, David L. *Literary Los Angeles: A Literary Anthology*. New York: Library of America, 2002.

Vargesson, Neil. "Thalidomide-Induced Teratogenesis: History and Mechanisms." *Birth Defects Research Part C: Embryo Today: Reviews* 105, no. 2 (2015): 140–56.

Vogel, Nelson J., Jr. "Constitutional Law—Abortion—1850 California Statute Prohibiting All Abortions Not 'Necessary to Preserve [the Mother's] Life' Is Unconstitutionally Vague and an Improper Infringement on Women's Constitutional Rights." Case Comments. *Notre Dame Lawyer* 45 (Winter 1970).

Wagner, Rob. *Film Folk: "Close-Ups" of the Men, Women, and Children Who Make the "Movies."* New York: The Century, 1918.

Ward, Thomas J., Jr. *Black Physicians in the Jim Crow South*. Fayetteville: University of Arkansas Press, 2003.

Washington, Harriet, et al. "Segregation, Civil Rights, and Health Disparities: The Legacy of African American Physicians and Organized Medicine, 1910–1968." *Journal of the National Medical Association* 101, no. 6 (June 2009): 513–27.

Watson, Wilbur H. *Against the Odds: Blacks in the Profession of Medicine in the United States*. New Brunswick NJ: Transaction Publishers, 1999.

Watt, Helen. *The Ethics of Pregnancy, Abortion and Childbirth: Exploring Moral Choices in Childbearing*. New York: Routledge, 2016.

Whiteley, Kate. "Monstrous, Demonic and Evil: Media Constructs of Women Who Kill." In *The Harms of Crime Media: Essays on the Perpetuation of Racism, Sexism and Class Stereotypes*, edited by Denis L. Bissler and Joan L. Conners. Jefferson NC: McFarland, 2012.

Wiebe, Robert H. *The Search for Order, 1877–1920*. New York: Hill and Wang, 1967.

Willis Kent Productions. *Road to Ruin*. 1934. https://archive.org/details/TheRoadToRuin_457.

Wilson, John Long. "Medical College of the Pacific Established in 1872 and National Efforts to Reform Medical Education." *Stanford University School of Medicine and the Predecessor Schools: An Historical Perspective*. http://elane.standford.edu/Wilson/index.html.

Wilson-Buterbaugh, Karen. *The Baby Scoop Era: Unwed Mothers, Infant Adoption, Forced Surrender*. Middletown CT: Karen Wilson-Buterbaugh, 2017.

INDEX

abortion: and "antenatal infanticide," 24, 94, 98; liberalization of laws on, 135–38, 142, 195; ring, xiv, 4, 109, 111–14, 141, 166, 172; specialist, 4–6, 21, 81, 99, 111, 113, 115, 137, 193; therapeutic, 2, 6, 56, 135, 141–44, 156, 162, 176, 179–80, 182–85, 188, 194; Tijuana, 2, 10–11, 139, 171, 175, 185, 189, 194

African Americans. *See* Black Americans

American Law Institute (ALI) model law, 175–77, 182–83. *See also* Therapeutic Abortion Act (1967)

American Medical Association, 17, 24–26, 46–47, 75, 80, 85, 90–91, 93–96

Arbuckle, Roscoe "Fatty," 58–60

Belous, Leon, 183–91. See also *People of the State of California v. Belous*

birth control. *See* contraception

Black Americans, 8, 47, 56, 73, 75–91

Browning, Margaret, 101–4

Bryant, Cheryl, 185–87, 189. See also *People of the State of California v. Belous*

Buffum, Roy L., 9, 166–69. See also *People of the State of California v. Buffum*

Burns, Inez, 106, 139–40, 220n1

childbirth, 19, 23, 94–96, 188, 196, 228n7

compulsory sterilization. *See* eugenics

Comstock Act, 22, 28, 43, 100–101

contraception, 8, 21–23, 25–26, 28–29, 55–56, 76, 80–81, 96, 100, 109, 136, 184, 187

coroners, 27, 30. *See also* Los Angeles County Coroner's Office

De Gaston, Paul, 117, 121–28, 219n28

dilation and curettement (D&C), 121

dying declaration, 30–34, 38, 42, 60–61, 63, 132

eugenics, 53–56, 78, 144–45

film industry. *See* Hollywood

gender norms and expectations: for men, 62, 145, 151, 180–81; for women, 10, 24, 66, 77, 97, 159, 178, 180; for young white women, 157–59

Hickock, Galen R. *See* Zangwell

Hollywood, 49–52, 56, 58–60, 66–67, 115, 122–24, 130, 150

immigration, 25, 54, 161, 164

251

Keemer, Edgar Bass, 81–82, 86
Kershaw, Laura. *See* Miner, Laura

Lanterman, Roy S., 60–64, 73
Los Angeles County Coroner's Office, 57, 68–72, 153–56, 166, 176–77
Los Angeles County Medical Association (LACMA), 46

Marmillion, Mathew, 8, 73, 84–90
Mexico, 1–4, 7, 9–10, 12, 49, 54, 57–58, 152, 161, 170–75, 185, 187, 189, 194; abortion law in, 1, 165–66, 170; American perceptions of U.S. border with, 161–66, 169, 189
midwives, 91, 93, 135
Miner, Laura, 107–10, 126, 131, 138–39, 145, 148–52
motion pictures. *See* Hollywood
Mottard, Henry Lee, 16–17, 40–42

National Medical Association (NMA), 79–80
Negro Project, 80–81
neurasthenia, 96

Pacific Coast Abortion Ring (PCAR), 4–6, 111–35
People of the State of California v. Belous, 7–8, 10, 186–91
People of the State of California v. Buffum, 10, 166, 169–72, 194
People of the State of California v. Reginald L. Rankin, et al., 4–6, 8–9, 11, 131–34, 137, 139–40

Planned Parenthood of Southeastern Pennsylvania v. Casey, 195–98
Prohibition, 15, 17, 42–43

quacks, 19–20, 23, 45–47, 50, 57, 94–95, 100
quickening, 18, 20, 24–25

Rankin, Reginald, 5, 9, 111–33, 138. *See also People of the State of California v. Reginald L. Rankin, et al.*; *State of Nevada v. Paul Cushing and R. L. Rankin*
Rappe, Virginia, 58–59
Reproductive FACT Act, 199–200
Rex v. Bourne, 141–42
Roe v. Wade, 2–3, 159, 193, 195–97, 199–200

Sanger, Margaret, 28–29, 54, 79, 81
State of Nevada v. Paul Cushing and R. L. Rankin, 145–48
steerer, 106–7, 115, 119, 122, 149, 166, 171
Storer, Horatio, 24–26, 97

Therapeutic Abortion Act (1967), 182–84. *See also* American Law Institute (ALI) model law

Watts, George E., 111, 113–15, 117–19, 124–26, 132–33
white race suicide, 25–26

Zangwell, 36–40, 41–42

www.ingramcontent.com/pod-product-compliance
Lightning Source LLC
Chambersburg PA
CBHW022003220426
43663CB00007B/944